Fiction with a Parochial Purpose: Social Uses of
American Catholic Literature, 1884–1900

Fiction with a Parochial Purpose

Social Uses of American Catholic

Literature, 1884-1900 *Paul R. Messbarger*

Boston University Press / 1971

FOR

Patricia

Rebecca

Rachel

Anne

Paula

Jessica

Preface

The origins of this study belong to a period in my life when I was first discovering the social sources of religious belief and behavior. The investigation that followed that discovery over the next several years was most often a sporadic private pursuit independent of my more deliberate preparation for the teaching of American literature; it was also a deeply personal one, owing to my long and intimate association with the Catholic Church. Eventually I was encouraged to develop these interests as a dissertation project at the University of Minnesota; the present volume is a revision of that completed project. What the reader will find in the following pages is then the product of both personal adventure and formal research.

To confront twentieth-century American Catholicism is to be immediately aware of two incontestable but apparently incompatible facts: by most indices of institutional health and vigor, Catholicism is the strongest denomination in America; but, by the most generous assessment of intellectual and artistic productivity, Catholicism is strikingly deficient. For years Church apologists have explained this paradox by reference to the social history of the institution, a history of material deprivation. The cogency of this argument, however, is challenged by a more specialized history of the American Church, a history of apostasy. The roster of literary giants of modern America is replete with the names of men and women who defected from the Catholic faith. A second list could be constructed of artists who remained loyal to the Church but whose growth and power seem to have developed only within heavily circumscribed limits. The inference is unmistakeable: Catholic culture in America could not (or did not) sustain and nourish the artistic sensibility.

The purpose of the present study is to examine this paradox of modern Catholicism by reference to its past, specifically to a period in the nineteenth century when the Church appeared first to have developed a direction, a moral authority, and a clear promise, and then to have lost that momentum—all within a single generation. The dates which frame the study are 1884–1900, known in Church history as the Americanist period. My access to the era is the literature—specifically popular fiction—that was read by the mass of Catholics of the time. The materials offer a special insight into the people who made up the subculture and serve as both source and reflection of their most intimate ambitions and apprehensions. In addition to providing an understanding of the period and the people, the study also seeks to examine larger questions: namely, the way a minority group accommodates itself to the greater society, how belief and behavior are conditioned by this relation, and how literature itself becomes a functional tool in the process of integration and assimilation.

My own long interest and labor in pursuit of this subject do not account entirely for the fruits of this investigation, such as they may be. My obligations to various friends and teachers are considerable, and only a small part of my total debt can be acknowledged here. My first serious investigation of the subject came at the direction of Professor Austin Warren of the University of Michigan. During my years at the University of Minnesota I developed what historical perspective and resources I have with the help of a variety of inspiring tutors, among them Professors David Noble, J. C. Levenson, Mary Turpie, and Timothy Smith. Professor Smith directed the doctoral dissertation on which this volume is based, and he is largely responsible for teaching me the standards of historical scholarship. Professor David O'Brien of Holy Cross College has read nearly the whole of the manuscript, and his critical comments have resulted in important organizational changes. To Boston University Press I am indebted for the opportunity of a wider readership than this study could otherwise have found. For their faith in the manuscript and for the generous editorial assistance of Mrs. Roberta Clark, I am especially thankful.

This study has claimed a large part of my life and that of my family for several years. Endurance alone would signify heroic qualities in a wife. My wife, Patricia, however, has practiced more active virtues; and for her inspiration and steady support, she can rightfully be called the co-author of this work. And finally, a special word of thanks to my parents. If ever I was moved to view Catholicism and its manifold influences on American life in a spirit of anger or disdain, I had always the steady recollection of the personal beauty and integrity possible within the Church because of those influences. These qualities define the lives of my father and mother.

Contents

Introduction   xiii

CHAPTER

1   The Politics of Americanism   1

2   The Social Origins and Consequences of
Catholic Literary Tradition   16

3   From Theory to Practice: Pre–Civil War
Fictional Conventions   32

4   The Emergence of Institutional Support, 1860–1900   50

5   Catholic Fiction with a Parochial Purpose   80

6   Cosmopolitan Expressions   96

7   Catholic Fiction: Literary Anomalies and
Excommunicates   114

8   Catholic Literature: A Topical Analysis   132

9   Varieties of Accommodation   159

Appendix   165

Bibliography   167

Index   175

Introduction

In the closing moments of back room debate over the presidential nomination at the 1968 Democratic National Convention, the focus of events converged on three men. To wrest the vote from Hubert Humphrey, the advocates of the "new politics" had to find a way to bring these three men into an alliance. All three were American-Irish; all three were Roman Catholic; but they were products of cultural forces so critically different as to make that alliance well-nigh impossible from the outset. The men were Richard Daley, Edward Kennedy, and Eugene McCarthy.[1] The present study is concerned, at least in part, with the nature and origins of those different cultural forces.

Of the three, Daley offers the casual observer an example of the simplest social classification. Born to the values—and the meager prospects—of turn-of-the-century immigrants, Daley fused his fortunes with one of the two-most-important instruments of immigrant advancement, the political machine of the Cook County Democratic Party. Working himself up through party ranks by means of his organizational genius and loyalty to the party leadership, Daley emerged in the 1950's as one of the most powerful political forces of the nation, a regional king and a national kingmaker. Throughout his remarkable career, Daley's personal qualities seem to have remained unchanged; increased power and influence have only illuminated them. A man of simple beliefs, severely chaste habits, and limited imagination, he is nevertheless profoundly skilled in the manipulation of social machinery. The role of religion in his life appears to be all of a piece with his ethnic, national, and party iden-

1. This account is taken from Theodore H. White, *The Making of the President, 1968* (New York, 1969), p. 332.

tity. Roman Catholicism, besides providing a link with the past—social, familial, and personal—gives a spiritual authority to the entire complex of values and allegiances of his personal and public life. He expresses to perfection that synthesis of religious and cultural forces that represents what might be called the tribal phase of American Catholicism.

Eugene McCarthy owns quite a different background and sensibility, although his public person appears to be even more sharply marked by the influence of the Catholic Church. McCarthy's rural origins, his training at the hands of the Benedictine Order, and his intellectual bias put him in a different tradition. Philosophically he appears equally comfortable with the ontological absolutes of Scholasticism and the pragmatic theater of compromise and uncertainty of Washington politics. His manner combines the colloquial wit of a Minnesota farmer and the refined urbanity of a Washington nabob. His special appeal is the result, I think, of combining seemingly contradictory qualities. A cosmopolitan citizen of the world, he knows precisely the impact on his constituency of a drop in wheat prices; a man profoundly aware of history, he uses that awareness to interpret the present and yet is convinced of a realm of meta-history, of the transcendental. In short, McCarthy is a man of large consciousness who appears to live on familiar terms with time *and* eternity, St. Cloud, Minnesota and the universe, in a state of mature equanimity. No one can fully explain the sources of such a personality, but surely his membership in a two-thousand-year-old religious community has something to do with it. The antique wisdom of that community, its poise amid the vicissitudes of time and events, is the sober foundation on which McCarthy has constructed a fully native American experience.

If Daley and McCarthy form the outlines for a modest typology of fixed and knowable elements, Edward Kennedy is the variant, the "sport" that may produce a new religio-cultural species. Ethnic identity is a powerful factor in the Kennedy family experience, and the tribal religion, Roman Catholicism, claims the full loyalty of all the Kennedys. Yet wealth, secular education, and constant traffic with the secular establishment have freed them almost entirely from the parochial perspectives of the mass of their fellow Catholics. By some mysterious process, both older Kennedys, John and Robert, shared an improvisational tendency that argues something quite new. Whether or not Edward Kennedy, the sole survivor, claims this unusual legacy, the design now has an existence independent of family. *Kennedy,* as a generic term, is a force in process—"becoming." Watching their vigorous pursuit of power and the mysterious methodology of public policy, one observes the workings of humane but pragmatic spirits, uninhibited by categorical imperatives, searching for the forms of things amidst the materials themselves. They represent a new and more dangerous barbarism or a sophisticated political analogue to developments in modern art—one can't be sure which. Somehow their personal force brings together various historical and cultural impulses in what appears to be a new design and enlarges radically the range of social and political possibilities in the United States.

Different as these three men are in style and philosophy, they yet can be said to have emerged from a broad but common cultural heritage; without denying the uniqueness of their special geniuses, one can say that each has found a mode of expression within a range of possibilities limited in part by his Catholic experience. Thus an observer at the 1968 convention might easily have inferred that the long-overdue ripening of the Catholic influence in America was at hand, as evidenced by this curious trinity. The John F. Kennedy victory of 1960 could be interpreted as a personal triumph; but the emergence of several powerful Catholic political figures in 1968— including the Democratic vice-presidential candidate, Edmund Muskie—suggests an institutional phenomenon, an era of great Catholic influence.

Such a development may well in fact occur, but if there is an era of Catholic dominance it will give witness to the strength of an already-disappearing subculture. For what is becoming clearer with each day is that the Catholicism which has remained virtually unchanged —except for enormous growth in numbers and wealth—for seventy-five years, will not survive another generation. What will replace it is not known, but certainly a fundamental reordering of the elements of American Catholicism is imminent. The forty million Americans listed on the roster of Catholic affiliation today are experiencing a crisis of confidence in the institutional Church as deep and as pervasive as that of any religious community since 1617. The internal tensions wracking the Church have produced a centrifugal movement so powerful that it threatens to break the hold of orthodoxy itself.

Not one sacred tenet of Church doctrine is now safe from attack or redefinition. Even that ancient mark of the Church's divine origin —the "one, holy, catholic, and apostolic Church"—is being challenged by new concepts of religious pluralism and ecumenicalism. In the meantime, the average Catholic layman, with numbing bemusement, witnesses the collapse of a system of signs and symbols, ritual and myth, from which he derived an integrated conception of his spiritual identity. In his view, his priests are compulsively confessing error, his nuns are shrilly condemning the religious life to which they conse-crated themselves, while his theologians drive him from the sanctuary of a fully revealed and minutely articulated faith into a shadowy arena of doubt and contingency.

Ironically, the force that has brought the Church to the brink of disintegration is the same one which ten years ago promised a future of health and creativity—the influence of the papal reign of John XXIII and the Second Vatican Council he convened. The documents of Vatican II and the encyclical letters of John, profoundly sensitive to the spiritual needs of the modern world as they are, worked more as catalyst than cause, however. The explosion of ideas, the realign-ment of forces, the growth of experimentation, the heady and radical-ly new departures that describe a large portion of current Catholic thought, have their origins in the pre-counciliar condition of Catholic life.

No one knows the eventual consequences of this movement. The most sanguine hope for a community of spiritual commitment, a much-reduced community to be sure, but one that will find the direction for apostolic work in the Gospel rather than in institutional preoccupations with behavioral and doctrinal uniformity; it will be a small elite perhaps but one galvanized by the hope of establishing the Kingdom of God. Others, steeped in the knowledge of history and severely disciplined by the apparent lessons of that history, see the current condition as a temporary loss of sanity, a hysteria resulting from millennial enthusiasm. In their view, once the period of excita-tion has run its course, historical parallels argue for a return to normality and a situation not unlike what prevailed before the explo-sion. As in 1545, 1850, and 1910, the highest and lowest orders of

Church membership will reaffirm their ancient alliance and place the Church back in the center of conservative orthodoxy. A third perspective, spiritually extramural and decidedly ironic, speaks in the voice of the Grand Inquisitor, pointing to man's fundamental fear of freedom.

To understand the current turmoil in Catholicism, if not to chart its future, one must pay a scrupulous heed to the past. In considering the three-hundred-year history of American Catholicism, one rather quickly sees a narrative in two parts. At least until the Civil War, the internal life of the American Church was marked by violent struggle, radical experimentation, and sectarian fervor. By the end of the nineteenth century, however, these characteristics had virtually disappeared; in their place was an elaborate apparatus for the regularization of belief and behavior, a well-organized ecclesiastical structure, and a vast and durable spirit of complacency. The watershed period for American Catholics occurred during the years following the Civil War to about 1900, and it offers, in its way, a mirror image of what was taking place in the larger American society. During that period, Catholics settled some of the more urgent questions of their institutional existence. Would they continue to be a small and fragile community on the edge of American society, or would they move into the mainstream of that society? We know the answer to this question: Catholics did assimilate and, given the immigrant status of so many members, at a prodigious rate. Another and more delicate question, however, still has not been adequately answered. What were the terms of the accommodation and the far-reaching implications of those terms?

A synthesis of volatile and disparate social and ideological forces during the last quarter of the nineteenth century was fashioned; that such a synthesis was possible is testimony to a kind of genius. The price of unity, however, is never small, and what one person may call a condition of creative flexibility, another may call static immobility. Whatever the language, the phenomenon itself is undeniable. The American Church did discover a formula for containing and deflecting the internal tensions of a large and culturally plural membership, at the same time absorbing millions of new members and suffering only a slight attrition. It is this formula especially that must be examined, both for its importance as an explanation to a singular historical puzzle and for the general insight it may supply into the complex process of acculturation.

The study conducted in the following pages is concerned with a period in the history of American Catholicism when a series of internal and external accommodations were invented to blunt the forces of institutional disintegration. It attempts to identify these accommodations and to assess their tactical value according to the immediate objectives. Somewhere to the side of the main path of inquiry, an influential if not controlling presence, is the anxious and slightly benumbed Catholic witness to the events of the last ten years. In many ways this is his story too. Destiny has assigned him the complex task of reordering his entire scheme of values; yet for the most part his emotional equipment is inadequate to that task. His cry of shock and amazement, his apostasy, his violent insistence on a return to the religiosity of his fathers, his incipient cynicism, his anti-clericalism, his headlong assault on a hundred chimerical windmills, a thousand contradictory causes—these are his instalment payments for a half-century of peace.

Fiction with a Parochial Purpose: Social Uses of

American Catholic Literature, 1884–1900

1 The Politics of Americanism

In the final year of the nineteenth century, Pope Leo XIII, then in the twenty-first year of his influential pontificate, issued the encyclical *Testem Benevolentiae* to the American hierarchy through its senior member James Cardinal Gibbons. This letter defined a number of heretical tendencies in the modern world. Although denying any special significance in the choice of descriptive titles, the Holy Father labeled these tendencies collectively "Americanism." By laboring to make absolutely clear the nature and destructive potential of these beliefs, while at the same time exonerating the American Church from any special attachment to them, Leo worked one of those familiar Vatican coups: the American bishops raced to declare their undiminished loyalty to Rome and to disclaim all taint of the heresies. Thus came to an end a lengthy and impassioned public debate over the theoretical possibilities of the Church in America. For several decades thereafter, American churchmen busied themselves by supplying the practical necessities of a burgeoning population.

The encyclical specifically associated with heresy a number of theological propositions: (1) that the Church should adapt itself to and embrace the modern world; (2) that divine grace works on the soul through agencies outside as well as inside the sacramental system of Mother Church; and (3) that a new personalism, as opposed to legalism, should be encouraged in the religious life of the faithful, especially in such matters as religious vows.[1]

1. Leo XIII, "Testem Benevolentiae," in John J. Wynne, ed., *The Great Encyclical Letters of Pope Leo* XIII (New York, 1903), pp. 441–53.

What the Pope had done, or thought he had done, was to crystalize in abstract and theological language the terms of a debate that had gone on for several decades in America; the discussion was to continue in Europe at least a decade longer, coming to a costly climax in the Modernist controversy. The American version of the debate can be judged heterodox only by the most stringent definition. It originated in and was dominated by the thinking of one man, whose published biography, translated into French, brought about the terminal confrontation. The man was Isaac Hecker, founder of the Paulist Order and the *Catholic World*. The papal document mentioned his name in connection with the influence of the biography and castigated an attitude toward authority that was peculiarly his.

It would be foolish to try to trace exactly the origins of Catholic Americanist sentiment—for it was only a sentiment and not an articulated philosophical position. Hecker's reaction to the work of the First Vatican Council, which ended in 1870, was a symbolic beginning. After considerable debate and not a few defections, the council enunciated the doctrine of Papal Infallibility, a position Church liberals found especially difficult to endorse. Hecker, who was an official observer at the council, might have been expected to join the dissidents; instead, he returned to America rejoicing in the new dogma. The reasons go far toward revealing his intellectual bent. Hecker argued that with the supreme authority of the pope in matters of faith and morals clearly defined, Catholics were free as never before to loose their imaginations, to speculate, to experiment, and to launch programs they would never have tried before for fear of leading the Church into error. Now, he said, Catholics knew that their faith was firmly anchored not only in the Scriptures but also in the living and ever-present person of the vicar of Christ, who was able to protect the Church from the dangers of heresy.[2] As Leo himself put it, without assigning the sentiment to any one person: "They say, in speaking of the infallible teaching of the Roman Pontiff, that after the solemn decision formulated in the Vatican Council, there is no more need of solicitude in that regard, and, because of its being now

2. Walter Elliott, *Life of Father Isaac Hecker* (New York, 1891), pp. 364–66.

out of dispute, a wider field of thought and action is thrown open to individuals." [3]

If Hecker's argument sounds naïve, it was also peculiarly American. It constituted a pragmatic and apparently instinctive abandonment of the philosophical complications of the problem in favor of a program of action. It was thus analagous to several splendid moments in American history, beginning with the founding of Massachusetts Bay and extending through the founding of the Republic and on down to the present, when an apparently insoluble conflict between freedom and authority found tentative resolution in a working compromise. Hecker was simply doing what Jefferson, Jackson, Lincoln, and Roosevelt did: defining an ultimate source of authority—Constitution, court, Bible, or intuition—that was itself predicated on human freedom.

This reaction does not, of course, mark the beginning of a national influence on Catholicism; but it is significant because of Hecker's involvement and because it so conveniently illuminates the alternatives open to American Catholicism in the post–Civil War period. The controversies that rocked the Church up until 1900, and which will be briefly described below, evolved from Hecker's position and the conservative reaction to it. To give this conflict a perspective that transcends the personalities which were important to that period, let me present a perennial dialectic within the Church, an abstraction from countless historical debates. I use the terms "liberal" and "conservative" to identify positions but as a mere convenience; the usefulness of these categories to denote well-defined philosophical positions is clearly disproved by recent history. The principal source of the ideas for this discussion is a speech by François Mauriac, given in 1961.[4]

The Church of Christ, by tradition and scriptural injunction, was assigned two crucial functions: to protect and interpret the "deposit of faith" and to spread the gospel throughout the earth. These are two radically different missions; many a divine during nearly two thou-

---

3. Leo XIII, "Testem Benevolentiae," p. 445.
4. François Mauriac, "Traditionalists and Innovators: Foes Within the Church," address delivered in Paris, 8 November 1961, translation in *Catholic Messenger*, Davenport, Iowa, 11 January 1962, pp. 5–6.

sand years of institutional history found that the difference between them amounted to a contradiction. Fulfilling the evangelical mandate requires confidence in the universal relevance of the Christian message and a willingness to test that relevance against any and all cultures. In contrast, guarding the Church's authenticity requires in watchdog fashion, constant vigilance against the ever-present threat of corruption from within as well as from outside the institution. The evangelical position I call liberal; the protectionist is, of course, the conservative.

One term by which Church historians know the latter position is "ultramontanism," and to its influence are attributed various historical developments: periods of retreat, retrenchment from the assaults of the secular world, and hardened resistance to change. Ultimately, in its most exaggerated form, the position is non-historical and otherworldly. The liberal excess is just as dangerous from a normative point of view. Its most exaggerated form is a kind of monism, a regard for all things, sacred and profane, as fundamentally alike and moved by the same spiritual principle. Through the evangelical's relation to the world, intimacy may truly breed kinship and even identity; the result is the denatured, even secularized, religion Will Herberg calls "religiosity."

It should be acknowledged that ideally the two positions exert a constant and corrective influence on each other. The history of Christianity can be read as a rhythmic alternation of ascendance by one or the other of these forces. The eventual and permanent triumph of one over the other would probably mean the end of the Christian Church.

Perhaps this general description will provide a background against which to understand the events of the Americanist controversy in American Catholic history. According to these definitions, Hecker represents the liberal position. His single ambition as priest, publicist, and preacher was to reconcile Catholicism with America. In his camp were found, first of all, the members of the order he founded, the Paulists, and particularly the converts Augustine Hewit and Walter Elliott. The intellectual leader of the group was Bishop John Lancaster Spalding, of Peoria, Illinois. Archbishop John Ireland of St. Paul led the shock troops; and in his command were Monsignor John Keane, first rector of the Catholic University of America, and Denis

O'Connell, rector of the North American College at Rome. Clearly in the liberal domain, but constantly obliged to work toward a united Catholic front, was James Cardinal Gibbons of Baltimore.

Their adversaries were a group of ecclesiastics who likewise owned no particular ethnic or geographical characteristic, although they are frequently referred to as the German–American faction. Led by Archbishop Michael Corrigan of New York and the German bishops of the Midwest, the conservatives drew their strength primarily from among the newer immigrants. The field of battle was American culture. The particular issues were numerous, and they multiplied with each year of the conflict; it reached the point in the late nineties when any policy recommended by a member of one side was sure to draw fire from the other. As examples of the range and depth of the split, a brief summary of five of the more abrasive confrontations follows. They are more than examples, for they supply an abbreviated history of the period.[5]

To begin with, consider the school question, an issue that had deep historical roots but which was most sharply defined in the last decade of the nineteenth century. The Plenary Council of Baltimore of 1884 had strongly endorsed a policy of parish schools, but the implications of the commitment were only gradually acknowledged. The debate sharpened in 1890 when Archbishop Ireland addressed the annual convention of the National Education Association on the question of public and private education. Endorsing fully the concept of public free schools, Ireland nevertheless lamented the fact that constitutional purists were determined to exclude religious instruction from tax-supported classrooms. His solution was wholly indigenous: the religion of the district majority should be taught in public-supported schools.[6] However unrealistic this compromise at the time, it reflected the Archbishop's personal blend of the native American and the Roman ecclesiastic. Ireland not only proposed the venture, he actually engineered it in one school system in his diocese.

The public reaction to Ireland's plan, both within and without the Church, was vigorous. Catholics feared that it would open the way

5. The flavor of this partisanship is perhaps most clearly evoked in Robert D. Cross, *The Emergence of Liberal Catholicism in America* (Cambridge, Mass., 1958).

6. John Ireland, *The Church and Modern Society: Lectures and Addresses,* 2 vols. (Chicago, 1896), 1: 217–32.

for state domination of religious instruction. The suspicion also grew that the measure would subvert efforts to maintain ethnic identity, a particular concern of the German clergy. Protestants and secularists read a papal conspiracy into the innovation. The experiment was short-lived, owing to a change in public sentiment in the Minnesota towns where it was tried; but it contributed to an intensification of the conflict among parties to the contest, the Catholic churchmen not the least.[7]

A second incident that exacerbated American Catholic tensions and one that had an international coloration, was the so-called Cahensley Affair. Peter Cahensley, a German philanthropist and statesman, in 1871 founded the St. Raphael Society, an organization to finance and guide the relocation of German Catholics in America. The organization typified the refined and highly effective nature of transnational relations between Old and New World Germans; it also suggested the complications arising from divided national loyalties. In ecclesiastical matters, this division produced a constant tension between German and Irish bishops. The bitterness found concrete expression in the fight over whether parishes and dioceses might have clergy whose nationality was the same as the dominant ethnic group. In 1890 a congress of St. Raphael Society delegates presented to Rome a document called the Lucerne Memorial, which articulated the sentiment in favor of ethnic leadership. The main proposal called for bishops to be selected according to the ethnic composition of the diocese, an obvious attack upon the Irish dominance in American Church affairs and upon the campaign of the liberals to naturalize Catholic immigrants as quickly as possible.

Rome apparently entertained this proposal with favor for a time, but Cardinal Gibbons sent word to the pope, in the name of the American hierarchy, reaffirming its support of giving no special privileges to any national group. Rome upheld Gibbons' judgment and denied the request of Mr. Cahensley in the middle of 1891.[8]

Ecumenicalism, a modern rallying cry, was in the 1890s hardly a theme to direct institutional behavior. Protestant denominations

7. For a full account, see Daniel F. Reilly, *The School Controversy, 1891–93* (Washington, 1943).

8. This conflict is given detailed examination in Colman Barry, *The Catholic Church and German-Americans* (Milwaukee, 1953), pp. 131–82.

found cause, after the Civil War, to unite on a number of issues, including temperance, missionary work, and religious education; but between the major religious groups there was little to relieve the traditional hostility. When the call went out, therefore, for a convention of all the world's religions on the occasion of the Chicago World's Exposition of 1893, and when important members of the Catholic hierarchy accepted it, a significant new departure seemed in the offing. When the Parliament of Religions was convened there in September of 1893, Catholics played a prominent role, not only in the ceremonial performances of the meeting but also in its official business. Twelve Catholics, including bishops, clergymen, and laymen, gave major addresses. Of course, the Catholic contribution to religious unity in no way suggested a lessening of the Church's exclusivism. What took place must be seen more as a gesture than as a substantial exchange. Still, in the context of interfaith history, the event was important and potentially laid the foundations for more fruitful dialogue.[9] Evidence of its significance appeared as much in the furor the parliament excited as in its actual work. Catholic participants came only from the liberal camp; not one conservative took part. This bespeaks a solid front on the part of both factions and provided a focus for the vigorous debate that went on before and after the convention.

Conservatives characteristically regarded the event as a public scandal, an occasion that would seriously confuse the faithful even if—and this was doubtful—the Catholic participants prevented any direct contamination of the Faith. The rift between the two parties was so severe that no local solution was even sought; the adjudication of difficulties was left to Rome. Conservatives forwarded a complaint to the Vatican. Papal response was both indirect and ambiguous, which is not surprising in view of the fact that the papal delegate to the United States, Archbishop Francisco Satolli, had attended the parliament. Shortly thereafter, at the Paris World's Exposition of 1900—inspired in part by the Chicago experience—French Catholics proposed a similar convention of continental religious bodies. This time, however, the injunction machinery was ready; before European liberals could work their will, the Pope intervened to prevent Catholic

9. John Henry Barrows, ed., *World's Parliament of Religions,* 2 vols. (Chicago, 1893). All speeches of the Parliament of Religions are reprinted in vol. 2.

participation and enunciated at the same time a policy of disassociation that prevailed until the middle of the twentieth century.[10]

This incident is more than a detail from a historical mosaic. It illustrates a number of characteristics of the American Church, but it also indicates a crucial change in the Vatican position as well. The parliament at Chicago was a gesture of accommodation much like the school proposal; Gibbons, Ireland, and the others were willing to accept a state of religious pluralism, at least at the level of public gesture. They would adopt a garb, a posture, a mechanism of compromise that was very American, even while denying the equality of the participants' claims.

The shifting attitude of Rome was exemplified by Archbishop Satolli, the emissary of Leo XIII to the United States. At the time of the Parliament of Religions, Satolli was the most enthusiastic Americanist among the Catholic delegates, remarking to the general assembly at the concurrent Columbian Catholic Congress: "Go forward, in one hand bearing the book of Christian truth, and in the other the Constitution of the United States. Christian truth and American liberty will make you free, and happy, and prosperous."[11] Shortly thereafter, as the factionalism became more clear to him and as he came to sense the future balance of power, Satolli's sympathies shifted to the conservative side. Within a year he was enlisted on the side of the German interests in the Catholic University struggle. From there on he was counted a partisan for the conservative cause, and he became an especially powerful lobbyist for the group at the Vatican.[12]

Parochial issues were not the only ones troubling the Church during these years. National problems provoked at least three other major controversies: the Knights of Labor issue (a conflict growing out of a general suspicion of the labor-union concept, but ostensibly based on a Catholic prohibition against membership in "secret societies");[13] John Ireland's activities on behalf of Republican candidates

10. Thomas T. McAvoy, *The Great Crisis in American Catholic History* (Chicago, 1957), pp. 83, 153–54.

11. Francisco Satolli, "Address," in *Neely's History of the Parliament of Religions and Religious Congresses at the World's Columbian Exposition,* Walter R. Houghton, ed. (Chicago, 1893), p. 894.

12. See John Tracy Ellis, *The Formative Years of the Catholic University of America* (Washington, 1946); and for one version of Satolli's ubiquitous loyalties, McAvoy, *Great Crisis,* pp. 82–83.

13. See Henry J. Browne, *The Catholic Church and the Knights of Labor* (Washington, 1949).

for public office in New York State; and the McGlynn–Henry George episode. Although no one of the conflicts can be accurately understood in isolation, only the last will be described.

Father John McGlynn was pastor of a New York City parish in the diocese administered by Archbishop Corrigan. During the years of greatest activity by prophet–economist Henry George, McGlynn gave him much public support, including help in the New York mayoralty campaign. In 1892, Corrigan ordered McGlynn to remove himself from public political debate and, when McGlynn refused, excommunicated him. Secular public opinion was nearly unanimous in support of McGlynn, although sharply divided over the economic views of George. The controversy divided the Catholic leadership but not on ideological grounds. In 1889 Gibbons had prevented public proscription of George's books by the Vatican, not because they reflected acceptable views, but because they were virtually harmless; he felt that their condemnation by Rome would only incite anti-Catholic sentiment in America. The Americanists too viewed the McGlynn excommunication pragmatically. His censure was not so much wrong as it was impolitic: McGlynn might become a *cause célèbre*, a martyr of the American Protective Association bigots, a prospect decidedly embarrassing to those working toward better Catholic–Protestant relations. The Ireland faction won the point, and McGlynn was restored to his Catholic and pastoral status in 1894.[14]

The occasion that produced the most severe crisis in Catholic affairs was the publication of Isaac Hecker's biography, written by another Paulist, Walter Elliott. In a sense, this event brings the account full circle. The book came out in 1891 bearing the *imprimatur* of Archbishop Corrigan of New York; it also ran serially in the *Catholic World*. In 1897 the book was privately translated into French, then presented to Abbé Felix Klein for his impressions. Klein thought the book worthy of publication in French and suggested some minor revisions. His edited version, with an introduction by him, was the edition circulated on the Continent, the book that produced a whirlwind of controversy throughout the Catholic world. [15]

The Americanist controversy thus took on a thoroughly inter-

14. McAvoy, *Great Crisis,* pp. 13–14.
15. McAvoy's entire book is concerned with this chronicle; the actual publication data is on pp. 113–27.

national cast, centering among French conservatives but including the ultramontanists of Italy, Germany, and the United States as well. Of special importance in the history of the debate was the Jesuit Order in Italy and its publication *Civilta Catholica*. For a year and a half the argument raged. To the participants, who exaggerated the melodramatic aspects, it sustained multiple intrigues and counter-intrigues, plots and counterplots, conspiracies, pseudonymous villains, monumental heroism and betrayals. In private letters, ecclesiastical meetings, pulpits, the religious and secular press, and even in parliaments, state houses, and embassies of the secular governments the debate went on. For insider and outsider alike it has the quality of a fabulous melodrama, with a cast of larger-than-life personalities, inflated language, and a coherent narrative structure.

The issues growing out of the translation and publication were listed at the beginning of this chapter, those questionable theological propositions cited in the papal letter. But when all is said and done, the issues become real and convincing only when seen in a political light. Hecker himself appears to have been an innocent party who, for a number of reasons—mainly his position in the liberal hagiology—became a pawn in the contest.

In reviewing this complicated history, filled as it was with strong personalities, the pressures of an anti-Catholic bias throughout the United States, and a multitude of exigencies that could not have been anticipated, the historian is grateful for an overriding theme or at least a continuity in party divisions. Scholars who have examined this subject are guided by two kinds of concern. One group looks to the data to discover whether or not there was any doctrinal deviation on the part of the liberals; in effect, to rehash the same argument carried on in the 1890s. Theodore Maynard offers a rather typical example of this approach.[16] The definitive study of the theological issue is Thomas McAvoy's book, *The Great Crisis in American Catholicism*. In a thoroughly scholarly fashion and in minute detail, he traces the debate leading up to the issuance of the papal encyclical. He concludes that, for all the emotional charges and countercharges, there is no evidence of doctrinal heresy on the part of the Americanists, that Americanism was truly a "phantom heresy," and that whatever

16. Theodore Maynard, *The Story of American Catholicism* (New York, 1941), pp. 498–521.

heterodox thinking there was on either side occurred outside America and only there.

A second group of historians has tended to regard the question of heresy as a red herring, and to look to that controversial period for the sources of twentieth-century Catholic development. They argue that the dominant force of modern Catholicism in America was shaped during and by the Americanist debate; their efforts are directed to identifying the parties, recording the progress of the exchange, and most importantly, awarding the victor's prize. The best of these historians is Professor Robert Cross, whose *The Emergence of Liberal Catholicism in America* is an optimistic account of the Americanizing influence in Catholic history. Cross reaches sanguine conclusions in part because he imposes a cowboy-and-Indian classification upon the events and personalities of Catholic history (i.e., he uses a rather simple index of party affiliation, thereby obscuring a range of attitudes in between the polar extremes) and partly because he regards a continuity in spirit as a continuity and even enlargement of influence within the Church. The genealogy of liberalism is traced from Bishop John England, of the mid-nineteenth century, all the way to Monsignor John A. Ryan and Father John LaFarge of the twentieth century. To tell the story of the Americanists, then, is for Cross an opportunity to document that period when momentum clearly shifted to (and was secured by) the progressive wing of the Catholic Church.[17]

A more recent examination of the same conflict, similar in design although less thorough than Cross's, is Andrew Greeley's *The Catholic Experience*. Greeley also describes the ideological split, and his sympathies are likewise with the Americanists; but his conclusion is quite the opposite. He sees the papal letter as fatal to the liberal cause, effectively stifling for several decades a sentiment that could have dramatically changed the course of American Church history.[18]

Historians, then, have looked to the period either to examine it on its own terms as a conflict between orthodoxy and heresy or, unwilling to play inquisitor, to discover the bias of institutional power and to trace it into the twentieth century.

17. Cross, *Liberal Catholicism*.
18. Andrew M. Greeley, *The Catholic Experience: An Interpretation of the History of American Catholicism* (Garden City, N.Y., 1967), pp. 150–215.

Yet another dimension to this investigation, a deeper and more complex phenomenon, has been largely ignored by historians of American Catholicism. I refer to a quality of religious behavior, apparent in the Americanist camp, traditionally known as Gallicanism, or more generally culture religion. Delicately alluded to by Commager in his book *The American Mind,* it has only recently come under the critical eye of younger institutional historians.[19]

This spirit, a triumphalism based on the manifest destiny of both America and Catholicism, is to be found, in latent or explicit form, in a thousand events, statements, and gestures. For our purposes, this spirit is best and most simply dramatized in the body of correspondence between John Ireland and Denis O'Connell, written during the Cuban crisis of 1898. (O'Connell was rector of the North American College in Rome.) One letter in particular, from O'Connell to Ireland, evokes these sentiments of manifest destiny most transparently.[20] It is dated May 24, 1898, and was occasioned by Ireland's assignment to mediate the Spanish conflict as both an official of the Church and a friend of the McKinley Administration.

For O'Connell, the Spanish–American War was being fought on two fronts, religious and secular. The United States was engaged in a war of liberation, lifting the yoke of foreign oppression from the islanders of Cuba and the Philippines, carrying out a mandate superior to international law, a mandate implicit in the nature of the country and its traditions. The American Church, in the person of John Ireland, was similarly engaged in a struggle to purify and redirect Roman Catholicism by infusing it with the vigor and values of that wing of the Church nourished in a climate of political liberalism. The letter, running to several pages at a high rhetorical pitch, develops these two propositions separately at first; midway, however, the parallel lines are abandoned and the elements merge: American Catholicism and national policy become one.

19. Henry S. Commager, *The American Mind: An Interpretation of American Thought and Character Since the 1880's* (New Haven, 1950), pp. 194–95. See also Dorothy Dohen, *Nationalism and American Catholicism* (New York, 1967); David O'Brien, "American Catholicism and the Diaspora," *Cross Currents* 16 (1966): 307–23; Thomas F. O'Dea, *American Catholic Dilemma* (New York, 1958); Joseph Fichter, "The Americanization of Catholicism," *Roman Catholicism and the American Way of Life,* Thomas T. McAvoy, ed. (Notre Dame, Ind., 1960), pp. 113–33; and Walter Ong, *American Catholic Crossroads* (New York, 1959) and *Frontiers in American Catholicism* (New York, 1957).

20. O'Connell to Ireland, May 24, 1898, Archives of the Archdiocese of St. Paul, Minn., reprinted in McAvoy, *Great Crisis,* pp. 206–10.

In the context of their friendship, Ireland's personal triumph is offered as the key to larger goals. Although "some are ready to sacrifice [him] and many would have laughed in joy to see [him] fall . . . [he] has put John Ireland to the front in America and Europe as no other American Bishop was ever put before." With his own eminence thus assured, the cultural revolution could proceed because Ireland represented a force that was "free and noble and open and true and humane [America]" against a civilization that is "old and vile and mean and rotten and cruel and false [Europe]." The lines were drawn, the issues were clear, so "on with the banner of Americanism which is the banner of God and humanity."

O'Connell welcomed the coming struggle as a purifying conflict of providential design, war being but one of Nature's means of purging the idle, the weak, and the decadent and revealing the "fittest." Out of this new order of reality would emerge a triumphant America, under the messianic inspiration of John Ireland. In rhapsodic language, O'Connell called to his friend: "Take the place God has destined for America and leave John Ireland's name imperishable among these achievements. You are the only man in America, lay or cleric, who can properly take in and give the right initiative to this design . . . . because for this were you born for this you came into the world."

O'Connell's tribute, which Ireland warmly acknowledged in return correspondence,[21] revealed a number of important attitudes: first among them was his blatantly chauvinistic interpretation of the international conflict. The overripe fruit of decadent civilization, he said, must give way before American vitality and virtue; the natural law of growth and decay—which sanctifies military conquest if necessary —requires this. Such a cause merely points to the manifest destiny of the American Republic, a destiny marked out by Divine Providence. In this highly emotional rhetoric, O'Connell invoked all the slogans of a debauched Americanism: jingoism, social Darwinism, adulation of war, the doctrine of inevitable progress. Voiced by an American Catholic prelate, these are remarkable ideas; but what is even more singular are sentiments which bespeak a kind of religious imperialism: The Church, in its international makeup, reflects all

21. Ireland to O'Connell, June 18, 1898, excerpts in John T. Farrell, "Archbishop Ireland and Manifest Destiny," *Catholic Historical Review* 33 (1947):300–301.

the same elements of youthful vitality and corrupt old age that are found in the secular world. The Church thus needs revivification—but only under the leadership of the American hierarchy.

This document needs no further explication; but its presence must, by the grossness of the sentiments expressed and the violence of the language, haunt these pages to the very end. And it is a ghost that defies all manner of ritual exorcism, be it theological or scholarly. In this study, the document serves to define the historical apex of the Americanist drive, a climax that is followed, as climaxes usually are, by a clear dénouement, the issuance of *Testem Benevolentiae* and subsequent American Catholic history.

In abbreviated form, therefore, this period of American Catholicism can be located in the larger context of Church history as follows: the Church in America found itself from the beginning of its American existence at a considerable disadvantage, owing to Enlightenment liberalism and the hostility of the Protestant majority. The Church grew from an isolated and rather fragile phenomenon in the first two hundred years of colonial and Republican history to one of considerable size and influence in the late nineteenth century. Along the way the institution took on certain native American characteristics and began to express a native idiom. But until the Civil War this direction was hesitant, tentative, and nearly always unstable. After the Civil War Church leaders initiated a deliberate campaign to link the Church with its secular environment—to make the apostolate more effective and to correct certain defects in the image of European Catholicism. This activity was most vigorously pursued during the years 1884–1900, as chronicled above; and it produced a countermeasure aimed at preserving intact the old-world character of Catholicism. This conflict progressed until 1899, when the Pope effectively curtailed all public exchange and political activity in the terms evolved during the preceding fifteen years. With that event, both parties to the question proclaimed a signal victory, and, in effect, quietly expired.

History, however, is society's genetic base; every least moment leaves its mark on that structure, and no mark is ever entirely expunged from the organism. The Americanist debate was a crucial experience for American Catholics. Its effects explain much of the shape and direction of twentieth century Catholicism. The social and ideological processes signified by this public debate, however, go forward at levels other than the political. The balance of this study will examine certain of those processes in order to paint a more intimate portrait of the Catholic subculture.

2 The Social Origins and Consequences of Catholic Literary Tradition

The struggle for cultural identity is conducted on a number of fronts and at several levels. For American Catholics, actual physical warfare was never necessary; but that fact in no way indicates the difficulties of forging a common religious identity out of a polyglot of nationalities and languages. Institutional policy was in the hands of the national hierarchy and Rome; doctrinal purity and an exacting discipline were rigorously maintained through the elaborate structure of the Church bureaucracy. The essential marks of Church membership thus being removed from the influences of time and place, there remained nonetheless a large area of community life reflective of the peculiar qualities of the American milieu. As we have seen, the overriding concern of Church leaders during the last quarter of the nineteenth century was to establish a viable national posture that would insure the loyalty of the faithful and reinforce an effective apostolate to the secular world. Community consciousness, however, is constituted of elements other than mandate and precept, doctrinal definitions, and statements of national policy. These other elements are the imaginative referents of a shared identity, a system of images, symbols, and myths by which a group encounters and understands its reality. To clearly apprehend the phenomenon of American Catholicism, one must consult some of the oblique documents of the imagination from which the American Catholic took the materials for a vital, functional self-concept; through them, the historian can hear something of what Lional Trilling calls the "buzz of implication" of a bygone era and understand more fully the impact of the Americanist controversy on the Catholic layman.

Among the records of a society are its artifacts, the things which are consciously fashioned to serve at least a partially spiritual purpose. In the case of American Catholicism, artifacts include a liturgy, forms of devotionalism, church art, architecture, and, not least, imaginative literature—the prose and poetry that has the interior as well as exterior markings of denominational identity. All of these materials offer a rich source of investigation for the social historian.

One class of artifacts in particular, however, claims a special significance, the theoretical basis for which will be indicated here and demonstrated throughout this study. The purpose is to examine the prose fiction of American Catholics during the final quarter of the nineteenth century as an institutional phenomenon, a publishing event, and a literary phenomenon. To prepare for that examination, the reader deserves an account of the supporting rationale—the author's theoretical assumptions, particularly with regard to the relations between art and society.

To begin with, an artifact combines in varying proportions the purely personal and the communal, the public and the private. This is true of the work of the most accomplished artist as well as of the more conventional workman. An artifact, considered as a cultural document, must be treated as an "event" in the sense that it is rooted in time and place. The tool, the building, the poem, are not completely meaningful in themselves; the act begins with the person of the fabricator and his environment and ends only with its impact on a community. The personal and impersonal mix is best understood, for analytical purposes, by the simple formula that the more gifted the artist and the more authentic his artistic vision, the less he is imprisoned in the ideology of his own culture. Basically this is an epistemological matter. It would be more properly articulated as a relationship between the artist and cultural reality: the artist functions prophetically in his milieu. He is *in* but not *of* the world of his inherited surroundings. Traditionally the artist has been regarded as more fully attuned to the present and the particular, the world of the concrete and ephemeral, than his contemporaries. But for all this, despite an interior commission to describe and interpret the world of his own time and place, the true artist is always an arm's length from that reality—sifting, selecting, critically controlling the flow of images according to a transcendent bias. To put this another way, no one is more contemporary than the artist; but also no one is more free of the ethnocentrism of his social environment. A Nathaniel Hawthorne is unthinkable outside the complex of values and history associated with America, New England, and Salem; but *The Scarlet Letter* is thematic quicksilver, infinitely various, impossible adequately to contain by the most thorough catalogue of that native ideology.

All of the foregoing suggests both the usefulness of art to the student of history and its limitations. There is a purely documentary value in art; one looks, with some reservation to be described later, to the novel, the drama, and painting of a period for a faithful rendering of the look, sound, and texture of life. But the greater value of art is much deeper, in a structure of thought, a set of attitudes, implicitly developed, that reveal not only the conventional *Weltanschauung* but also a criticism of these same values. The tools of such an analysis, of course, are by no means easy to achieve. As Erwin Panovsky describes the preparation needed for an iconographic study, the analyst must be not only intimately aware of the conventional historical records of the era, but also have a professional critic's understanding of the artistic genre. [1]

The corollary to the above assumption is that the less gifted the artist, the more he is controlled by the conventional attitudes of his society. However, just as no serious artist is ever entirely free of the culture in which he lives, so too no one is entirely dominated by his culture to the point that his thoughts and feelings are exactly one with society. In between these hypothetical extremes is a spectrum along which the various possibilities descriptive of the relations between the individual and society can be located abstractly.

Yet two more factors that should be cited are the conventions connected to an artistic tradition and the deliberate exploitation of these conventions for nonaesthetic purposes. Of the first, without fully explaining its operation, one can say at least that art has its own history, quite apart from the development of civilizations and institutions; or, perhaps better, that art is itself an institution with tradi-

1. Erwin Panovsky, "Iconography and Iconology," *Meaning in the Visual Arts* (Garden City, N.Y., 1955).

tions that are neither wholly separate from other institutions nor wholly explained by them. This is true of particular genres as well as motifs, of aesthetic theories as well as technical conventions: the sonnet and the theme of the quest, the Romantic theory of prosody and the interior monologue—all are conventions that are the heritage of every subsequent literary artist. What for one artist or one generation may be an innovation becames part of the accepted body of conventions for the next. While a given property may have profound implications for a particular society (e.g., Goethe's sorrowing Werther), most conventions are virtually incidental to the culture; together they form the techniques of the artist's craft within which he works. They are his language, a vocabularly that he fashions into statements as fresh or as hackneyed as his own skill and insight can make them.

The better artist renews, revivifies the tradition each time he successfully invokes it; the poorer artist merely repeats it. The historian who would learn from these artistic materials must know the tradition and the variations it makes available. For example, predominance of blonde heroines in the literature of a given generation of writers is not particularly meaningful if the convention has a precedent in previous generations. On the other hand, the very existence of a Catholic novel in the early nineteenth century is a matter of great significance.

Finally there is the matter of deliberate fabrication for nonartistic purposes, a phenomenon to which we are sensitive in an era of the industrial production of mass entertainment. But even in earlier ages such a phenomenon was not unknown; the hack is a perennial figure in the world of art. Without attributing complete cynicism to such a person, one can at least note that he works from a certain awareness of what has immediate currency, and he manipulates his materials to exploit that condition. Henry Nash Smith has described an early form of this market in mass fantasy, the assembly-line manufacture of the pulp Western over a century ago.[2] Hollywood's "B" movies and radio and television soap operas are more recent examples of the same process.

For the cultural historian, such manufactures are not valueless.

2. Henry Nash Smith, *Virgin Land* (Cambridge, Mass., 1950).

However, they must be understood for what they are—pure exploitation. Our new understanding of the ability of the dream merchants not only to satisfy but to create a market, makes it apparent that innovation and change are as likely to result from industrial and technological factors as from a simple competitive reach for a piece of the market. The entertainment industry, for all its competitiveness, requires a degree of rationalization in order to produce pre-tested elements which can then be put together in a variety of ways to suit an ever more standardized, if ever more whimsical, public. The well advertised variety of models of Detroit-manufactured automobiles is a good example of this control over mass taste in another field.

Thus far, this discussion has referred only to individual, commercially motivated fantasy merchants. A more common—and frequently more sinister—person is the writer-agent of an institution who tailors his materials to give metaphoric reinforcement to ideology. The American Church, as this study will show, rapidly realized the power of didactic art to catechize and discipline the faithful.

If human expectations are both a cause and an effect, if the popular artist is both creator and satisfier of the desires of a community of patrons, cultural inferences can be adopted only with great caution. One temptation, of course, is to consider popular art as some kind of latter-day folk art, a purely unselfconscious expression of the culture in the singular but impersonal voice of the artist, a communal liturgy as well as a community literature. This romanticized understanding of folk art is widely accepted, and in postliterate civilizations such attributions are apt to be assigned to the bestseller. In considering American Catholic fiction, however, different assumptions about the relations of literature and culture are necessary.

The first condition that must be acknowledged is that American Catholic fiction during the period of this study is almost completely without serious artistic merit. The religious motivations of the writers are not in question; their artistic objectives as well as their accomplishments are subliterary. Given the quality of such material, the historian is forced to adopt a formula for evaluation and interpretation that is at least partially quantitative. Frequently the meaning of a fictional element is determined largely by its numerical incidence. A theme, a characterization, a particular narrative strategy, a rhetoric, become important for their commonness to a large number of works rather than for their singularity. Obviously, the influence of the purely literary tradition of an era must be assessed before any inferences can be made about either the writer or his readers. Thus, for example, it is important to realize that an explicit appeal to versimilitude was characteristic of the English novel of the early nineteenth century before making a great deal of this feature in a particular group of novels. The vogue of the historical novel coincides with the period under discussion; the uses to which a Catholic novelist put this convention must therefore be measured against the secular or non-Catholic novels of the same period.

It is not entirely accurate even to describe Catholic novels according to canons of popularity, for it is doubtful that many of them would have found a readership of any size without the official *imprimatur* and the urgings of an institutional publishing apparatus. A good Catholic was expected to read and promote Catholic literature. Thus one does not ordinarily look to this literature for profound and highly personal insights into the character of the American religious situation. What one can hope for is an institutional view, a view that is as much the product of the public organization as it is of the artist's private self.

One could ask at this point what advantage there is in studying such materials instead of other, more conventional, documents. If the American Catholic novel of the late nineteenth century is so much a product of the institution, if individual works are indistinguishable, why not use direct and expository materials for a cultural analysis: statements of the hierarchy and diocesan councils, editorial content of Catholic newspapers and magazines, Catholic scholarship on cultural subjects as well as theological? The answer is simply stated, not so simply demonstrated. It is true that most of the authors of the period wrote very much as though they were quasi-official spokesmen for the Church. The critical reviews in leading Catholic journals make this abundantly clear.

The advantage of studying the fiction, however, is at least twofold. For one thing, this material was bought and read by the mass of American Catholics, which was certainly not true of the official documents and records of the Church, however widespread their promulgation. Because of their large and varied readership the novels give access to the literary experiences of the ordinary layman in a way that few other records do. More important, fiction imposes certain formal necessities on the writer, and these necessities combine to make available revelations not found in any expository equivalent. Discounting that element of a novel governed by convention and those parts explainable by the explicitly didactic purposes of the novel, what remains is at least partly the result of selection—conscious or unconscious. In other words, there is no perfect rendering of a philosophical or theological point of view into metaphor; the transformation is always slightly openended. Character, incident, setting, and above all language may be dictated by habits connected with the genre, as well as by their convenience for embodying a moral or theological point; but they are not entirely controllable. The metaphoric, which refers to the entire range of mimetic elements in imaginative literature, is volatile; it is laden with emotional as well as rational content. Taken together, these elements reveal, in ways which the author is never entirely aware of himself, attitudes, values, biases that go considerably beyond the abstracted and rationally developed elements of a formally articulated confession of faith. These elements, however, cannot be labeled and assessed with anything like the precision of a doctrinal analysis. It will be necessary, therefore, to regularly check the hypotheses emerging from literary studies against the evidence of nonliterary sources.

Given these assumptions about the relation between literature and culture, one can proceed to consider more directly the phenomenon of American Catholic literature (particularly the foundations of that literature) insofar as this is important to an understanding of what occurred in Catholic fiction at the end of the nineteenth century. The immediate problem is the presence of a specifically Catholic literary tradition and the necessity to assess that tradition. Traditions, of course, are not inert historical constants; they have a life and character that grows and changes according to a myriad of circumstances and influences. The American Catholic literary tradition is shaped by a number of important factors; the most important are the European heritage imported by Catholic immigrants, the development of a publishing and distribution apparatus, the growth of a body of critical and theoretical statements defining Catholic literature, and the novels themselves. To be sure, no one of these determinants operated in isolation: publishing patterns followed critical acceptance; rare popular successes forced an adjustment of norms; and European Catholicism was not entirely immune to influence from American developments. These factors will be dealt with separately, however, for the sake of clarity, beginning with an account of the place of prose fiction in the literary attitudes of European and American Catholics at the beginning of the nineteenth century.

The nineteenth century Church historian John Gilmary Shea described the critical reception Catholics accorded the earliest popular Catholic novel, *Father Rowland* (1829), whose author, Charles Constantine Pise, was a priest, poet, editor, and chaplain to the United States Senate. "Like many good works," Shea wrote, "this work at first found many assailants and borne down by the fierce criticism of Catholic reviewers the publisher of these popular Catholic works was compelled to stop the publication." He concludes the passage in a manner indicative of fifty years of changing attitudes toward the novel: "All, however, now admit the necessity of a literature of this kind, of which Dr. Pise must be considered the founder." [3]

Shea's observation supplies us with at least a general notion of the reception given the novel by American Catholics, official and popular. The hostility toward Pise was not, however, particularly remarkable, nor, for that matter, a reaction peculiar to the Catholic minority. Historians of the novel in America agree that the art form continued to be held in disrepute at least throughout the first half of the century. The reasons for this are various. According to one survey of attitudes of late eighteenth-century America, the novel struck root at a time when the intellectual establishment of America was thoroughly enamoured of the Scottish philosophy of commonsense realism, a philosophy so given to an objective, wholly historical, and nonimaginative view of reality, as to be inherently opposed to works of the imagination. [4] The American tradition that supported this philosophy

3. John Gilmary Shea, *History of the Catholic Church in the United States,* 4 vols. (New York, 1886–1892), 3:407–08.
4. Kenneth J. Meyer, "Social Class and Family Structure: Attitudes Revealed by the Earliest American Novels, 1789–1825" (Ph.D. diss., University of Minnesota, 1965), pp. 104–10.

clearly runs through puritanism and deism, but its most vehement expression came at about the turn of the nineteenth century. Novels continued to be read in America and to be written by Americans, but not without some concession to the prevailing bias, primarily modification of the art form itself: by making it more "realistic," by exaggerating the didactic purpose of the fable, and most effectively, by insisting that the evils associated with the genre were in reality confined to works of foreign authorship, the novel gained acceptance. Advocates of the novel were thus able to convert the attack into an endorsement of American fiction, the reading of which was seen as a moral and patriotic act.[5]

This antipathy, whatever its sources, and whatever its effects on the development of American fiction, is here a "given," one that I will not seek to demonstrate. Every social or ideological group reflected it, some certainly more than others. This differentiation is especially notable among religious groupings: antifiction sentiment appeared strongest among evangelical Protestants to whom reading novels was akin to other dangerous forms of idleness such as drinking and dancing; the more tolerant Protestant response was found in denominations closest to Anglicanism, one of the first groups to recognize the polemical uses of prose fiction.[6]

Among Catholics, however, a still deeper and more fundamental factor was at work to color their response. European Catholic culture had developed certain literary traditions which were inimical to the kind of prose we call the novel. An antipathy existed between the novel and Post-Reformation Catholic culture, and this antipathy had to be removed or sublimated before there could be a Catholic novel or a significant Catholic readership. To explain why this is so, however briefly, requires a foray into literary sociology. The elimination of this antipathy is an indirect index of Catholic Americanization, or at least of the growing influence of certain middle-class values.

If it is accurate to say that social profiles issue from the religious persuasion of a group, then it seems equally true that social and

5. James Hart, *The Popular Book: A History of America's Literary Taste* (New York, 1950), p. 54.

6. See Herbert Brown, *The Sentimental Novel in America, 1789–1860* (Durham, N.C., 1940); Kathleen Tillotson, *Novels of the Eighteen-Forties* (Oxford, 1954) describes the proliferation of religious novels.

religious experience affects the development of literary traditions.[7] Ian Watt declares the novel form to be the child of the middle class, a product of the break-up of the medieval order. His observation is the result of an analysis of both the ideology and formal innovations to be found in the early novels and of the social environment in which they flourished. Briefly, Watt claims that the novel began as a celebration of a new ideal and a new dramatic geography. Earlier forms of literature in Western Europe were regarded unselfconsciously as ritual reenactments of traditional cultural myths—timeless materials given force and shape by the imaginative power of the individual artist. Like a religious service, the epic and the drama provided the audience with a reassuring explication of the mysteries of reality in forms which were utterly familiar, no matter how moving the enactment. The literary experience of the time might be termed, variously, initiation or exorcism: initiation into community experience; exorcism of fear of the unfamiliar. The purgative function of literature was achieved by the communal nature of the event, as well as the familiarity of the material. Watt names this literary theory "classical," although it could well describe most of Western literature before the age of the novel.[8]

In contrast, the novel of the eighteenth century middle class revealed a new point of view and a different set of materials. The first was characterized by the primacy of the individual consciousness, newly released from the constraints of society and its traditions, facing life autonomously and carving out terms for existence outside the institutional apparatus of conventional society.[9] Private and subjective apprehensions of reality took precedence over the conventional. Where classical literature had depicted the universality of significant human events and the unchanging character of truth, the novelist emphasized the uniqueness of these events. The *materials* of the novel reflected a similar departure from tradition: plot elements found a higher degree of particularity, of "realism," of fidelity to the literal transcript of time and place. In addition, in language, classical

---

7. For a narrow but provocative example of recent scholarship on socio-religious factors, see Gerhard Lenski, *The Religious Factor* (Garden City, N.Y., 1961).

8. Ian Watt, *The Rise of the Novel: Studies in Defoe, Richardson and Fielding* (London, 1957).

9. The name of the new genre itself suggests this contrast with the past.

literature was abstract and conventional, its norms based on rhetoric and decorum; by contrast, the novel found a value in linguistic idiosyncrasy.[10]

Perhaps the most singular difference between the two traditions is the concept of time. Classical literature is ahistorical: writers of that tradition said, in effect, that there is nothing new under the sun. Change, innovation, process—these are but chimeras; stripped of the impact of their immediate presence, they yield up a character of sameness, the common patterns of timeless human experience. Like the seasons, life is a changeless cycle, a pendulum movement that brings each foray into the apparent unknown back to its starting place. But, as Leslie Fiedler says, the "Richardsonian novel of contemporary life had discovered the present for fiction, made time a medium in which characters moved." [11] Time in the novel was not only explicit, it was functional in a new way. The past became a causal force in the action of the plot, explaining events in the present, whereas the older literature had relied on coincidence.[12]

The progenitor of this new literature was Defoe's *Robinson Crusoe,* which employed a plot device placing the drama of self on a deserted island. As an expression of the ideology of the new middle class, Defoe's novel is an almost perfect vehicle, dramatizing as it does the insularity of life cut off from all normal human ties and conventions and the effort to fabricate an existence out of resources drawn from the individual alone.[13]

While traditionalist critics of the novel did not always discriminate among these various innovations or see them as manifestations of a single thrust, they consistently showed an uneasiness about them. But the element that worked most profoundly and perhaps most consciously to alienate the Catholic mind from the emerging ideology was secularization. Watt's analysis takes the now familiar translation of Puritan religious fervor into mundane morality one step further. Just as economic and social progress resulting from the Puritan discipline undermined the otherworldly ideals of the sect, so too the realism and individualism on which the novel was based inevitably

---

10. Watt, *Rise of the Novel,* pp. 13, 21–27, 28–30.
11. Leslie A. Fiedler, *Love and Death in the American Novel* (rev. ed., New York, 1966), p. 136.
12. Watt, *Rise of the Novel,* p. 22.
13. *Ibid.,* p. 62.

caused a degree of secularization. Generalizing broadly, Watt writes. "the novel requires a world view which is centered on the social relationships between individual persons; and this involves secularization as well as individualism, because until the end of the seventeenth century the individual was not conceived as wholly autonomous, but as an element in a picture which depended on divine institutions such as Church and Kingship for its secular patterns." [14]

Without attempting to certify these claims for the novel, claims with which in general I agree, one might mention one manifestation of this unhappy relationship between the novel and Catholicism, the Catholic *Index Librorum*. Harold Watson, a student of French literature, in a study of lists of proscribed books, concluded that the Vatican censors have always had a special antipathy for the novel: "The novel has been king of Western literature for well over a century, but Rome still rejects it as a legitimate art form." [15]

If Watt's analysis is correct and if the literary traditions congenial to European Catholicism were hostile to the development of the novel, then it is a matter of some importance to show how and to what extent the novel was received by American Catholics. Acceptance, of whatever degree, would be one index of the Americanization process. The development of an attitude toward the novel, the beginnings of a Catholic theory of the novel, and the early organization of machinery for publishing and distributing Catholic novels are the essential factors in that index.

The condition of Catholic literary criticism in early nineteenth century America was chaotic, and necessarily so. The principal practitioners—newspaper and magazine editors were mostly untrained for such activity and often poorly educated in even a general way. Episcopal reins were loose, often to the point that editors enjoyed virtual independence from bishops on issues as uncertain as imaginative literature.[16] Reading through the review columns of these early periodicals, one can find no common principle of evaluation; what was shared was a general lack of sophistication and a tendency to use simple-minded formulae to reckon value. Before the founding of the *Catholic World* by Issac Hecker in 1866, only one person appears to

14. *Ibid.*, p. 84.
15. Harold M. Watson, "French Authors and Roman Indexers," *America*, 114 (1966):83.
16. Robert C. Healey, *Catholic Book Chronicle* (New York, 1951), p. 31.

have seriously considered the need for a literary theory for the Catholic minority in America—the convert Orestes Augustus Brownson.

Brownson, like Isaac Hecker, was one of the central personalities of nineteenth century Catholicism. His zeal to fight solitary battles on several fronts at once may have resulted in a certain dilution of intellectual substance in his work.[17] Nonetheless, for an articulate contemporary opinion on almost any aspect of American culture, Brownson is a reliable resource. Judging from the volume of material he produced on the subject, literature was a serious issue for the midcentury Catholic. His review essays are at once a lengthy checklist of pre–Civil War fiction, a chronicle of changing personal taste, and most important, a serious and honest attempt to formulate a philosophical rationale for the Catholic novelist.

At one point in life Brownson declared flatly: "We set our face against all novels."[18] The exasperation in this remark, though characteristic of one desperately committed to rational discourse, was only momentary. In more amiable moments he approved novels, especially religious ones, and labored to describe their nature and purpose. Brownson's writings dramatize the chronic dilemma of the Christian critic—his uncertainty about the relations between nature and the supernatural. Scholastic theology teaches that the redemptive act of Christ achieved a reconciliation of these two orders of being, that the doctrine of grace is an affirmation of nature—not its repudiation. Sanctification is a process that works through nature. Historically this ontology has been attacked by a number of heresies, all in some degree Gnostic and all growing out of a need to emphasize discontinuity in being, to make the life of the spirit a thing apart from and transcendent to nature. Christian aesthetics faces the same difficulty as theology: how does one dramatize the process of salvation without abandoning the order of nature altogether?

Brownson, characteristically, met the difficulty head on. At one point he wrote that since nature and grace are unalterably opposed, to represent the natural at all is to war with the spiritual: "All that is profane, or not religious, is hurtful in a greater or less degree; and none is religious, save in so far as it embodies the supernatural life

17. See Arthur M. Schlesinger, Jr., *Orestes A. Brownson: A Pilgrim's Progress* (Boston, 1939).
18. Orestes A. Brownson, "Women's Novels," *The Works of Orestes A. Brownson* (hereafter *Works*), ed. Henry F. Brownson, 20 vols. (Detroit, 1882–1898), 19:599.

of religion, as the principle of the interest it excites or of the gratifica-
tion it affords." He specifically enjoined the religious novelist not "to
paint actual life or life as we actually find it, but to idealize, and raise
it, as far as possible, to the Christian standard." [19] Doubtless this
exhortation would have been applauded by the great majority of
Brownson's contemporaries, but the restraints it would place on
novelists are all too obvious. Moreover, as a principle of composition,
such idealization of life invited the sentimentality of which Brownson elsewhere complained.

Brownson was vulnerable then to charges of inconsistency, but he
was also a very astute critic of most of the types of fiction that called
themselves religious. He was weary of polemic disguised as fiction,
books that "appear to be written on the principle, that they must be
filled with arguments for the Church, or have a good Catholic moral
tacked on to the end, or they will not be recognized as Catholic." [20]
This artificial combination of fiction and theology and an even more
questionable combination of religion and sentiment, were Brownson's
two principal hates; by temperament he was disposed to dislike the
latter more. Religion and romance caused the degradation of the
former, according to Brownson: "We would . . . recommend the
discontinuance of such religious novels as seek to entice, through
interests which center in love, to the meditations of what is serious,
pious, and holy." The favorite gambit of contemporary writers of
fiction, religious or secular, was to make the moral structure of the
novel a matter of sexual difference; Brownson said that his results
from a convention that is the very "curse of the age," betraying the
writers lack of virility, rather than his freedom from barbarism. "It
is an age of women worship," he wrote; "women are angels; men are
demons. . . . All the virtues are feminine and all the vices masculine."
The same moral division led to the convention of "employing beautiful and fascinating young women for the conversion of sentimental
young men." Given these developments, the religious novel becomes
merely a "vehicle of sentimentalism." [21]

19. Brownson, "Novel Writing and Novel Reading," in ibid., p. 565; idem, "Review,"
ibid., p. 430.
20. Brownson, quoted in C. E. McGuire, ed., Catholic Builders of a Nation, 5 vols.
(Boston, 1923), 2:190.
21. Brownson, "Religious Novels," Works, 19:150, 154; idem, "Literature, Love and
Marriage," ibid., p. 497.

Although this negative critique permeates Brownson's reviews and accurately sums up what he thought of existing religious fiction, he also frequently described what the Catholic novel should be, particularly in America. Both as critic and as standard-bearer his ideas are especially significant because they point up an important difference between himself and Isaac Hecker and between the two quarters of the nineteenth century that each dominated. Brownson was convinced that using the novel as an evangelical tool was a dangerous expedient, dangerous not for the novel but for the Faith. Using the novel as an agent of conversion, he said, makes the writer "adopt too low a tone, and seem to be afraid to present the Church in all her imperial dignity and glory, as claiming always to be all or nothing." In opposition to the liberal spirit characteristic of his day, Brownson wanted the Catholic author to accentuate the exclusiveness of the Church, in fact to write for Catholics alone and "make them supremely conscious of their own spiritual community." [22] Hecker, as later pages will show, had no such scruples about either the frankly didactic or sentimental, so long as the Faith was served.

The American Catholic writer of fiction received almost no support from Brownson. He believed that because American culture was still Protestant, literature professedly Catholic had to show much of the Protestant element even though "no explicit statement in a particular novel may be shown to be heterodox." Because of this overpowering predominance of the Protestant spirit, he wrote, "we confess that any direct efforts to call forth a domestic literature, a popular literature we mean, strike us as premature, and not at all desirable." Until Catholicism has matured in America, "other nations will supply us with books, and better books than we can write for ourselves." [23]

Brownson thus systematically repudiated the elements most commonly found in the fiction, religious or secular, of his time: sentimentality, didacticism, and any combination of the two that made conversion the consequence of sentimental attraction. He made no concession to popular taste, whatever its propaganda benefits. Recognizing that the artist must draw on his own cultural environment for materials, Brownson said that the Catholic writer of novels would be forced—however strong his intellectual resistance to Protestant cul-

22. Brownson, "Recent Publications," ibid., pp. 164, 167–69.
23. Brownson, "Review," ibid., pp. 134, 137.

ture might be—to reflect, largely by unconscious processes, the underlying attitudes of that culture. Brownson's caution was not misplaced. Another generation of American Catholics would embrace the novel, not only to describe the Faith but also to demonstrate the modernity and even Americanism of Catholics, with what effects we shall see.

3   From Theory to Practice: Pre-Civil War Fictional Conventions

The grist for Brownson's critical mill was a small and heterogeneous body of novels of foreign and American authorship. It seems fairly obvious, however, that without the establishment of a specifically Catholic publishing industry and the conditions under which it was established, there would have been even fewer. Although Matthew Carey, one of America's first and most successful publishers, had proposed the establishment of a Church-sponsored publishing house as early as 1791, and although such proposals were repeated throughout the nineteenth century, the Catholic hierarchy consistently refused to support such ventures.[1] Despite these rebuffs, Carey himself began to promote what might be called a selfconsciously Catholic reading public early in the century; after his initial success, other privately sponsored Catholic publishing houses proliferated. By 1850 over fifty Catholic publishing firms were operating in the United States.[2]

The place of fiction in this publishing scheme is not easy to ascertain: checklists are for the most part incomplete, and exact classifications by literary genre difficult to determine. Oscar Wegelin mentions, for example, that Caleb Bingham published Chateaubriand's *Atala*—that curious blend of French Romanticism and Catholic pastoralism—in

1. Matthew Carey, circular addressed to the First Synod of the United States, Baltimore, Nov. 7, 1791, *American Catholic Historical Researches* 16 (1899): 135–36.
2. Sister Mary S. Cavanaugh, "Catholic Book Publishing in the United States, 1784–1850" (masters thesis, University of Illinois, 1937), p. 30.

this country in 1802.[3] Of more orthodox Catholic fiction, however, except for the few novels to be discussed below, we can accept Sister Mary Cavanaugh's conclusion that the staple publications of the Catholic press were the Bible, catechisms, missals, devotional books, histories and biographies, philosophical and theological works, poetry, and hymns. Only toward the middle of the century, she says, did fiction for children and adults appear. One publisher, Edward Dunnigan of New York, was responsible for most of the earliest novels and short stories. He issued fewer reprints and more American originals than any other house.[4] Dunnigan's Home Series included a number of novels during the 1840s; most of the authors remained anonymous (e.g., *Father Felix, a Tale,* 1846, by the author of *Nora Carmody;* and *Victorine, A Tale from Real Life,* 1844).

Perhaps more than any other media, the newspaper launched the novel among Catholic readers. Patrick Donahoe, who founded the Boston *Pilot* in 1836, helped several Catholic writers to an audience, primarily by printing a good deal of fiction in his newspaper. A marital combination seems to have exerted an important influence on the industry generally through the firm of Dennis and James Sadlier; founded in 1832, the house was funded for several years from the profits of Mrs. James Sadlier's novels.[5]

By 1850 the congenital suspicion of the novel, a general attitude of reluctance if not outright hostility, had gradually given way before the insistent demands of an ever-enlarging and demanding reading public. The new market was created partly by developments within American society. It was also affected by certain key events abroad.

Two publishing events proved of immense importance to English-speaking Catholics and especially those interested in a respectable pedigree for the novel: the publication of novels by English prelates John Henry Newman and Nicholas Wiseman. The circumstances leading to these two works were greatly different, and the novels themselves vary considerably in merit and topicality. Their importance for the American Catholic, however, was nearly identical; they conferred a virtual *imprimatur* on Catholic novelistic ventures.

Next to the pope himself, no two men of American acquaintance

3. Oscar Wegelin, *Early American Fiction, 1774–1830* (New York, 1929), p. 11.
4. Cavanaugh, "Catholic Book Publishing," pp. 95–96, 123.
5. Madeleine B. Stern, *Imprints on History* (Bloomington, Ind., 1956), p. 112.

commanded quite the same respect as these two English princes of the Church. They expressed different but equally admirable modes of response to life in a religiously indifferent if not hostile environment. Newman attracted perhaps the greatest sympathy from his coreligionists, if only because he seemed the more courageous. Moreover, his conversion offered living proof of the intellectual claims of the Church, an event of singular importance in an age characterized by the retreat of orthodoxy from intellectualism. A conversion from among the Oxford leaders, the very cream of England's academia, served to quiet charges of intellectual obsolescence made against the Church. And Newman, like Brownson, in effect had converted himself, or as he said: "I was not converted by Roman Catholicism; I was converted by Oxford." [6]

As one might expect, Newman had a genuine horror of the sentimental novel as well as "all books in which the glory and beauty of Christian behavior is not related to the actual roughness of the Christion life." Sentimentality in fiction he likened to pietism in religion —baseless emotion, feeling that fed on itself.[7] At the same time he decried the "cruel realism" of Jane Austen's portraits of life, a cruelty he blamed on her lack of a "dream of the high Catholic ethos." True to his Dissenter background, he tended to look on books in a "sternly utilitarian" manner, with the "moralist's sense of what is useful." [8] There is nothing very surprising in all this; what is singular, at least on the surface, is the fact that Newman turned to the novel as a means of self-expression. A partial explanation for this phenomenon is provided by his milieu; Newman was drawing on a convention that the Oxonians and their antagonists had firmly established, i.e., using the novel for polemical purposes.[9]

Newman wrote two novels: the earliest, *Loss and Gain* (1848), has a contemporary setting; the latter, *Callista* (1856), is a dramatization of life in the Early Church. The latter novel won greater success in America and for that reason deserves to be briefly discussed.

Callista is a story of conversion and martyrdom during the earliest

6. Quoted in Josef L. Altholz, *The Liberal Catholic Movement in England: "The Rambler" and Its Contributors, 1848–1864* (London, 1962), pp. 3–4.

7. Quoted in Sean O'Faolain, *Newman's Way* (London, 1952), pp. 155–56.

8. Ibid., p. 117.

9. See Joseph Ellis Baker, *The Novel and the Oxford Movement,* Princeton Studies in English, no. 8 (Princeton, 1932).

years of Christianity. Newman's choice of time and locale is not accidental, for the concern to rediscover the ancient roots of Christianity was the most important basis for the Oxford critique of contemporary Anglicanism. The heroine, Callista, is a Greek, beautiful, witty, and urbane. Weary of the pale intellectualism of the neo-Platonic philosophies then in vogue, Callista is repelled nonetheless by what she regards as the passivity of Christianity. Her conversion comes about through contact with a saintly Christian bishop and reading of the Scriptures. Circumstances require that the process of assent be greatly compressed, but Callista manages wholesale inversions of conventional wisdom in convincing fashion. Although there is a good deal of sophisticated philosophical debate, the thematic burden of the novel seems to rest on a simple contrast between arrogant intellectualism and acquiescence. These polar positions are also rendered symbolically, primarily in the opposition of city to farm. The pastoral theme implicit in traditional Christianity is not so much argued as assumed. The hero, Aegelius, tends a vineyard; and although his faith is weakened by lack of instruction and priestly ministrations, yet the spirit survives and is nourished by the felicitous conditions of his rural environment. His twin brother, on the other hand, grows up in the city, loses his faith, and develops a skeptical regard for life as he becomes correspondingly morally corrupt. The conflict of intellectualism and anti-intellectualism is very neatly resolved by the development of an affection between Aegelius and Callista. Rationalism is thus properly chastened, while Christianity is shown to be intellectually respectable.

Callista enjoyed great popularity in America all through the nineteenth century, and American Catholic *litterati* frequently invoked *Callista* as a model for the developing native literature.[10] The appeal of Newman's novel for American Catholics is only partly accounted for by the author's ecclesiastical eminence and the scholarly quality his name conferred on the Catholic cause. Of even greater significance, I think, was his choice of materials. Catholics in America and England, unlike their continental brethren, faced a situation in many ways similar to that of sixteenth century Protestant reformers. They were a religious minority, living in an environment religiously and culturally hostile; and they were engaged in the very difficult

10. Maurice F. Egan, *Confessions of a Book Lover* (New York, 1922), p. 28.

problem of retaining spiritual integrity while influencing the secular world toward a condition of perfection. This is not to suggest that the Catholic Church in America became a perfectionist sect like the Anabaptists or the Quakers. But from their experience certain patterns of thought and behavior developed for which the nearest historical parallels are the dissenting Protestant sects of the sixteenth century. The parallel can be discovered not only in the theological critique of orthodoxy mounted by the dissenters, a critique based on an interpretation of the Primitive Church, but more importantly in the emotional identification with early (pre-establishment) Christianity. The Oxford Movement supplied the intellectual thrust for the critique; a renewed interest in the lives of the early Christians, often in the form of historical fiction, provided the imaginative referents. *Callista* reflected this tendency and reinforced it.

Of similar importance was Cardinal Wiseman's calculated adventure into the arena of fiction, *Fabiola*. Like Newman's, Wiseman's career interested American Catholics. Presiding over the English Catholic Renaissance as its chief engineer, Wiseman demonstrated an effective administrative response to the widespread distrust of the Church.[11]

Fabiola was written in 1854, according to the author's preface to answer his own frequent pleas for a fiction based on Catholic history. The title character is the pagan daughter of a Roman noble, learned and beautiful. Under the influence of her friend Agnes (St. Agnes), Fabiola tests Epicurus and Lucretius against St. Paul and Christ. The result is her conversion. The drama of the novel derives from the Diocletian persecution of Christians, and most of the emotional effort is expended on the celebration of martyrdom.

Of special significance is Wiseman's treatment of the church–state issue. The Christian community in third-century Rome was nothing so much as a secret society. It met in underground compartments, members were identified by a system of occult signs, worship was conducted by mysterious rituals, and the society was passionately committed to revolutionary social goals. This aspect of Christianity— suggesting a conspiracy against the state—fuels the sense of outrage of the secular spokesmen in the novel. The frequency and intensity of the anti-Christian violence increase proportionate to the paranoia

11. See Altholz, *Liberal Catholic Movement,* especially chap. 1.

of officialdom. Sebastian (St. Sebastian), a centurion (later a martyr), not only indicates the success of Christian infiltration into positions of civic import; it is also his duty to argue the absence of a Christian threat. Throughout the novel, the elements of the debate remain the same: secular officials cannot conceive of a religious movement not directly subversive of the good of Rome. Sebastian insists, however, that the conflict is imaginary, that the Christian is by virtue of his faith a more conscientious worker and a more loyal citizen than the pagan. All the Christian asks is freedom of worship; his duty to the state is but reinforced by Christianity since that duty is a divine command. Sebastian dies after prophesying the coming of the Christian establishment, that intimate church-state alliance subversive of the legitimate goals of both powers. The author appears to be unaware of the irony, an inconsistency generally characteristic of nineteenth century American Catholics who, on the one hand, shouted their devotion to the republic and, on the other, looked to the eventual establishment of a state church.

Fabiola has a long publishing history. P. J. Kenedy and Sons first introduced the novel in America in 1854, the year it was published in England; the same company still had an edition out as late as 1930. Testimonies to its polemical power and literary excellence can be discovered throughout the half century. Maurice Francis Egan, the high priest of American Catholic literature, called it "a very great book."[12] Perhaps the strongest tribute to the novel was the publication in 1890 of a sequel, *Fabiola's Sisters* by E. L. Clarke.

Wiseman and Newman gave respectability to Catholic fiction at a critical period. But their influence went beyond endorsement. The subjects of their books, particularly their use of early Church history, their handling of sensitive contemporary issues such as the relationship between Church and state, and Christian intellectualism worked a deep influence on their readers. Their works also demonstrate one feature of Catholicism peculiarly suited to the early novel. Almost universally the central conflict of these novels grew out of a love relationship. But for all the power of sexuality in the novels, writers found it almost impossible to make a mature sexual relationship

12. Egan, *Confessions,* p. 12; see also the remark of Lawrence Kehoe, Catholic book publisher, who in 1886 said that *Fabiola* was having "a greater run than almost any other book." Interview in London *Register* (June 12, 1886) reprinted in *Publishers' Weekly* 30 (1886):37.

compatible with the idealized conception of their heroines. Various evasions were practiced: usually the heroine was killed off in a spiritually charged last chapter, or the girl was allowed to take a vow that precluded marriage. A powerful amount of sexuality was often generated during the course of the tale, a force subsequently translated into a religious or at least sacrificial (and non-sexual) commitment. Such a translation (in psychological terms, "sublimation") had the effect of legitimizing or transcendentalizing a "gross" human urge. And the Catholic novelist had two very well known ideals of Catholic behavior to draw on to effect a similar result: celibacy and the cloistered life. Wiseman's novel extols virginity and the early sisterhoods; and although his heroine does not take formal religious vows, she does live a celibate life. In Newman's novel, Callista is martyred, and the man who loves her becomes a priest. Later novelists drew on this convenient dénouement rather frequently.

Turning to the earliest American Catholic fiction, one would hope to find, of course, a literature definable by theme and treatment as the Americanist period. This is not so simply discovered, however, and for rather obvious reasons. In the absence of a tradition, with a small literate readership, and in the face of hostility from the leaders of the Catholic community, the novel could hardly be said to have a secure existence, let alone a self-conscious rationale developed from past experience in writing. Beginning with Father Pise's early novels, through the works of "lady" practitioners like Mrs. Mary Ann Sadlier and Mrs. Anna Dorsey, one can point to slight literary accomplishment. For the most part these novels were modest moral tales or thinly disguised autobiographies of conversion—convent literature that only incidentally betrayed American authorship. Maurice Francis Egan illustrated the sentiment of much of this fiction by quoting from a biography of St. Rose of Lima given him when he was quite young: "So pure was the little Saint, even in her infancy, that when her uncle, who was her godfather, kissed her after her baptism, a rosy glow, a real blush of shame, overspread her countenance." [13] This early period generated no geniuses, no novelists who in some half-conscious way created an imaginative synthesis of American Catholic thought. But there were glimmerings of what was to come, and there were figures who stand out as precursors.

13. Egan, *Confessions*, p. 11.

The father of the American Catholic novel is Pise.[14] His first novel, *Father Rowland*, was written in 1829, a calculated response to an anti-Catholic novel then making the rounds called *Father Clement*.[15] Although quite explicitly written for polemical purposes, *Father Rowland* nevertheless betrays an awareness of the conventions of polite fiction: eyes are induced to tear—discreetly or in torrents—at least once per page at provocations as slight as a line of poetry and as powerful as a well engineered religious tableau. But the most interesting quality of the novel is the image it conveys of Catholicism, intended apparently for non-Catholic readers.

Father Rowland is the story of the conversion of three female members of an aristocratic Virginia family, the Wolburns. The agent for their conversion is a Jesuit priest, Father Rowland. Most of the novel is given over to catechism sessions during which Rowland answers what are presumably the most important objections to Catholicism: doctrines concerning the transubstantiation, confession, the supremacy of the Church's interpretation of the Bible, and surprisingly, the doctrine of the exclusiveness of salvation. Of the latter, Father Rowland offers a most liberal explanation and magnanimously exempts from damnation all but the deliberately wrongheaded! Even more important concessions to the non-Catholic reader are made by suggestion and indirection. For example, General Wolburn, a genial Deist, encourages the pursuit of truth by his wife and daughters but persists in his own easy beliefs. The author accords the general the utmost deference and at one point suggests that as he had spent his energies in the Revolutionary War—a cause not greatly different from holy religion—he might hopefully look forward to a saintly crown. The linking of Roman Catholicism with republicanism is not exhausted in this characterization; it is also suggested that the Protestant minister, because of close English ties, was moved to side with the rebellion only because of expedience.

With the general's convictions thus protected, Pise goes on to depict

14. The claim is made that the first novel written by an American was the work of a Catholic, Thomas Atwood Digges. Digges, a Marylander and patriot whose work was honored by Washington and Jefferson, is said to have written *The Adventures of Alonzo,* a partly autobiographical account of the Revolutionary War as it was debated in Europe (London, 1775). This discovery is attributed to Robert H. Elias of the University of Pennsylvania in a letter to the editor, signed T.F.M., *America* 65(1941):718. Wegelin, *Early American Fiction,* p. 5, lists the book as having an anonymous author.

15. Charles Constantine Pise, "Foreword," *Father Rowland,* (New York, 1870), p. iv.

a religion that is strongly aristocratic and feminine. The badge of authenticity argued by the priest consists of the four marks of the True Church; but the most dramatically effective credentials are courtliness, learning, and breeding. Father Rowland's manners come to be quite as persuasive an index of the true ministry as his holiness. When the question of the "lower classes" is brought up, the reader is assured that Catholic servants are more reliable and industrious than others; a Negro servant of the Wolburn's submits, on his deathbed, to a quiz to demonstrate the understanding his class has of the Faith.

What seems to count most among the sentimental ladies of the novel are three or four artful tableaus that exhibit the picturesqueness of Catholicism: the servant's deathbed affirmations; a scene at a local convent when the sacrament is suddenly exposed and all drop to their knees while a choir of angelic nuns spontaneously intones a chant; and the Mass itself. Father Rowland is a parody of the kind Evelyn Waugh would have mercilessly satirized in our generation; but for Pise he is obviously the ideal bearer of good news. The fact that his mission appears to be exclusively to women and the poor suggests that Pise chose to make his appeal on the most acceptable—and conventional—grounds.

Two other male novelists, who are of interest beyond the parochial limits of American Catholicism, and who made serious attempts to dramatize the spiritual and cultural possibilities of Catholicism in America, are Jedediah Vincent Huntington and Orestes Brownson. The former was primarily a novelist, the latter, of course, a novelist only incidentally. Both were converts, both were intellectually sophisticated, but in their approachs to the writing of fiction they were quite different. Of special interest to this study is the fact that both Huntington and Brownson wrote novels before and after conversion to Catholicism; the revelations available depend a great deal on a before-and-after comparison.

Jedediah Vincent Huntington (1815–1862) is now an obscure figure in American literary history, but a century ago he was one of the more remarkable members of that incredible Huntington family that produced generals, railroad builders, artists, and merchants. Huntington was the grandson and namesake of the Revolutionary War general. After being educated at the University of the City of New York and the University of Pennsylvania, he entered the Episcopal ministry in 1841. Deeply interested in the Oxford Movement, Huntington made a trip to England, then to Rome. On his return to America in 1849, he announced his conversion to Catholicism. The same year he published his first novel, the complications of which hint at his preconversion state of doubt and confusion.[16] The novel was entitled *Lady Alice, or The New Una.*

Lady Alice contains all the elements of a nineteenth-century romance. The plot defies summary, so various and circumstantial are its complications; realistic details are embroidered to a fantastic degree. A constant sense of "presence"—supernatural and preternatural—lends a charged atmosphere to the most ordinary scenes. In the language of a modern critical equation, sensibility overwhelms the fable.

This style is perhaps to be expected in a novel of the time, even one ostensibly devoted to a religious theme. What is not to be expected, however, is the development of the theological debate. Lady Alice is a High Church Anglican, a devotee of the Oxford group, and the wealthiest heiress in Europe. Her lover, Clifford, is blueblood and English, but a Roman Catholic. The resolution of this intellectual and amorous dilemma is complicated and confusing, an indication of Huntington's Oxford ambivalence as well as his apprentice skills in fiction writing. In debate, the Roman position triumphs, yet Clifford becomes an Anglican. At his defection, Alice romanizes herself, to a point just delicately short of submission to the pope. When Clifford returns to the Catholic Church, they are married in an Anglican ceremony, a dispensation having been acquired on the basis of Lady Alice's "invincible ignorance." Love then is shown to be the solvent of all antipathies, thorny theological difficulties among them. Huntington appears to be arguing the authenticity of both churches if not their oneness—a remarkably liberal view for its time and one that he rejected after his conversion.

In 1851 and 1853, Huntington published two more novels—the second a sequel to the first—that gave full witness to his new faith. *Alban* and *The Forest* trace the intellectual and romantic career of a native American from Congregationalism to Catholicism. Alban

16. Richard J. Purcell, *Dictionary of American Biography* 9: 417–18; James J. Walsh, "Dr. Jedediah Vincent Huntington and the Oxford Movement in America," *Records of American Catholic Historical Society* 16 (1905):241–67, 416–42.

Atherton is a wealthy New Englander and a graduate of Yale. His society, people of some wealth and breeding who are mostly Protestant, provides the frequent occasion for religious debate. The polemical element is relieved only by the hero's courtship of Mary DeGroot, the daughter of a wealthy New York patroon and herself a convert. The debate that runs through both novels centers on the question of authority—biblical, ecclesiastical, or individual. Needless to say the Catholic position is victorious. The victory, however, is not achieved by strictly logical means. Huntington gets his strongest endorsements by working a few miracles (e.g., a Catholic priest rids a home of an assortment of playful demons after a host of Protestant ministers has been ineffectual).

Huntington moved beyond an English-Roman accommodation in these later novels. More importantly he demonstrates, like Pise, an aristocratic bias that is quite representative of the Catholic position in America at the time. The bias projects an image of the Church as a civilizing, stabilizing, and conserving force rather than an agent for a supernatural power. Alban confronts sin, error, and ugliness with taste, breeding, and the tranquillity of one aware of centuries of tradition—caste and aesthetic appeal make up his formula for Catholicism. At one point in *Lady Alice* Huntington says of Clifford that "he united two qualifications not generally found in his shopkeeping and heretical country—an incontaminate faith and an immaculate pedigree." [17]

This identification of Catholic sensibility with an old-world social ideal had a constricting effect on the writer's imagination. The materials of the American social environment, a Protestant middle class environment, are patently unsuitable—except in a negative way —for Huntington's purposes. Since in the Atherton novels he does not move the action abroad, he is left with but two alternatives: one technical and the other involving his choice of materials. In *Alban* he makes use of the first of these; in *The Forest* he chooses the latter.

Because the character Alban is a Catholic convert in a Protestant society, Huntington is severely limited in his story to the drama of individual conversion. The social ramifications of Catholicism as he envisages them simply can't be dramatized; polemic alone must

17. J. V. Huntington, *Lady Alice, or the New Una* (New York, 1849), p. 64.

convey the social dimension. Structurally then, *Alban* is picaresque, a series of intellectual and spiritual adventures in which the hero's discoveries are played against a social background of ignorance, bigotry, and democratic small-mindedness. Fortunately for Alban, he can both fulfill his class obligations and preserve his religious exclusiveness by means of a romantic entaglement with the well born Miss DeGroot.

In *The Forest,* however, Alban's conversion is secure and the possibilities for debate are nearly exhausted. Huntington turns to a social referent congenial to both class and religion—a settlement of Indians under the spiritual guidance of a missionary priest. Beyond the limits of white Protestant settlement the Catholic influence can be depicted in a setting entirely free of the influence of American institutions. The Indian village (reminiscent of Chateaubriand's missionary settlement in *Atala* and some of the accounts preserved in the *Jesuit Relations*) with its simple routines, the childlike dependence and piety of the natives, the fatherly role of the missionary, suggests a social milieu at least faintly feudal. Here on the edge of the wilderness lies an island civilization, an idealized community of Christianized natives and their white religious leader, patent if implicit criticism of the coastal societies developed by the white settlers. Here the blending of primitive naturalism and ritual formalism is demonstrated in the conduct of a whole community living a a kind of sacramental existence. Here one finds order, stability, peace, a quality of life that can only be called pastoral, where passivity and humility are the cardinal virtues. As one might expect, the chief dangers for such a society come not from the villagers themselves (from any latent atavism), nor from the heathen native, but rather from the white man: the pathfinder, the builder of cities, and harbinger of change and complexity.

In these three novels, particularly the last two, Huntington provides an example of the peculiar position of the American Catholic writer of fiction. The cultural conflict described and the imaginative solutions (or evasions, if you will) that Huntington worked out, are indicative not of a mid-century phenomenon but of a tendency that recurred in Catholic fiction as late as World War I. This tendency was the result of an inability to construct a fictional world out of native materials.[18] The Catholic writer was forced to locate his imaginative creations in another environment or another time—in Europe or in the ancient past, in the uncontaminated forest societies of the Catholic missionary, or, in a later period, in the self-contained world of the urban Catholic ghetto. The hardihood of this line of fiction could be described in terms or numbers. A conservative estimate woud place at least sixty per cent of the novels written by American Catholics in the nineteenth century in this category of fiction. Huntington's career thus illuminates the dilemma of the American Catholic writer, and his novels provide a prefatory definition of one typical response.

Huntington's inventions, however, do not exhaust the early models of Catholic fiction. A more significant development, a native fiction based on native materials, came about in part as a result of a deliberate, organized campaign, a development that, as later chapters will show, links the world of Catholic fiction to Catholic politics. One of the two writers to be considered who were able to apply a Catholic point of view to decidedly American materials, was the ubiquitous Orestes Brownson. His two novels, although often ignored by his biographers and critics, contain some of his best writing. The earliest, written in 1840 shortly before Brownson became a Catholic and during that time of his greatest spiritual anxiety, is *Charles Elwood: or the Infidel Converted*.

Structurally the novel is little more than a series of vigorous exchanges between the protagonist and a group of evangelical ministers who refuse to debate theological issues, but who rely on revivalist slogans to call Charles Elwood to the Christian life. Elwood refuses this appeal; and, presumably because there is no available spokesman for the Church, he disengages himself entirely from institutionalized Christianity. In this state of unbelief, Elwood turns to the study of

18. It should be noted that the dilemma of the Catholic writer, who could bend the materials of American society to literary uses only with difficulty, was shared by other American writers. Throughout the century, novelists as different as James Fenimore Cooper and Henry James lamented the poverty of American culture, especially as it constricted the artistic imagination. Democracy and other leveling influences in America, they said, gave a flatness, an insipidity to life that made the writing of fictional romance nearly impossible. They too were forced to adopt stratagems to overcome this deficiency and, not unlike Catholic writers, used the past and Europe to supply a remoteness suitable to the "idealizing" faculty of art. For a brilliant account of this problem for major and minor American writers of the middle decades, see Perry Miller's *The Raven and the Whale* (New York, 1956).

society and its amelioration, to which he comes passionately committed. Immersed in this activity, he comes upon a philosopher–philanthropist who argues that Elwood's devotion to humanity, although devoid of creed, makes him a spiritual Christian. The wealthy Howard, who is obviously spokesman for Brownson, defends the earnest infidel as morally superior to the nominal Christian. While granting the necessity for ecclesiastical institutions, he warns that they frequently lead to empty formalism and authoritarianism. Significantly, he acknowledges the validity of the Catholic Church but finds it thoroughly priest-ridden and too enamored of its own bureaucratic prerogatives to recognize the necessity of individual responsibility in matters of faith and morals. The program of the future —a program that could have been proposed only by an American and a democrat—must be directed toward the education of the layman. The novel prophesies a religious Utopia analogous to Brownson's political Utopia of a few years before. When men have been convinced that they themselves constitute the Church and not the visible bureaucracy and code, not priest and precept, then indeed the formal ecclesiastical structure will wither away.

This first novel enunciated a theme that characterized a radical wing of American Catholic thought throughout the century: that the future effectiveness of Christianity depends upon the influence of democratizing elements already present in contemporary political life. The historical claims of Catholicism are unchallenged, its doctrines affirmed; but its institutional posture is criticized for reflecting an image of society obsolete since 1776. With the growing influence of domestic ideals, specifically the ideals of American democracy, the old Church will once again invigorate secular life. This, of course, describes the position later adopted by Hecker and the Americanists, although certainly their language was less strident, their images more equivocal.

Charles Elwood was one of Brownson's last attempts to synthesize the disparate intellectual and spiritual elements that attracted him. After his conversion, his world view became more and more dualistic: good and evil, truth and error, were polarized. A system of absolutes eventually eliminated the possibility of a dialectical process; ten years later he would condemn Newman's *Development of Christian*

Doctrine for suggesting that theological truth was in any way susceptible to an evolutionary process.[19]

Brownson's second novel, *The Spirit-rapper* (1854), is something of a political allegory in the form of a fanciful bit of science fiction. The story concerns an American Faust who with the power of hypnosis alone engineers several of the liberal European revolutions of 1848. The failure of the liberal cause is attributed to the power of the Church, a power demonstrated not so much by the political machinations of the papacy, as by the simple loyalty of the great mass of peasants and urban laborers who refused to rise up in support of the radical leadership. For the protagonist the defeat is a bitter one; but the most painful evidence of his failure is the defection of the woman who had served as a kind of portable transmitter for his hypnotic powers. She had circulated within revolutionary circles communicating the will of the American leader. With the help of her husband and a kindly priest, she rediscovers herself and her capacity for personal involvement.

Although a minor effort as novels go, *The Spirit-rapper* was nevertheless a powerful attack on contemporary liberalism, as cogent in some ways as the work of Hawthorne and Henry James. Brownson demonstrates first the liberal's inordinant reverence for science (in this case rather occult) and his singleminded belief in progress based on the manipulative power of science over society. With only a very simple definition of good and evil, having emancipated himself from tradition and conventional values, Brownson's liberal is left with an attitude toward power "purified" of human concerns. In *The Spirit-rapper,* the protagonist comes to regard people as units to be exploited for an abstract vision of the future. In the fashion of a Hawthorne character, he loses the capacity to love.

In this second novel Brownson represents liberalism as a dangerously inhumane philosophy. As an American document it is interesting in that it associates the revolutionary aspiration of American radicals with those of continental Europe. (This is not a picture of the innocent American abroad.) As a document of religious history, it demonstrates his all-or-nothing assumption about the relation of Church and state (a far cry from the democratic utopianism of *Charles*

19. O.A.B. to W. G. Ward, Sept. 29, 1847, in Henry F. Brownson, *O.A.B., The Middle Years,* 3 vols. (Detroit, 1899), 2:53–58.

Elwood). The shadowy characterizations of the novel define in a wholly abstract way the claims of orthodoxy and liberalism, claims which for Brownson at this time were mutually exclusive. Although the drama is concerned primarily with European politics, its implicit comment on the American situation is a sobering reminder that in the face of pressure for radical change this country had no bastion of orthodoxy such as the Vatican on which to fall back.

These novels show only two of the admittedly many faces of Orestes Brownson, but they conveniently reveal the almost inevitable direction of Catholic fiction. Once Brownson is solidly within the Catholic camp, his theological and political line becomes hardened, his Americanism more qualified and tentative. The proposition that the Church must be democratized undergoes an inversion. Significantly, he shifts the scene in the latter novel to Europe where the triumph of orthodoxy can be shown to be the result of an organic community force.

The final example of pre–Civil War fiction is a little known novel called *Grace Morton, a Catholic Tale,* by Mary L. Meany, originally published in 1864.[20] The tale is modest and derivative of contemporary popular forms and conventions. It nevertheless is one of the earliest Catholic novels to examine the relationship of the American Catholic to his Protestant environment and to do so sympathetically. Miss Meany shows sufficient good will for the non-Catholic to grant him a measure of genuine conviction and at least an equal status in a ranking based on ethical behavior. What makes this all the more remarkable is that the author was writing prior to that period when Catholic critics and polemicists were calling for such sympathy and tolerance.

The setting of the novel is rural Pennsylvania, where Mr. Apthorpe, scornful of all religions, lives out a life of great bitterness and loneliness because of the marriage of his only son to a Catholic and the son's subsequent conversion and disinheritance. To fill the void, Apthorpe adopts Grace and her brother, both orphans. When Grace learns of Apthorpe's harshness and makes the acquaintance of the younger Apthorpe's disinherited widow, she too becomes a Catholic and suffers a similar exile. When Apthorpe dies, his estate goes to the Catholic widow because of a flaw in the will. One of the Apthorpe grandchildren becomes a priest; another marries Grace's brother; and

20. Published under the initials M.L.M.

Grace herself marries a congressman from Virginia, but not before he too has been converted.

The novel attempts to describe the painful circumstances of life facing a Catholic in Protestant America. This conflict plus the several conversions make up a formula to which nearly every Catholic writer paid some heed. One of the subplots, however, departs from the convention. After Grace has been driven out of Apthorpe's house, she takes a position as schoolteacher in a small Pennsylvania town. There one learns of the small-mindedness and bigotry of backwoods America, the chief stimulus for this pettiness being, of course, Grace's Catholicism. But this is not the whole image reflected by the community, for Grace is championed by one of the townspeople, a woman of warm and sympathetic inclinations. The woman and her son own no other distinction in the town than their independence of mind; their virtues are those of the community when not threatened —openness and ready trust, a love of plain talk, an aversion to pretensions of any kind. The earthy good humor of the woman is a welcome contrast to the stagy posturing of the heroine—inevitable as it may be—but her characterization is remarkable for another reason. The author describes her evangelical piety in neither a critical nor a patronizing way. In this one adventure, the author seems to suggest that Catholic and Protestant can coexist without undermining the validity of the other's religious belief. Only the unbeliever is criticized in this story.

What has been described in this chapter are the earliest attempts by American Catholics to use prose fiction. By the time of the Civil War, a solid group of Catholic publishers had materialized, not a few of whom were sensitive to the market appeal of the novel. This development was accompanied by an incipient criticism, spearheaded by Orestes Brownson, the one American Catholic of his age willing to consider freshly and in the light of new cultural conditions the teleological assumptions of religious literature. The novels themselves, however, provide the most suggestive material, and they illustrate a number of structural and thematic patterns that can be only partially explained by prevailing literary conventions. The most important of these patterns was the inability to portray comfortably or convincingly a Catholic social reality in Protestant America. Two kinds of social ideals were presented, the dominant one aristocratic and conservative, a proud force seeking to restrain democracy from the last short step to anarchy; the other at least faintly approving of egalitarianism and pluralist norms. The literature of subsequent periods continues this division and works a near balance, with what wider implications and effects I hope to show.

4 The Emergence of Institutional Support, 1860–1900

The American Civil War produced, among its more powerful and lasting effects, a truly national consciousness. That conflict, fought in the name of unity and continuity, put to rest the claims of regional sovereignty. The tools fashioned for the war effort—a national network of commerce and industry—solidified the political solution achieved by military means.

American Catholics were the religious communion perhaps least affected by the political issues of the war. Neither slavery nor secession created even a temporary schism in the Church.[1] Both the hierarchy and the laity reacted to the war according to regional identity, and this division appears not to have even momentarily threatened Catholic loyalties either to the national hierarchy or to Rome. Following the war, however, pressures from within—immigration and shifts in population—and without—non-Catholic suspicion and even hostility—forced on hierarchy and laity alike a kind of identity crisis. This crisis was analogous to the one occurring in the bastions of the secular power: while the Lodges and the Adamses were anguishing over the threats to the continuity of American institutions posed by immigration, urbanization, and industrialization, Catholics were examining more intensely than ever the threats and opportunities their faith confronted in American life.

The days of slow-paced, pragmatic, and largely decentralized planning were at an end; for the next forty years at least, events would

1. John Tracy Ellis, *American Catholicism* (Chicago, 1956), pp. 90–99.

shape Church policy. Between 1866 and 1884 the Catholic population doubled, from over three and a half million to eight million.[2] At the same time there was an extensive turnover in the episcopal leadership of the country. Ahead, in the last sixteen years of the century, lay the promise of growth as awesome and frenetic as the period just ended. The total population of the Church in America would exceed twelve million by 1900. But numbers alone do not describe the enormity of the problem: new immigration accounted for at least half of the general increase, and the percentage of foreign-born in the Catholic population remained at about one-third throughout the century.[3]

To face these accelerating changes the Church, like secular America, turned more and more to centralized planning and administration. This development is best seen in the work of the Second and Third Plenary Councils of Baltimore, 1866 and 1884. The latter, falling midway in the post–Civil War epoch, resulted in the formulation of organizational programs that were in effect well into the twentieth century. At a critical meeting held in Rome in 1883, the pope expressed a preference for the continued missionary character of the American Church. Cardinal Gibbons, however, prevailed on the pontiff to assent to his plan, later formulated in the council's sessions.[4]

What the Amrican hirarchy did in 1884 has been described by one historian as the building up of the institution. Specifically, beyond the fundamental legislation for uniformity in doctrine and discipline, this meant the implicit endorsement of a Catholic subculture. The faithful were urged, for the preservation of the Faith as well as its extension, to band together in all significant activities of their social and religious lives. The Council's best-known endorsement of this sort concerned the parochial schools. Although some controversy now exists over the exact intentions of the bishops, it

2. Although the *Catholic Directory* for 1866 gives no summary figures, John Gilmary Shea makes these estimates in his *History of the Catholic Church in the United States,* 4 vols. (New York, 1886–1892), 4:715, and his essay "The Progress of the Church in the United States, from the First Provincial Council to the Third Plenary Council of Baltimore," *American Catholic Quarterly Review* 9(1884):495.

3. Gerald Shaughnessy, *Has the Immigrant Kept the Faith?* (New York, 1925), pp. 172, 190.

4. Robert H. Lord, et al, *History of the Archdiocese of Boston in the Various Stages of its Development* (New York, 1944), pp. 88–91.

seems fairly clear from council documents that the hierarchy envisioned something like a national network of Church schools, running from elementary grades through graduate school.[5]

Even so, one can detect a certain ambivalence towards the isolationist position in the council proceedings, and this is illuminated by a writer who interpreted the event for the readers of the *Catholic World*. The writer was convinced that what took place best showed that "the United States is the Church's true home," that "when the institutions of this nation are let to do their work they unconsciously favor the triumph of Christianity, which in its concrete organic existence is the Roman Church."[6] While nothing so enthusiastically expansionist as this judgment found expression in the written conconclusions of the council, there were indications of a similar thinking in the terms of accommodation. Consider, for example, the question of a Catholic press. The bishops plainly favored a much enlarged institutional press. From the language of the section describing that development ("Christian Doctrine") one can infer a number of objectives: the laity should be insulated from non-Catholic influence; non-Catholic representations of Catholicism should be systematically and repeatedly corrected; and the public image of the Church should be so shaped by its press as to attract non-Catholic sympathies. At one point, the bishops went so far as to suggest that the marks of Church affiliation be removed from certain publications so that a non-Catholic readership might be cultivated.[7]

These various objectives, at once isolationist and expansionist, mark nearly every public activity of the American Church for the balance of the nineteenth century, including its imaginative literature. The remainder of this chapter will describe the growth and emerging character of the post–Civil War Catholic publishing industry and the development of organizational methods to engage and enlarge the Catholic readership. Following that, the changes and refinements of Catholic literary opinion governing fiction will be examined, in-

5. Title VIII, *Acta et Dicreta,* in Peter Guilday, *History of the Councils of Baltimore* (New York, 1932), pp. 241–42; Robert Cross, "Origins of the Catholic Parochial Schools in America," *American Benedictine Review* 16(1965):194–209; Guilday, *Councils of Baltimore,* p. 238: "almost one-fourth of the decrees of the Council are devoted to the subject of Catholic Education."

6. "Catholic National Council," *Catholic World* 40(1885):714.

7. Guilday, *Councils of Baltimore,* pp. 240–41.

cluding the attitudes of the novelists themselves and the larger literary context in which these developments occurred.

In July of 1886, a summary of an interview with Lawrence Kehoe by the London *Register* appeared in *Publishers' Weekly*. Kehoe for the previous ten years had been director of the Catholic Publication Society, a venture sponsored by the Paulist Fathers. In this capacity he had been, and was for the four remaining years of his life to be, the prototype of an important kind of American Catholic publisher. In the interview, Kehoe surveyed the Catholic publishing situation candidly, albeit bleakly. Because of the shortage of a literate readership, he said, but more particularly because of the difficulties of book distribution over a huge territory, the Catholic publisher was constantly faced with financial failure. Only prayer books and manuals of instruction could be counted on to pay for themselves; aside from these even "the best books couldn't be counted on to sell a thousand." Kehoe concluded the interview with an appeal to Catholic writers to market their works through Catholic publishers and to the clergy to establish parish libraries as a remedy for the ills of the trade.[8]

What is interesting about this interview is that Kehoe at once accurately diagnosed the Catholic market and, in his appeal, prescribed the exact manner in which that market would be tapped—or, more accurately perhaps, created. These next sixteen years, critical years in the American Catholic experience, saw the proliferation of associations, sodalities, societies, fraternal and professional groups—all with the denomination Catholic. For Catholic publishing too it was a time for organizing.

As one might expect, one of the earliest Catholic spokesmen to endorse an association for the promotion of Catholic literature was Isaac Hecker. In 1866, shortly after he founded the *Catholic World,* Hecker announced the formation of the Catholic Publication Society. Its objective was "to issue short tracts and pamphlets conveying that species of instruction required by Catholics, in the most entertaining form, so as to engage the attention, affect the heart and suit the wants of all classes," especially the poor, who could understand

8. *Publishers' Weekly* 30(1886):37. In a parenthetical note of some interest to this study, Kehoe mentions what he calls a freak of current publishing, namely that Newman's *Apologia Pro Vita Sua* had sold more copies in the last two years than it had in the previous sixteen.

only "simple narration and dialogue." Elaborating the aims of the new organization, he named three important features: the society must seek to appeal to an unsophisticated readership by means of a narrative form of instruction; such a form should be modeled on the work of Protestant publications; and the work should be carried out mainly by laymen. Two months later another article appeared, adding the final defining characteristic of the enterprise: while the society was regarded as a rather exclusive publication venture by and for Catholics, at the same time it would seek to extol the health of American institutions in order to foster Catholic progress.[9]

The idea of a national publishing concern officially identified with the Church leadership was, after Matthew Carey's earlier abortive attempt, proposed in a letter from Archbishop Martin J. Spalding to Archbishop Kendrick in 1855, in which he wrote: "While the Methodists and other sectarians have their vast book concerns and all-pervading tract organizations, it is a shame that we children of light should be inert. Let a Catholic institution be established with its headquarters in Baltimore, the Bishops all to be honorary members and Doctor Ives to be secretary, charged with the publishing of books and tracts."[10]

Pursuing the same plan eleven years later, Hecker moved for official endorsement from the bishops meeting at the Second Plenary Council of Baltimore. Individual bishops gave him strong encouragement and committed themselves to some financial support, but the council did not agree to an official establishment. In 1872, the proposal was finally abandoned and the Paulists took full control. One last attempt was made before the century was out to centralize Catholic literary activity through the founding of the Catholic Press Association in 1894. Under the administration of priests and laity, endorsed by the hierarchy and the apostolic delegate, the association's aims generally were reminiscent of Hecker's original proposal for the Catholic Publication Society. But the Catholic Press Association endured for only a few years, managing to publish a total of twenty-three titles before 1900.[11]

9. "The Catholic Publication Society," *Catholic World* 3(1866):278, 280; "Use and Abuse of Reading," ibid., p. 472.

10. In John Lancaster Spalding, *Life of the Most Reverend Martin J. Spalding* (New York, 1894), p. 342.

11. Guilday, *Councils of Baltimore*, pp. 213, 219; Paul J. Fullam, C. P., "A History of the Catholic Publication Society and its Successors from 1866 to the Founding of the Paulist Press

The failure of an official publishing venture did not, however, mean failure for Catholic publishing generally or a decline in attempts to minister to the reading needs of the Catholic population. In effect, Catholic leaders gradually abandoned the printing and merchandising side of the book business. Individual publishers of Catholic books continued to compete for official favors—publishing rights to certain popular and official prayerbooks and textbooks and the right to use titles such as Benziger Brothers' "Printers to the Holy See"—but the rise and fall of publishing houses did not follow the pattern of patronage. Like the Sadlier firm noted in the previous chapter, the most powerful publisher to emerge from the nineteenth century, P. J. Kenedy and Sons, succeeded by attending more to the market than to patently evangelical schemes. Kenedy sponsored no daring innovations but prudently bought up a dozen or so failing or bankrupt houses along with their stock of plates. This enlightened opportunism contrasts with the always vulnerable idealism of Kehoe of the C.P.S.[12] When Kehoe died in 1890, his firm was turning out over fifty titles a year, but his profit margins were always narrow; and when he died the firm folded, a victim of business habits dictated by religious zeal.[13]

On the business side, therefore, Catholic enterprises were subject to the same rules of operation as secular publishers, despite attempts to ignore or evade them. The overwhelming subject of discussion and debate within the publishing industry during the post–Civil War years was the practice of price-cutting. It is significant that the association formed by Catholic publishers in 1883, the American Catholic Publishers' Association, quickly went under for reasons of mutual mistrust growing out of the practice of price gouging. In an obituary, the *Publishers' Weekly* quoted one of the members: "The Association had done much in one year to elevate and give

in 1916," (master's thesis, Catholic University of America, 1956), p. 31; "Christian Press Association," *Publishers' Weekly* 45(1894):432; and Patricia Feiten, "A Survey of Catholic Americana and Catholic Book Publishing in the United States, 1896–1900," (master's thesis, Catholic University of America, 1958), p. 5.

12. Robert C. Healey, *Catholic Book Chronicle* (New York, 1951), pp. 37–40. An analogous pattern of success and failure is described by James P. Shannon in his book on the western colonization schemes for Catholic immigrants during the same period. Those which produced viable settlements were founded in some measure on hardheaded business principles. *Catholic Colonization on the Western Frontier* (New Haven, 1957).

13. Feiten, "Catholic Americana," p. 5. For a pathetic account of Kehoe's career, see his correspondence maintained in the archives of the University of Notre Dame Library, parts of which are included in Fullam, "Catholic Publication."

character to the business of publishing Catholic books, but the bad faith shown by two members . . . so disgusted the others that they concluded to disband and let 'the devil take the hindmost'." [14]

While Catholic publishers were discovering a workable formula for commercial success, the number of Catholic titles continued to rise through the eighties and nineties. Between 1876 and 1880 a total of 558 Catholic works appeared in America; the five years leading up to 1890 saw the issuance of more than 1,300 titles.[15] These figures are a little misleading, however, as 1890 appears to have been the high-water mark, at least in terms of the number of titles published. It was also the year during which the largest number of specifically Catholic publishers were doing business; and eleven of them issued at least ten titles.[16] After that point production began to stabilize: marginal companies fell off; the pamphlet literature, which was of slight literary value and ephemeral interest although increasing at an astounding rate, became more and more the work of small seminary presses. The few houses that survived the century generally grew stronger (Herder of St. Louis, Benziger Brothers of New York, Kenedy and Sons of New York), but survival involved liberalizing policy and gradually adding works not exclusively tailored for the Catholic market. This diversification was not confined to the Catholic presses; in fact, a Catholic bibliographer says that turn-of-the-century non-Catholic firms began increasingly to publish Catholic works. Between 1900 and 1950 secular publishers handled twice as many Catholic titles as Catholic firms.[17]

During this period of development within the publishing industry, the Catholic leadership occupied itself by creating a readership and a method of advertising. In the early days the usual procedure was to ask parish priests to serve as jobbers; according to Kehoe, it was the only way the Catholic publisher could hope to survive. This method of distribution, however, was only suited to serving existing

14. "Literary and Trade Notes," *Publishers' Weekly* 24(1883):187.

15. Margaret Anne Fahey, "A Survey of Catholic Americana and Catholic Book Publishing in the United States, 1876–1880," (master's thesis, Catholic University of America, 1954), p. 165; Mary Patricia Ruskin, "A Survey of Catholic Americana and Catholic Book Publishing in the United States, 1886–1890," (master's thesis, Catholic University of America, 1952), p. 72.

16. Feiten, "Catholic Americana," p. 5.

17. Joan Mary Lonergan, "Publishing Trends Reflected in Works of Academy Members of the Gallery of Living Catholic Authors," (master's thesis, Catholic University of America, 1955), p. 139.

needs; what people like Hecker wanted was to greatly increase the Catholic reading public. Such a goal was aided by the parochial school system, where students could be systematically introduced to Catholic literature and where it became a staple of both classroom and non-classroom diets.[18]

Of equal importance were the various catechetical, self-improvement, and social organizations that sprang up during the eighties and nineties. The impetus for this development was provided by the pastoral letter emanating from the Plenary Council of 1884: "It is obvious that our young men are exposed to the greatest dangers, and need the most abundant helps. Hence . . . we desire to see the number of thoroughly Catholic and well-organized associations for their benefit greatly increased, especially in our large cities . . . and we appeal to our young men to . . . band together under their pastor, for mutual improvement and encouragement in the paths of faith and virtue."[19]

By 1900 a number of social, educational, and religious agencies for the Catholic layman had been formed, and they all contributed to the growing market for Catholic literature. The type of organization most directly connected with literary developments was the reading circle. Hecker had initiated the first program as a book circulation scheme in the late sixties. At that time the Paulists were running a sunday school in New York City; the faculty provided students with books and a forum for their discussion. Apprehensive about students after they left the school, the Paulists decided that continuing education was necessary; thus began the "post-graduate" Ozanam Reading Union. Several years later, in 1889, the *Catholic World* announced the formation of the Columbian Reading Union, a loosely federated association of reading circles throughout the country. The association served mainly as a clearing house for ideas, which were regularly published in the *Catholic World*. A second organization, founded shortly thereafter by Warren E. Mosher and called the Catholic Educational Union, obliged its membership to adopt certain organizational rules, to consider fixed discussion topics, and to subscribe to the union publication, the *Catholic Reading*

18. This claim is based on a survey by the author of high-school literature textbooks published for use in Catholic schools.

19. Peter Guilday, ed., *National Pastorals of American Hierarchy, 1792–1919*, 2 vols. (Washington, 1923), 1:261–62.

Circle Review. At the Chicago Exposition of 1893 a report submitted to the World Parliament of Religions cited a membership in both organizations of over 10,000 in more than 250 local units.[20]

The purpose of the two associations was much the same throughout the century. Hecker had wanted to provide some means for self-improvement, particularly for young Catholics who had received academy or college training; but the promotion of Catholic literature was almost as important a goal. As a layman wrote to the *Lowell* (Massachusetts) *Sun,* the Catholic Reading Union wanted principally "to get Catholics to read Catholic literature."[21] Understandably, a great deal of the organizations' efforts were bibliographic; at a time when only a few Catholic writers known widely in the United States could get their work published, it was very difficult to obtain a list of authentic Catholic writers to govern schools and libraries in their choice of reading materials. The *Catholic World,* therefore, devoted a great deal of space to publishing lists of authors and titles in almost every volume after 1885.[22]

A rarely stated but obvious secondary intention of these activities was the subsidization of Catholic writers. The prospects for a would-be author, particularly if he did not have the financial security of holy orders, was somewhat frightening—obscurity was hardly the worst of his dilemmas. Thus a managed market helped to solve the bread-and-butter problem for Catholic writers and to attract new talent into the profession. The word "patronage" was never used, but no word could better describe this system, the effects of which will be discussed later in this chapter. As one of the novelists said in 1893, "the point of all this is not only to raise Catholic intellectual standards, but also to create a market for Catholic lecturers and writers."[23]

Although the reading unions most directly promoted a literary

20. Thomas McMillan, "Growth of Reading Circles," *Summer School Essays* (Chicago, 1896), pp. 131–33, 139; John H. Burrows, ed., *World Parliament of Religions* (Chicago, 1893), p. 1415.

21. James B. Troy, letter reprinted in *Catholic World* 51(1890):415.

22. This effort has been a characteristic activity of American Catholics until very recently. One could compile a sizable bibliography of bibliographies from the American and British journals over a fifty-year period. The fact that the lists include a number of writers whose affiliation with the Church is at best nominal suggests their largely promotional function. See Appendix.

23. Katherine Conway, "Catholic Summer School and the Reading Circles," in *World's Catholic Columbian Conference* (Chicago, 1893), p. 110.

establishment, there were other important Catholic organizations, including the parochial schools, the Young Men's Catholic Associations, and various local societies and sodalities. One development that deserves special attention here is the Catholic Summer School, an outgrowth of the reading unions and originally suggested by the head of the Catholic Educational Union, Warren Mosher. A candid imitation of Methodist Bishop John H. Vincent's New York Chautauqua, the Catholic Summer School was referred to as "Catholic Chautauqua" well into the twentieth century, even though some condemned this all-too-obvious mark of imitation. Beginning in 1892 when the school convened in New London, Connecticut, the Summer School mounted an impressive array of lectures and social events that annually drew from three hundred to a thousand members for the balance of the century.[24]

The final event in this narrative is the founding of the Guild of Catholic Authors in 1898, the purpose of which was frankly sectarian. Called somewhat optimistically a trade union, the guild by the end of the century had managed to produce little more than an annual meeting at which writers exchanged ideas on their mission as well as on more pedestrian issues such as publishers' royalties and copyright law.[25]

It was no accident that most of these activities imitated Protestant successes. As early as 1870 a writer in the *Catholic World* was urging programs like those of the Methodists, and throughout the next thirty years this cry was echoed again and again. In 1888 an anonymous writer in the *Catholic World* spoke of the necessity for imitating Chautauqua and the Agassiz Association, particularly for setting up discussions of Catholic literature.[26] Sometime later Katherine Conway, a writer for the *Boston Pilot* and herself a novelist, wrote of the need to borrow organizational ideas from the YMCA, the Christian Endeavor Societies, and other non-Catholic groups.[27]

24. See "Observations on the Catholic Young Men's National Convention," *Catholic World* 52(1890):404–10; James Addison White, *The Founding of Cliff Haven*, U.S. Catholic Historical Society, monograph series XXIV (New York, 1950).

25. "Guild of Catholic Authors," *Publishers' Weekly* 53(1898):63; a report of the third meeting is summarized in the "Columbian Reading Union" column of *Catholic World* 69(1899):142–44.

26. J. R. G. Hassard, "Catholic Literature and the Catholic Public,"*Catholic World* 12(1870):400; "Reading Circles," ibid. 48(1888):418–19.

27. Conway, "Catholic Summer School," p. 106.

The extent of this imitation is nowhere more clearly demonstrated than in the founding and development of the Catholic Summer School. The rural setting, the curriculum of studies that blended religious training with humanistic studies, the roster of speakers that added up to a veritable educational and professional Who's Who, and the extention of summer school activities to include home study programs and regional summer and winter schools—all bespeak an awareness of and an endorsement of the Chautauqua pattern.

To further illustrate this comparison, consider the hypothetical Methodist or Presbyterian child of the 1870s. He would normally be a member of a local sunday school class which was part of a national organization; and probably he would subscribe to a sunday school magazine (e.g., *The Pansy,* edited by Isabella "Pansy" Alden). His older sister might be taking a correspondence class or belong to a discussion group, both administered nationally by the Chautauqua organization. The whole family might save for a summer vacation at the New York Chautauqua. All the family would be enrolled in the local church temperance and missionary societies; and they would combine piety with recreation in family readings of the fiction of Mrs. Alden, General Wallace, or Grace Livingston.

Somewhat later, his Catholic counterpart, especially if a child of better-off parents, would probably be enrolled in a sunday school class or in the parochial school of the parish. He would receive *The Young Catholic,* a sunday school paper for children.[28] His older brother would belong to the Young Men's Catholic Association. If he lived near the East Coast, he might attend the Catholic Summer School at Plattsburgh, New York, and follow up this activity by joining a reading and discussion group, e.g., the Columbian Reading Union. His reading, needless to say, would be guided by lists printed in Catholic magazines and carried on the shelves of the parish library.

At the producing end of this process, another phenomenon, also loosely parallel to features of Protestant groups, is apparent. The Catholic who emerged as a public figure in one activity was likely to find himself engaged eventually in the entire spectrum of

28. A monthly, *The Young Catholic,* first appeared in 1870, edited by Mrs. George Hecker, Isaac's sister-in-law.

Church-related efforts. The same people who worked on the lecture circuit for the Columbian Reading Union also wrote novels, engaged in religious controversy, and wrote articles of every description, literary, political and apologetical, for the Catholic press. Such interlocking activities were the rule rather than the exception on both sides of the religious dividing line. Once admitted to the establishment, one was expected to embrace the apostolate in all of its myriad endeavors: to write poetry as well as biblical exegesis; to help manage lay congresses as well as serve on editorial boards; to teach at the Catholic Summer School as well as turn out short stories and novels.[29]

The upshot of this was the emergence of a curious kind of writer novelist Wilfred Sheed calls the religious hack—a professional Catholic whose versatility is indicated by writings on every conceivable church-related subject.[30] A machinery had been created and it appeared to be almost self-perpetuating: a Catholic readership was brought up to read only Catholic works; Catholic writers were conditioned to write for a ready-made public, using formulas which guaranteed a measure of popular and financial success. Unfortunately such a system worked to prevent the serious kind of writing for which it was established. Superficiality was a by-product of the system itself; and public recognition was tantamount to the kiss of death for any serious aspirant.

But the most appalling fact of all is the absence of public dissent, of virtually any questioning of the complacency evinced by this establishment. In all the vast and self-congratulatory literature on the subject of reading unions, fraternal associations, summer schools, extension societies, etc., only two public personalities sounded discordant notes: Arthur Preuss, editor of *The Review* of St. Louis, and William Henry Thorne, editor of a New York magazine, *The Globe-Review*. Thorne, who is virtually unmentioned in accounts of Catholic journalism and controversy, regularly attacked the activities, at one point writing: "I am perfectly convinced that any one issue of this *Review* published during the last four years has done more for the advancement of Catholic truth and Catholic cul-

29. See, for example, the public career of Kate Conway in "Authentic Sketches of Living Catholic Authors," *Catholic World* 63(1897):281–82.
30. Wilfred Sheed, *The Hack* (New York, 1963) is the tragic story of a modern religious writer.

ture than has been done by all the meetings and all the lectures of all the Catholic or Protestant Summer Schools, yet held in this land." His principle objection was made on professional grounds, claiming that "not one in a hundred of the lecturers lecturing before such a body is competent to instruct them on the themes set down for him." [31]

What has been described so far is the growth of an institution through the proliferation of interconnected agencies. In spite of the rationale for such a development, its effect on the writer was generally fatal. For the Catholic people it meant, notwithstanding numerous disclaimers, increased parochialism. Isaac Hecker's plan for a Catholic publishing industry to serve as a gateway to communication with non-Catholic America had led instead to a reinforced wall of separation.

A final note to this story of institutional growth is supplied by three otherwise insignificant publishing events of 1898. In that year Benziger Brothers of New York issued three books of somewhat unusual content: *A Game of Quotations from American Catholic Authors, The Pictorial Game of American Catholic Authors,* and *A Catholic Speller.* From that point, it is no great distance to a Catholic dictionary and even Catholic applesauce!

Literary theory, even when it has the force of an institution of growing self-consciousness behind it, is always a few steps behind literary fact. It has already been suggested that Catholics and prose fiction were not by cultural tradition very compatible, and for some time the relationship was forced and unnatural. Brownson had attempted to give the union a philosophical basis, but for the most part the affair progressed quite independently of official benediction. People (Catholics or otherwise) would read novels; that was a clear fact. All the Church could hope to do was bless the arrangement and try to guide the future development of the form. As an anonymous writer in the *Catholic World* wrote in 1870: "Stop novels, we cannot. Let preachers thunder as they may, they will be written and they will be read. It is for us to seize upon that weapon and turn it to our purpose." [32] Among those not seriously engaged in writing

31. William Henry Thorne, "Summer Schools and Catholic Culture," *The Globe-Review* 6(1896):116.
32. "Catholic Literature," p. 405.

or criticizing, this attitude gained currency and was comparable to accommodations made among most Protestant communions. The novel had become a part of the routine recreational diet of a great many Americans; there was little to do except to sanctify it, Catholicize it. An index of the result is the contrast between ex-transcendentalist Isaac Hecker and social philosopher John A. Ryan. Hecker once said that he had not spent over one-half day in his lifetime reading novels, but for that period he had made them objects of intense study.[33] This remark, with its obvious irony, was the response of one generation. Hecker's spiritual heir, Monsignor Ryan, told his friends that one of the most important influences in his early life was the novel *The New Antigone* by English author William Barry.[34] Between Hecker and Ryan a new consensus had developed within the Catholic community.

In articles appearing in Catholic magazines over a period of twenty-five years, this new consensus is fairly well represented. In 1866 the prospectus for the Catholic Publication Society proposed "narrative prose" as appropriate for the religious instruction of the poor and ignorant. Twenty years later Francis Lavelle was writing in the *Catholic World* that the novel was the most persuasive art form then practiced; and he encouraged Catholics to turn to it for evangelical purposes. Convert, he said, through the instruction of the novel.[35] In a column of the "Columbian Reading Union" section of the *Catholic World* of October 1889, the literary editor of the magazine remarked that novels were useful to the discussion groups as relaxing and entertaining reading to be alternated with "hard" books. The first article published in the *American Ecclesiastical Review,* which began in 1889, discussed the responsibility of the clergy toward Catholic literature and concluded that priests must not only promote but write the literature that their flocks should read, to the end of upgrading the general cultural level of the Catholic people. Shortly thereafter, the *Catholic World* reprinted a letter arguing the propagandistic value of the novel and citing the work of British religious novelists. Finally, in a similar vein, the reviewer of

33. Walter Elliott, *Life of Father Hecker* (New York, 1891), pp. 59–60.
34. Told to the author by the late Monsignor Michael Shanahan, librarian at the archdiocesan library of St. Paul, Minn., July 1964.
35. "The Catholic Publication Society," *Catholic World* 3(1866):279; Lavelle, "Novels and Novel Writing," ibid. 43(1886):521–22.

a book of short stories by American Catholic Mary Mannix wrote: "Some of the stories are truly effective as sermons." [36]

The common theme in all these exhortations is a strong utilitarianism: imaginative literature is a useful teaching device, in some ways and for some readers more persuasive than exposition. This rationale is hardly surprising; didacticism is usually the first defense of a literary *fait accompli*. Katherine Conway recognized a secondary function of literature when she said of the effect of the blue-chip roster of speakers at the Catholic Summer School: their presence helped break down the self-doubts of Catholics "by showing them Catholic luminaries in the flesh." [37]

These two objectives illuminate the reactions of any culturally underdeveloped group sensitive to its minority status, particularly one for whom religion is the chief mode of identification. At first the world of art is almost foreign to the group and certainly an object of suspicion, especially as it appears to be the especial province of the dominant culture. This suspicion, plus a normal fear of something as volatile as art, may lead to an unofficial ban on or discouragement of artistic experience. But subsequent to this wholly negative phase, a timid rationale develops, based on the potential of art to influence: i.e., if a person can movingly project an imaginative conception of matters vile and erroneous, why cannot a believer turn the same power to good? Once accepted as a legitimate expression of a religious point of view, art becomes enmeshed in the act of debate in two ways. First and most obviously, such writers produce materials designed to reinforce the convictions of the faithful and to convert or undermine the beliefs of the gentile; their art is polemic, pure and simple. Meanwhile, more subtly, artistic eminence begins to be seen as authenticating belief, and the reputation of its writers in the larger culture becomes a factor in the Church's own battle for self-respect. So, in spite of the availability of a rich and ancient artistic tradition, nineteenth century American Catholic writers conformed in significant ways to a minority culture pattern. The constant inflation of claims to artistic merit also reflects this pattern.

For Catholics like Brownson and Hecker, who combined rigorous

36. Troy letter, ibid. 51(1890):416; review of *The Tales Tim Told Us, Ave Maria* 48(1899):86.
37. Conway, "The Catholic Summer School," p. 110.

critical judgments with tremendous faith, the question of religious art had been relatively simple. Just as the free competition of ideologies in an environment of political and intellectual *laissez faire* would lead inevitably to the triumph of Catholicism; so too in artistic accomplishment, Catholics could expect to be superior to writers of other faiths as long as they worked within a civil society that permitted an aristocracy of talent. The truth of their religious belief would guarantee their artistic superiority. For Brownson and Hecker this conviction did not get in the way of critical judgment. Brownson especially would not let shoddy work pass for better because of the religious credentials of the author. The same was not true, however, of lesser and later spokesmen for Catholic literary norms. For the reviewers of Catholic magazines of the eighties and nineties, religious affiliation came to be the ensign of literary talent. Ideological assumptions obscured fair and accurate assessments: works whose authors were Catholics must by definition be superior to those of non-Catholics. The result of this critical attitude was a harvest of mediocrity. More and more second-rate writers moved into the Catholic market; promising writers either broke with the system or adjusted gradually to a species of subliterature; perhaps worst of all the readers themselves were taught a method of discrimination that avoided literary criteria. One contemporary who saw this development all too clearly, Brother Azarias Mullaney, complained that "it is not necessary to establish two weights and two measures for our Catholic authors;" and that Catholic reviewers, for their work, "must plead guilty to the impeachment of having been in the past too laudatory of inferior literary work." [38]

The review sections of the most widely circulated Catholic magazines of the period—*Catholic World, Ave Maria, Messenger of the Sacred Heart*—are perhaps the best source of the critical assumptions of American Catholics. Reviewers were often anonymous, but there is so little difference in their enunciated principles that this anoonymity does not affect interpretation. In addition, these magazines offered the Catholic writers themselves a popular podium from which to explain their objectives.

During the post–Civil War years one finds judgments offered in scattershot fashion. Critics praised or condemned a writer for any

38. Brother Azarias Mullaney, *Books and Reading* (New York, 1890), pp. 138–41.

number of qualities, including grammar and spelling. Consider this conclusion to a review of William McDermott's *Cremore* in *Catholic World:* "his unfettered soul . . . seems to have scorned the beaten path of correct grammatical construction and punctuation."[39] But the two norms most frequently invoked, idealism and realism, are themselves somewhat contradictory. In an extended review of the work of William Dean Howells in the *Catholic World,* "R. P." wrote of an artistic objective which should motivate all serious writers: "Art is ever pointing upward, and the influence of true art upon man is to make him look upward, too, to that vast [*sic*] where his ideal sits . . . where all is beautiful, where all is immeasurable by him until he beholds it with his glorified intelligence." The writer concluded that people "look to their novels to take them out of themselves, out of their everyday lives, and to lead them into other worlds for the time being."[40] This language formed a veritable refrain in the journal reviews. James, Howells, Norris, and Crane were regularly panned for their lack of idealization, for their preoccupation with the grim and sordid; whereas the female writers of England, Ireland, and the Continent were regularly extolled for their celebration of the pure, the good, and the refined. "High-bred tone," "ideal sentiments," "pure and high aims of the writer," and similar phrases formed the linguistic currency for Catholic criticism.[41]

The appeal to realism was of a rather special kind. For the most part it was based on an exacting knowledge of Catholic doctrine, canon law, and the rubrics of the liturgy and Church offices. A novelist who assigned a wrong title to a member of the hierarchy, gave a misleading explanation of the Pauline privilege, or provided certain priestly faculties to a character in minor orders was treated with intramural contempt. Critical essays frequently dealt with nothing but an elaborate correction of the text. Approval was expressed typically in statements such as this one from a review of John Talbot Smith's *Saranac:* "that it possesses genuine positive merit, as well as the negative one of containing nothing detrimental to faith and morals, need hardly be said of a writer whose previous

39. "Chats for Book Lovers," *Catholic World* 42(1886):858.
40. R. P., "Novel Writing as a Science," ibid. 42(1885):287, 279.
41. See the reviews of works by Mrs. Oliphant and Mde. Craven in *Ave Maria* 23(1886):314 and 24(1886):307.

stories have proved so deservedly popular." [42] "Sound and whole-some," "a good Catholic story," were the plaudits which announced a literary success; "depressing," "questionable grasp of Church doctrine," "nothing to identify the author as Catholic" were the marks of failure.

Literary embellishments were also suspected by the guardians of Catholic taste. For example, consider the complaint of a novel reviewer in the *Messenger of the Sacred Heart* that there were too many literary allusions, which hindered the writing's effect on "the earnest men who desire to do good or work in the world and have not time to waste on the mere accomplishments of literature." [43] Readers were often warned about writers who strained after "artistic effect."

Novelists themselves practiced a species of criticism not unlike that of reviewers for Catholic periodicals. In public revelations of trade secrets, Catholic writers showed considerable respect for the therapeutic function of their work: a penchant for looking on the smiling aspects of life, a habit of offering superficial versions of reality—religious and secular—and a respect for the catechetical possibilities of fiction were their literary baggage. Isabel C. Clarke in an essay revealingly titled "The Apostolate of the Novel," argued that the Catholic author should never forget that he writes more for those without than for those within the fold. "He was," she wrote, "as responsible as the preacher" to demolish age-old prejudices, the long accepted untruths which continue to vilify the Church. Her contemporary, Eleanor C. Donnelly, sister of the Minnesota politician, Ignatius Donnelly, and author of at least eighty-five volumes of poetry and prose, had a special distaste for the literature of her own century. She told an audience at the World's Catholic Columbian Congress of 1893 that "the dove that goes forth from the saving ark of a purified literature must not pause to dissect the putrid carcasses tossed upon the rocks by the preceding deluge of human passions." For Frank H. Spearman, whose following was considerable in secular circles as well as Catholic, the Catholic novelist had a number of choices; but the principal one was his decision

42. Ibid., 37(1893):79.
43. Review of M. F. Egan, *The Disappearance of John Longworthy*, in *Messenger of the Sacred Heart* 6(1891):304.

to write for a Catholic or a non-Catholic audience. Because the novel was "a medium through which millions of readers reach conclusions concerning the vital questions of life," writers loyal to the Church had a "glorious opportunity to instruct the faithful and the heretic alike." This being the true objective, he must concern himself with the tactical problems of meeting the expectations of his particular readers.[44]

Maurice Francis Egan and Brother Azarias, who devoted nearly the whole of their adult lives to the teaching and promotion of Catholic literature, produced more studied and elaborate discussions of literary theory and strategy for American Catholics. Egan, himself a prodigious writer of novels, drew on a rather shapeless eclecticism in his innumerable critical reviews. Because of his central importance to a wide range of Catholic responses, he will be discussed at length in a later chapter.

Brother Azarias Mullaney (1847–1893), during a short life, wrote several books and lectured frequently on a Christian philosophy of literature. But as thorough and cogent as these studies are, their relevance to the story of American Catholic literature is slight. For one thing, Brother Azarias rarely wrote directly of prospects for an American Catholic novel. Moreover, his conception of literary form, like his conception of philosophical truth, was a static, "classical" one. The main job of the artist in his eyes was to rediscover the purity of perfected forms, and these are available primarily within the Christian tradition.

After dismissing the influences of the Reformation as pernicious and destructive of all hope of cultural progress, Brother Azarias identified all things "genuine and lasting in literature" since that time as "either reversionary or reactionary." Similarly, he regarded nearly all the poetic energies of the Romantic period to be abortive, if not degenerate. Wordsworth, Shelley, and Coleridge failed their readers because they wrote "not to give the reader objective reality" but "to promote some view or speculation of the author." Exhibiting a knowledgeable if unsympathetic acquaintance with the intellectual influences of his time—evolution, positivism, pessimism, and

44. Isabel C. Clarke, "The Apostolate of the Novel," in F. X. Talbot, ed., *Fiction by its Makers* (New York, 1928), pp. 129–30; Eleanor C. Donnelly, "Women in Literature," in *World's Columbian Catholic Congress* (Chicago, 1893), p. 87; Frank H. Spearman, "The Catholic Novelist," in *Fiction by its Makers*, pp. 104–07.

even Freud—Brother Azarias dismissed all of them as excesses of the rationalist or romantic tendency of the man who does not accept the Christian resolution. That resolution was, according to his understanding, an ontological dualism made coherent only through the good and infallible offices of the Roman Catholic Church. Sublimity, moral edification, a sense of what lies behind the veil—these are the crucial criteria by which one judges the literary act. Significantly, his roster of acceptable models virtually ends at the Renaissance. He did, however, concede the mantle of literary respectability to a number of American Catholic writers, including several who appear in this study. Generally, however, Brother Azarias avoided reference to specific contemporary works. His person, rather than his particular views, was important; he lent a certain philosophical ballast to the movement to found a native Catholic literature. But his theory, insofar as it worked an influence, served mainly to canonize the forms of the past.[45]

A summary diagnosis from a contemporary critic, the editor of a Catholic newspaper, is most instructive. Speaking to the Catholic Lay Congress of 1889, Condé B. Pallen claimed that there were four impediments to progress in American Catholic letters: Catholics had always to face the "distracting cares of a pioneer career, the want of an audience, the lack of a stimulus, and above all, the attitude of self-defense into which the Church has been forced by an aggressive prejudice." He concluded by asserting that the seige mentality was no longer warranted, that "the long night, which for three centuries has hung over us, is lifting its blankets of darkness, and the dawn draws near." Though the diagnosis is amazingly perceptive, the prophetic note reflects a painfully erroneous reading of the times.[46]

Sixty-two years later, an eminent historian of Catholic literature, John Pick, came to roughly the same conclusions concerning the failure of Catholic writers during the intervening period. Catholic writers, he said, cannot deal with Catholic life on any but the most

45. See especially *A Philosophy of Literature* (Philadelphia, 1899), pp. 142, 164, 205–08 and *Books and Reading,* pp. 54–56. The one serious study of Brother Azarias as a literary critic is in Edward J. Drummond, "Catholic Criticism in America: Studies in Brownson, Azarias, and Egan, with an Essay for Catholic Critics" (doctoral diss., State University of Iowa, 1942).

46. Condé B. Pallen, "Catholic American Literature," in *Official Report of the Proceedings of the Catholic Congress, 1889* (Detroit, 1889), p. 141, 142.

superficial level; they treat the novel as polemic; and out of excessive prudence they fear to depict sin. Pick too predicted the dawn of a new era in Catholic letters. The similarity of these two judgments is more than a historical curiosity. It points to a special continuity in American Catholic thought which is being challenged only in the present generation.[47]

What has been said so far describes the development of a sectarian *belles lettres* and a theory to support it. These developments can also be measured in numbers, for the American Catholic novel had a prodigious growth during the 1880s and 1890s. After the Civil War there was a bare handful of Catholic novelists; by 1880 over forty novelists were writing for Catholic publishers and a few others for non-Catholic firms. By 1900 well over a hundred American Catholics had written and published at least one novel. In 1891, Benziger Brothers of New York, the largest publisher of Catholic novels, advertised a list of 116 novels, of which 77 were written by Americans. By 1899 the number of adult American novels published that year alone had exceeded fifty.[48] In early 1896 Benziger issued five books of American Catholic fiction; within three months all were in second editions.[49] The same year, the firm issued a collection of short stories triumphantly titled *Round Table of Representative American Catholic Novelists.*[50] In 1898, Charles Wilderman of New York began a series of "one-half dime" issues called the Library of Choice Catholic Stories.[51]

Merchandising was not confined to hardcover publications. With an inflated market, popular magazines such as *Ave Maria, Catholic World,* and *The Messenger of the Sacred Heart,* carried a full complement of fiction.[52] A new children's monthly, *Our Boys and Girls' Own,* was announced in *Publishers' Weekly* November 26, 1898. The Catholic newspapers, of course, had been carrying fiction

47. John Pick, "The Renascence in American Catholic Letters," in Norman Weyand, ed., *The Catholic Renascence in a Disintegrating World* (Chicago, 1951), p. 172.

48. These figures were compiled from advertising lists appended to various Benziger Brothers novels: Francis Finn, *Tom Playfair,* 1891; Mary E. Mannix, *Pancho and Panchita,* 1899.

49. "Columbian Reading Union," *Catholic World* 65(1897):142.

50. Eleanor C. Donnelly, ed., *Round Table of Representative American Catholic Novelists* (New York, 1896).

51. Noted in "Columbian Reading Union," *Catholic World* 67(1898):431.

52. In fact, according to my own calculations, about a third of all American Catholic fiction published during this period first appeared in print as magazine serials.

in their pages for years. A sampling of two diocesan papers during the eighties and nineties, the *Northwestern Chronicle* of St. Paul, Minnesota, and the Cincinnati *Telegraph*—the first Catholic diocesan newspaper published in this country (beginning in 1831)— shows that fiction was printed throughout the period. Ambitious serial fiction appeared prominently in both papers from about 1885 to 1895. After that date serials virtually disappeared, but short fiction, mostly reprints from magazines, remained important features.[53]

While much of this activity can be adequately explained by what was going on within American Catholicism, these developments were not isolated phenomena. Although perhaps not determinative, a number of trends in the wider context of religious and secular literature were at least influential. The most worthy literary products of the age were the work of the realists. Responding to the new science, to powerful hypotheses that described the nature of the individual and collective mind as well as matter, America's most gifted writers soon forged a coalition to force a change in the direction of the country's art. In the name of truth and literary democracy, William Dean Howells argued for a literature purged of sickly romanticism, a literature brave enough to record life's events in all their ordinariness; language would be direct, forceful, in the vernacular, encasing the elements of the fable within a thematic structure based on probability and common sense. Howells' concern was to create a literature suitable for a democracy and the common man. While he articulated the premises of the movement, his colleagues (Frank Norris, Hamlin Garland, and Stephen Crane) best exemplified them. In the process, their work acquired the hard cutting-edge of both indigenous and imported naturalism.

Custodians of public taste, however, are rarely persuaded by the claims of the artistic avant-garde. The time lag between literary innovation and its permeation to all levels of a society's literature is a familiar phenomenon. Not until the 1920s did anything like a mass following develop for the literature of social realism. This is

53. Although this study is not concerned with the foreign language press, it is relevant to point out here that serial fiction from works written in foreign languages or translated from English made up a sizable part of the journals and papers read by the immigrants.

not to say that the popular mind was unaffected by the intellectual and artistic currents of the Gilded Age, but that the reaction was in the opposite direction. At least three major trends can be identified in the popular literature of the period, and all three bespeak an accommodation to the intellectual and scientific assaults on orthodoxy. One, marginal in relation to the total literary output of the period but sizable with respect to its own publishing history, was the utopian novel. Looking at a checklist of all such fiction issued between 1850 and 1950, one can discover a dramatic increase in this type of writing beginning about 1875, the surge continuing until World War I.[54] The most famous of these, Edward Bellamy's *Looking Backward* (1888) and Ignatius Donnelly's *Caesar's Column* (1890), reached bestseller status and illustrate a state of profound discontent with the state and future prospects of American society.

A second category was the continental or historical romance. Called by literary historians *"Graustark* fiction" after the title of a popular novel by George Barr McCutcheon (1901), these novels enjoyed a large following, primarily because of their escapist plots and old-world atmosphere. *Graustark* itself offers the standard elements: an imaginary European kingdom, palace intrigues, melodramatic sword fights, plus a strong dose of Americanism. The hero, a Yankee, marries the princess but not before giving her lengthy and tedious instruction on the superior virtues of the free citizen of the American democracy.

A third class of fiction with special significance for this study was religious in subject and theme. Frank Luther Mott estimates that at least one-third of American bestsellers before World War I could be called religious works, and a fair number of these were novels.[55] The market for religious fiction was especially lively at the turn of the century. To be sure, most of these works bore the marks of secularization, combining subjects of great contemporary interest with a sometimes facile pietism. For example, in the seventies and eighties, E. P. Roe, an ex-Presbyterian minister, wrote the equiva-

54. Glenn Negley and J. Max Patrick, *The Quest for Utopia* (Garden City, 1962), pp. 18–22.

55. Frank Luther Mott, *Golden Multitudes: The Story of Best Sellers in the United States* (New York, 1947), p. 286. For a further account of religious fiction, see the contemporary study "The Influence of the Religious Novel," *Nation* 47(1888):329–30; and Arthur Schlesinger, Sr., "The Changing Church," *The Rise of the City, 1878–1898*, vol. 10, History of America Library (New York, 1933).

lent of religious Horatio Alger stories for an eager audience. Lew Wallace's *Ben Hur* (1880) combined the appeal of historical romance, dramatic spectacle, and religious fervor. A spectacular case of this splicing of the sublime and the genteely sensational was Henryk Sienkiewicz's *Quo Vadis* (1896), a vivid dramatization of pagan decadence and Christian courage. All of these novels sold in great volume and obviously touched the imaginations of a large section of the American reading public.

In the meantime, the Protestant press (insofar as it can be distinguished from the general publishing establishment) praised General Wallace's book and others like it. Protestant publishers also found a growing market for their own religious titles, and during the balance of the century the staple of denominational fiction was little different from what had pleased readers as far back as the 1850's—Home-and-Jesus novels centering on family life and the trials of Christian belief in an increasingly secularized world. Two prolific novelists of the last quarter of the century whose works illustrate Protestant preoccupations were Isabella Alden (1841–1930) and Emily Clark Miller (1833–1913). Between them they wrote over 140 volumes of fiction and poetry, the largest percentage of which was directed to the sunday school market. Avoiding appeals to narrow sectarian interests, both women dramatized the broad tenets of evangelical Christianity, describing the remedial effects of Christian affirmation on contemporary social problems. The novels, generally free of suggestions of institutional reform, reduced social issues to the simple confrontation of individualistic pietism with godlessness and despair. Late in life, Mrs. Alden confessed to a niece her personal motivation for writing novels, a rationale that goes far toward explaining much of the literary activity of the period: "When things went wrong, I went home and wrote a book to make them come out right." [56]

Although works of this kind provided routine fare for the average Protestant's literary diet, a more strenuous image of contemporary religious life also began to be fashioned and to find a large readership. Undoubtedly the social gospel movement of Washington Gladden, Walter Rauschenbusch, and Henry George had much to do with this phenomenon; quite likely they are parts of the same

56. Quoted in "Obituary," *New York Times,* Aug. 6, 1930, p. 13.

phenomenon: the anguished awakening of sensitive Christians to the spiritual disorders of the era. While George was advancing a revolutionary and Christian solution to the nation's economic problems in campaigns for public office and in his book *Progress and Poverty* (1879), Charles Sheldon, a Kansas minister, published a dramatic fable that argued for a radical reorientation of personal values. In this novel of legendary popularity, *In His Steps* (1897), Sheldon described a town shocked, then challenged, by the question "What would Jesus do?" as the norm for their everyday behavior. Originally a series of sermons, *In His Steps* in published form won an enormous following. Like Bellamy's novel, Sheldon's work was followed by numerous imitators, all of them circulating the idea that Christianity might find American society seriously deficient—a courageous judgment in an age of exaggerated nationalism.[57]

Two additional aspects of the general literary situation of which Catholics were aware are the image of Catholicism projected in non-Catholic fiction and the works of foreign Catholic writers who commanded an American readership. It has already been noted that the first known Catholic novel in America was written to refute calumnies against the Faith spread through the novel *Father Clement*. In fact, the justification for a native Catholic fiction was the need to counteract anti-Catholic stories. It is true that the more vicious attacks had only an underground circulation, but occasionally such a piece would surface to precipitate a public controversy, like Maria Monk's *Awful Disclosures* (1836). It is the respectable literature, however, that offers the more significant history of the developing image of Catholicism.

Gifted writers such as James Fenimore Cooper and Nathaniel Hawthorne created without apology dangerous and sometimes frightening representatives of European Catholicism, especially in their priest characters. Cooper's novel *The Prairie* (1827) describes a Spanish priest of the Louisiana Territory who wars for the soul of the hero Middleton; but all his doctrinal subtleties are ineffectual against the native common sense of the Yankee. Father Ignatius is a semi-comic character, an example of the "compliant minions of absolute power (Catholics)," and Cooper's anti-Catholicism is more

57. See Mott, *Golden Multitudes*, pp. 195–98.

cultural than theological.[58] Hawthorne too used the Latin priest as an image of European decadence, a foil to American innocence. In the *Marble Faun* (1860), although his attitude toward Catholicism remains ambivalent, Hawthorne creates the character of a Capuchin monk who haunts the edges of the novel's main action, conveying such sinister qualities that the hero is led to destroy him. The monk, a Mysteries-of-Udolfo figure of melodrama, does not so much represent contemporary Catholicism for Hawthorne as a version of the solitary and autonomous man who owes allegiance only to himself—a type that in another novel bears the name Roger Chillingsworth.

By the 1860s the novelist's rhetorical uses of Catholicism had become more deliberate and politically conscious; the numerical presence of Catholics in the United States was a factor that could not be ignored. Thus Oliver Wendell Holmes' satiric portrait of an Irish pastor, Father McShane, in *Elsie Venner* (1861), although based on cultural assumptions similar to those of Cooper and Hawthorne, was gratuitously insulting. In much the same fashion but toward different ends, Harriet Beecher Stowe's novel, *Agnes of Sorrento* (1862), presents a picture of exotic Italy during the time of Savonarola. While cautious of Catholic feelings, Mrs. Stowe's New England bias shows itself, not in sneering deprecations of Catholicism, but in a supercilious and patronizing tone.

A European, Ludovic Halévy, entered the picture in 1882 with *The Abbé Constantine;* according to Mott, the novel was the first sympathetic account of Catholicism to become popular among American readers. Two years later, Helen Hunt Jackson's novel *Ramona* (1884) found a similarly large circulation for a story highly complimentary to the Church and its ministers. It is true that in the same decade Mark Twain wrote his biting indictment of the sixth century Church, *A Connecticut Yankee in King Arthur's Court* (1889); but his real target appears to have been all established religions rather than the Church of Rome in particular. At about the same time his friend and competitor for the literary leadership of the country, William Dean Howells, wrote a novel in which a priest had a minor, but warmly sympathetic, role. In *The Quality of Mercy* (1892), Père Etienne, a French-Canadian pastor, is confidant

58. James Fenimore Cooper, *The Prairie* (Rinehart edition, 1964), p. 178.

to the self-exiled hero. Earlier Howells had depicted a less attractive priest in *A Foregone Conclusion* (1875): Don Ippolito is a Venetian who falls in love with an American girl and is ready to flee his vocation and his country to prove his love. Partly out of respect to Catholic feelings, however, Howells is said to have altered his original conclusion to permit the priest to become reconciled to his vows.[59]

Anti-Catholicism in literature, then, did survive the century, but in a much muted form. Its more virulent expression either disappeared or seeped down to a level below the surface of respectability. Of course, a contemporary Catholic reader could hardly be expected to react complacently to even the milder forms of culture criticism for which Catholicism offered a convenient symbol; today, however, we can regard this anti-Catholicism much as historians interpret the anti-Semitism of a Kansas Populist of the 1890s—as a convention which served more of a rhetorical than an expository function. Like the terms "eastern" and "European," "Catholic" came to stand for a complex of cultural values and attitudes that contrasted with the individualistic and egalitarian ideals of American democracy. That there was a relationship between this functional symbol and individual Catholics or contemporary American Catholicism was very nearly incidental.

An altered and more attractive image of Catholicism in American and European novels might be indicative of a significant change, one supposes, in secular attitudes toward Catholicism. The novels described here, however, all dramatize a kind of Catholicism far removed from the life of the immigrant congregations. All find a setting for acceptable versions of Catholicism outside the conventional limits of American middle class life—in Italy, Canada, or, in the case of Miss Jackson's novel, the Spanish–American West. The familiar storybook accounts of Catholicism—simple rural peasants living idyllic if ignorant lives, super-subtle Church hierarchy acting out roles appropriate to Renaissance princes; the quaint, the exotic, and the remote—these were palatable, even attractive, versions of Catholicism. If they fostered a change of sentiment among

59. Edwin H. Cady, *The Road to Realism: The Early Years, 1837–1855 of William Dean Howells* (Syracuse, 1956), p. 191.

non-Catholic Americans, this change must be understood within the limits of the narrative form.

Catholic reaction to this literary image is more difficult to assess, and the Catholic journals convey no clear idea of it. Certainly the Catholic readership was at least vaguely aware that much of Catholic fiction was written to combat explicitly anti-Catholic literature. And the convention, noticeable in the novels discussed, of using glamorized European settings for Catholic life, was quickly taken up by American Catholic writers and was to become very familiar indeed to the Catholic reader, as later chapters will show.

A final note should be taken of Catholic literary influences from abroad. Besides Wiseman and Newman, whose contributions were discussed in Chapter 3, there were two later British novelists highly regarded by Americans, Robert Hugh Benson and Miles G. Keon. Benson (1871–1914) was the son of the Archbishop of Canterbury and an ordained Anglican minister until his conversion to Catholicism. His numerous novels, although now forgotten, still occupy the shelves of many Catholic libraries. Contemporary testimony was lavish in its praise. Isabel Clarke, a prolific Catholic novelist, wrote that "he did more than anyone to popularize the Catholic novel." [60] Keon, whose fame rests largely on *Dion and the Sibyls* (1866), which appeared serially in the *Catholic World,* also helped shape the literary taste of American Catholics.

Other favorite imports were the writings of French Catholics René Bazin (1853–1932) and Paul Bourget (1852–1935), both of whom achieved celebration beyond Catholic circles. Bourget, a follower of Zola until his conversion in 1889, sometimes employed American themes in his novels. Together the influence of these four writers on American Catholics was, in two respects, unfortunate. First, they helped preserve a condition of American dependence; second, compared to the best secular American fiction of the time, the imports were pale idealizations of life, interesting, sometimes delicately written, but ultimately backward-looking. But from another point of view, this influence may have had a salutary, if delayed, effect. When the giants of European Catholic literature

60. Cyril C. Martindale, *Life of Monsignor Robert Hugh Benson* (London, 1916); Clarke, "Apostolate of the Novel," p. 129.

emerged in the twentieth century—Bernanos, Greene, Mauriac, Undset—they found a hesitant but eventually willing audience among Americans who could not accept a Hemingway or an O'Neill.

Throughout this chapter I have made use of patterns of cultural adaptation to be found in secular or non-Catholic America in order to describe what was going on in American Catholicism in the eighties and nineties. Thus, the move toward a nationalized consciousness and centralization suggested a parallel development in Catholicism, as did the elaboration of educational and evangelical organizations in the Protestant churches. However, to make these comparisons central to an understanding of Church history is in important ways misleading; for in the last analysis, mainstream America and the Catholic Church in America were moving in opposite directions, and somewhere during the twentieth century they exchanged positions.

Henry May, in his analysis of the post–Civil War changes in America, concluded that the philosophical fabric of American society remained of a piece, however damaged, until World War I.[61] According to May, surviving cultural assumptions of the eighteenth century were under constant siege by proponents of a new science and a new theology, but they were not abandoned until the 1916–18 cataclysm. May's account is one of disintegration, falling apart, beneath a facade of complacency, even optimism; and as the nineteenth century wore on that complacency was urged with an insistence that approached hysteria. If there was a single motif for this period, it was change, flux, realignment, a bottom to top restructuring of American ideology and myth; and this reordering of values is nowhere more powerfully suggested than when Dreiser's Sister Carrie disembarks from her train in the Chicago depot to begin a career in the city, a cultural event that can be dated 1900.

The Catholic subculture, however, was following a quite different path. Subject to the forces and influences of the Gilded Age no less than the non-Catholic, the Catholic population nevertheless responded differently. There were, it is true, incipient forms of a truly sectarian thrust throughout the eighties and nineties, individual schisms. But the main movement in American Catholicism was toward a stiffening of boundaries of thought and action, a harden-

61. Henry May, *End of American Innocence* (New York, 1959).

ing, a solidifying of policy and possibility; and this occurred at the same time that the Irelands and the O'Connells were indulging in the most enthusiastic and even millennial rhetoric.

I do not propose to endorse the theory that institutionalization inevitably constricts the range of creativity. Yet that formula appears at least partially to explain the developments described in this chapter. Certainly in the areas of publishing and literary criticism, the Catholic population gradually developed its own literature and its own norms. Although there was never absent from the verbal encouragements of such a literature the wish to penetrate and eventually dissolve the wall of separation between Catholic and non-Catholic, the practical effect was an even more pronounced separatism. Ironically, however, as the life of the Catholic became ever more parochial, his values and aspirations became ever more American. Despite the wholesale duplication of social and educational facilities, despite the exoticism of medieval vestments, ritual, and symbol, the American Catholic was in many ways by 1900 a veritable caricature of the American. Aggressive dissociation gradually had turned into aggressive accommodation.

While the function of a semiofficial imaginative literature in all this is not as clear-cut as that of other, more directly observable phenomena, one can at least say that by the mid-eighties American Catholicism had the machinery for its own literature, including a publishing and promotional network of sizable proportions. How a separatist development could ultimately effect a measure of Americanization will be the concern of a later discussion. At this point it is necessary to move on to a consideration of post–Civil War literature itself, the subject of the next four chapters.

5 Catholic Fiction with a Parochial Purpose

Intramural literary reactions to conditions in the eighties and nineties, in spite of the increasingly denominationally-centered scope of Catholic social life, were not undifferentiated. The theoretical and organizational developments discussed in the last chapter suggest at least two different kinds of literature. Insofar as a writer was committed to the Americanist version of contemporary social reality and of its strategy for integrating the Faith into the national culture, he tended to draw on materials that fused Catholicism and Americanism. He wrote fiction demonstrating directly or indirectly the compatibility of the two supposedly hostile forces. He might suggest peaceful coexistence (pluralism), a program of Romanization of American life (triumphalism), or even the Americanization of Catholic institutions. In short, he chose to deal with the immediate and local problem of a Catholic presence on American soil. A second type of writer, persuaded that Catholicism was an alien force on contemporary American soil and that the true and natural habitat of the Church and Catholics was in Europe or in the remote past, was concerned to give his reader a representation of an authentic Catholic culture and the triumphs of the past. Such a writer was, in fact, often incapable of dealing convincingly with Catholic and American materials, and he wrote novels which avoided the Americanist issue altogether. He located his stories in a geographical and historical context utterly different from the America of the 1880s and 1890s.

These appear to have been the two options for the Catholic writer, for which we will use the terms Parochial and Cosmopolitan. This division, however naturally it may have developed—and few Catholics seem to have commented on it—represents the closest American writers came to a war of novels. It was an undeclared war conducted with good will on both sides, and it left no clear-cut victors. In this chapter the Parochial fiction will be examined. Later chapters will explore the Cosmopolitan writers and a third group that chose not to identify themselves as "Catholic" writers.

One should begin with Maurice Francis Egan, whose career itself defines the term Parochial. His name has appeared throughout this study about as often as that of Orestes Brownson. Egan's career was as prominent as Brownson's, his influence on contemporaries as great, and his ultimate impact on American Catholicism in some ways greater. Egan's funeral eulogist described him accurately as "the pre-eminent representative of Catholicism in American letters."[1] He pursued a number of careers during his long life—professor of literature, magazine editor, ambassador, poet, critic, lecturer, and novelist. His acquaintances included presidents and bishops, artists and entrepreneurs. He was probably the best-known and most-admired Catholic layman of his generation.

Egan was born in Philadelphia in 1852, the son of an intense and ascetic Scotch-Irish mother and an expansive, colorful Irish father. Before he was old enough to attend school, his mother had a conversion experience and enrolled him in a program of home reading and study of a religiously emotional kind. Having survived that regimen, Egan embarked on a career of study and work that became a pattern for several generations of Catholic lay leaders. He attended a parochial prep school, then LaSalle College. After a period of teaching at Georgetown University, he joined the staff of a Catholic magazine, *Freeman's Journal,* and became its editor in 1888. There followed, in succession, appointments as professor of English at Notre Dame and Catholic University, and, in 1907, an ambassadorship to Denmark. Throughout this period, he published dozens of novels, short stories, book reviews, essays, literary commentaries, and poems.[2]

1. Very Rev. P. J. Healy, "Funeral Sermon for M. F. Egan, Philadelphia, Jan. 9, 1924," reprinted in *Catholic Historical Review* 4(1924):118.
2. For details on Egan's life see Allen Westcott, *DAB* 6:49–50; and the autobiographical

Philosophically Egan was a genial eclectic—by turns romanticist and pragmatist. Perhaps he never sorted out his convictions in any systematic way. He reacted to people with the liberality of a saint and to ideas with unsophisticated common sense. Thus, he could claim the friendship of Walt Whitman, yet call Whitman's poems "excrescences." His lifelong friend and companion, James Huneker, was an apostate from Catholicism and an avant-garde critic of the arts. Egan had great respect for the French Catholic liberal Lamennais, yet could not comprehend Lamennais's break with the Church.[3] Few people, including Teddy Roosevelt, could resist Egan's charm; that, perhaps more than his writings, is the measure of the man.

Egan's *Introduction to English Literature,* published in 1900, was probably his most ambitious scholarly work. A review in *The Nation,* a journal not particularly known at the time for the severity of its critical standards, said: "It does not rise to the level where serious criticism can touch it."[4] This was an accurate, if harsh, evaluation, for Egan's critical abilities were comparable to his philosophical achievements: his judgments were shallow and often inconsistent, and his opinions of specific writers tended to be simplistic and even whimsical. He admired *Moby Dick* and *The Scarlet Letter,* but he claimed the English author Mrs. Oliphant as the greatest novelist of his generation. He praised the works of W. D. Howells, but thought both Tolstoy and Dostoevski poor artists. Henry James lacked, for Egan, a quality of "idealization," and he considered F. Marion Crawford's *Saracenesca* better than anything Howells or James ever wrote. He thought Mark Twain wrote the most egregiously vulgar fiction and would be a public menace were it not for the antidote provided by Booth Tarkington. And Thomas Hardy "on a pedestal could not reach Thackeray's base."[5]

What consistency appeared in Egan's hundreds of reviews and critical generalizations, sprang from his sense of the essential disassociation of the sacred from the secular. He would concede tech-

---

works, *Confessions of a Book Lover* (New York, 1922) and *Recollections of a Happy Life* (New York, 1920).

3. Egan, *Confessions,* pp. 89, 99.

4. *The Nation* 53(1891):472.

5. See Egan, "Chats with Good Listeners," *Catholic World* 43(1886):134,44(1887):559, and 45(1887):317,638; idem, "Some American Novelists," *American Catholic Quarterly Review* 17(1892): 621; and idem, *Confessions,* p. 143.

nical genius to James and Howells, but he reserved the supreme accolades for writers of a clearly Catholic imagination, such as Cardinals Wiseman and Newman. His criteria, expressed or implied, began and ended with proscriptions of anything that would wound the most narrowly-conceived ideas of Catholic morality and doctrine. Literature is, or should be, morally and spiritually uplifting, he wrote; beyond this, all one can ask is a modicum of grace and wit.[6]

The record thus sketched is perhaps too one-sided; yet except for one additional factor it is a fair account. Egan's own self-assessment in a large measure shows him in a very different light. In a collection of lectures, Egan characteristically referred to his own fiction as "sheer pot-boiling." He wrote that his youthful ambitions as a magazine editor were to refurbish the Catholic image "now in the hands of Mrs. Sadlier and J. V. Huntington."[7] Together, these comments point to a reasonable and fair judgment of his own role. Egan wrote potboilers, yes; but more importantly he domesticated the Catholic imagination. Together with the other writers discussed in this section, he helped to create a native American Catholic fiction with American locales, subjects, and themes. His novels are thus important not for their literary merit, but for the extent to which they turned Catholic readers and writers away from the exotic fantasies of Europe and the past and from the bias that regarded such exoticism as the true environment of a Catholic culture.

Egan's adult fiction (at least a third of his stories were for children) has three constant characteristics: it is melodramatic, apologetical, and depicts the varieties of life experienced by contemporary urban Catholics. The melodramatic aspects are the result of conflicts of conscience arising from temptations to wealth and social prestige, to "illicit" love (namely, for a non-Catholic), or to intellectual pride. Conflicting claims of religious and non-religious ideologies frequently exaggerate or reinforce such conflicts. Finally, a variety of urban social types, especially the immigrant Irish, crowd the stories.

A good example is the novel *The Vocation of Edward Conway*

6. Egan, *Confessions*, pp. 12,28,241.
7. Egan, *Lectures on English Literature* (New York, 1891), p. 148; idem, *Confessions*, p. 96.

(1896). Wondrously complex, the novel includes a long obscured theft, attempted murder and suicide, an amnesiac, a deathbed conversion, and a convenient call to the priesthood. To unravel such complications, Egan employed miraculous events and tissue-thin logic. He causes a child near death from smallpox to rise from his deathbed and walk several miles in the cold to discover his pagan father attempting to drown himself (an event which had been communicated to him in a feverish vision); the boy wrests an act of faith from the father before they both drown.

Despite dependence on such denouements, Egan always managed to build in a number of spritely theological debates, slanted unfairly by the faults given to the non-Catholic disputants. In *Edward Conway* four popular contemporary positions which recurred regularly in most of Egan's fiction are satirized mercilessly. One character, a young High Church Episcopalian minister, is enamored of a mannered medievalism. Though persuaded of the claims of his church, he is filled with uncertainty about his own sacerdotal powers. When one of his parishioners contracts smallpox and calls for him, the minister is fearful and finally declines to go. The local Catholic priest then visits the boy and converts him, proof of the superior claims of the Catholic Church. The boy's father is a grassroots transcendentalist, contemptuous of all formal creeds; his mother is a member of an evangelical sect. By setting off the incivility and pride of the father and the gross emotionalism of the mother against the gracious and reasoned person of the priest, Egan directs the religious argument toward rather obvious conclusions. He had most fun describing and brutally lampooning a group of women joined in the study of Eastern mysticism. The mixture of feminine fuzziness and unfeminine assertiveness provides a genuinely humorous interlude. Obviously Egan did not consider this belief a serious threat to his orthodoxy. If all this was not sufficient to bolster the self-image of his Catholic readers, the characters of two Catholics, the hero and the priest, are replete with piety, good sense, and robust Americanism.

Egan repeated this formula over and over again. The youthful hero in the *Success of Patrick Desmond* (1893) is tempted by the prospect of enormous wealth to give up his religion. Another succumbs to the lures of political advancement and adopts a comfortable agnosticism. Yet another is corrupted by the material comforts conferred by a large legacy, then redeemed in one night by an old woman dying of poverty and neglect whose faith has made her life an act of beauty. A young college graduate breaks a lifelong vow and ruins his life by marrying a non-Catholic. The religious representation remains similarly fixed, the list already described occasionally enlarged to include an Ingersoll agnostic, a higher-criticism modernist, or a confirmed atheist.[8]

The element Egan does not repeat, but which develops and grows and gives a special value to his fiction, is the social milieu of the urban Catholic. Most notable is a cast of characters he followed throughout several novels written in the 1890s, beginning with the *Disappearance of John Longworthy* (1890). This novel and its sequels depict a microcosm of Irish Catholic society in America and suggest a variety of promising as well as false avenues to social reform and Americanization. *John Longworthy* operates on several levels; primarily it is a quiet discussion of America's urban problem, using the sure-fire narrative device of disguised identity. In the guise of a ghetto photographer, the hero, a wealthy student of social problems, roams the metropolitan slums. Appalled by the conditions of slum life, conditions relieved only by the Church and the saloon, Longworthy concocts a plan to ameliorate the urban miseries, a plan which betrays the myopia of his upbringing and the gulf between the classes. The plan, which calls for massive doses of cultural uplift through free music concerts in a magnificent hall, leads to disastrous results: the concerts become occasions for brawls, flirtations, and buffoonery.

Longworthy's rescue and education comes at the hands of two Irish sisters who have managed to avoid the soul-bruising effects of their environment because of their Catholic schooling. Despite their lofty and pure gentility, however, the Gilligan sisters are astute tutors to Longworthy, arguing the tenets of Progressivism with the force of experience, common sense, and feminine charm. They persuade Longworthy that the community needs are more fundamental than he has imagined: better and cheaper consumer goods,

8. Egan, *The Success of Patrick Desmond* (Notre Dame, Ind., 1893); idem, "How Perseus Became a Star," *Round Table of American Catholic Authors* (New York, 1896); idem, "Heart Speaks to Heart," *Messenger of the Sacred Heart* 12(1892):255–67; idem, "The Packet with the Anchor Seal," *Ave Maria* 20(1884):1007.

more jobs, popular and healthful recreation, and the chance to learn skills for job and home.

In a subplot, the novel describes the career of a far more typical inhabitant of the slum, Miles Gilligan, a lazy, harddrinking, and unprincipled political hack. Miles' wife Nellie is the one masterpiece of characterization in the novel; loud and tasteless, transparently ambitious of imitating the manners of the newly rich, she is also a great vital force, strong, courageous, and loyal. Her pathetic mimicry of fashionable society is counterbalanced by her ability to see things from the point of view of the lower classes and to articulate that view in the authentic and universal idiom of the poor. Nellie is not only resourceful and cunning according to her kind, but she also has a native dignity and character that is luminous in comparison to the wholly proper sentiments of the lace-curtain Irish. She not only endures the aberrations of Miles over a long period of travail, she actually grows. Unlike the cretin passivity of Crane's Maggie, the simple biological cunning of Dreiser's Carrie Meeber, or the pale evanescence of a thousand more conventional heroines of Victorian fiction, Nellie Gilligan's moral resourcefulness is singular indeed.

Egan's literary achievements by any objective standard are slight. Yet within the context of American Catholic fiction, as a writer and critic, he not only reflected the taste of a great many American Catholics, he shaped that taste and judgment. For the historian he is a precious exemplar of consensus Catholicism. To say this is not to deny his personal graciousness and wit, his liberality of spirit, his power to mediate the conflicts between the Church and America. To say this is to affirm the opinion of the only contemporary—a priest and fellow novelist—who questioned Egan's literary and intellectual achievements. Father William McDermott ("Walter Lecky") during the period of Egan's greatest prominence characterized him as a "pioneer in American Catholic literature . . . an institution or part of an institution, and his work drew critical praise from half a hundred headless petty journals." [9]

Nevertheless, his novels served an important social function. On one level they offered a simple and basic social identity to Catholics, a prideful posture based on the right of American Catholics to a

9. William McDermott, "Maurice Egan," *Down at Caxtons* (New York, 1895), p. 61.

full and equal share in the American experience; they educated the Catholic to his rightful expectations and aspirations as an American citizen (in somewhat the fashion of Horatio Alger) and in the means to achieve these goals (hard work, sobriety, cleanliness, and propriety). More generally, Egan redeemed the domestic and the contemporary scene for his fellow Catholics, not only by making it congenial to the Faith but also by investing it with a vast potential for Catholic life.

The effects of his work were not miraculous; the urge to recapitulate traditional conceptions that owed virtually nothing to the American experience continued to be a powerful force in Catholic fiction. But Egan did partially undermine the hold of the tradition. His contemporaries and those who came after him were henceforth freer to cultivate with greater and greater confidence this territory he had cleared.

Within the body of fiction by writers classified as the Parochials, one can find several kinds of fiction, most of them distinguishable by their social utility. A large number of novels and short stories are thinly disguised instruction books on the manners of polite society. To some degree all fiction serves this socializing purpose, as I have argued previously; but such instruction was the central focus of the work of a writer like Lelia Hardin Bugg. Her earliest writings were commentaries on polite conduct for Catholics (for example, the Catholic woman always precedes her husband into the church pew, eyes downcast, hands folded). Later she integrated these rubrics into short stories and novels. *The People of Our Parish,* subtitled "The Chronicle and Commentary of Catherine Fitzgerald, Pew-holder in the Church of Saint Paul the Apostle," records the emotion-laden affairs of congregational life during a brief period of the ancient narrator's life.[10] Readers learn of the tensions in the parish and the social origins of these tensions; the associations one can join (the Brownson Debating Society, the League of the Sacred Heart, the Boys' Blue Ribbon Society—which promoted temperance —and the Society of Angel Guardians—which cultivated a special devotion to angels); of the necessity for absolute pastoral authority;

10. Lelia Hardin Bugg, *The Correct Thing for Catholics* (New York, 1891), p. 82; idem, *People of Our Parish* (Boston, 1900).

and of the varieties of class behavior within the parish. An earlier novel, *The Prodigal's Daughter* (1898), takes this concern for sectarian etiquette into a wider context involving romance. A breach of decorum generates the drama; the heroine inadvertently appears in public with a woman of ill-repute. Catholicism intrudes most explicitly when the heroine insists that her marriage to the town banker be delayed until after Easter.

An even larger body of fiction can be classified generically as cautionary tales, improbable vignettes that call into play one or more specific church sanctions and their effects. These are perhaps the dreariest reading in the entire canon; yet their function in reinforcing Church discipline cannot be overstated. One finds here such stories as that by Eleanor Donnelly which depicts the dire effects of an offense against modesty: an aspiring opera singer unwisely wears a low-cut dress to her professional debut, takes a chill and is ruined. A similar story by John D. Barry records the fate of a circus performer whose unmaidenly costume attracts an unworthy suitor and initiates a chain of calamitous events. Other frequent occasions for moralizing are mixed marriages, ignored vocations to the religious life, consorting with non-Catholics and going to non-Catholic schools, and temptations to wealth and power. Linked with these stories are accounts of the miraculous effects of certain devotions which work as barriers against an army of threatening disasters.[11]

Another small group of novels and novelists avoided simple social utility and the absurdly pious to develop small, strong, independent voices along the lines established by Egan. They deserve special mention here for their ability to integrate Catholic and American materials almost naturally. Father John Talbot Smith was one writer of adult and children's fiction whose experimentation with rural–urban tensions and their impact on Catholic attitudes reached the level of prophecy in more than one novel. Another was Kate Conway, mentioned earlier for her work as publicist and organizer, who in at least one novel dramatized in convincing fashion the social

---

11. See Eleanor Donnelly, "The Last Prima Donna," *Round Table;* John D. Barry, *Mademoiselle Blanche* (New York, 1897); Egan, "The Packet with the Anchor Seal"; L. W. Reilly, "The Mother of a Priest," *Messenger of the Sacred Heart* 30(1895):973–85; Marion A. Taggart, "A Round Year," *Catholic World* 62(1895):352–76; Francis Finn, "My Strange Friend," *Round Table;* William Seton, *A Poor Millionaire* (New York, 1884); and Reilly, "In His Name," *Messenger of the Sacred Heart* 31(1895):1012–18.

and political exploits of Irish Catholics in New England.[12] A third writer of distinction was Marion Ames Taggart, a convert from New England Congregationalism, whose writing career stretched over fifty years. Like the others, Miss Taggart was often confronted with a choice of materials sadly overworked. She redeemed the clichés, however, and gave them new vitality. Her story "Peace Hath Her Victories" brings together a priest doubtful of his vocation and a married parishioner uncertain of her vows. In the fashion of a Brownson, she argues (metaphorically) for more hardheaded rationality and less dependence on magic or the stirrings of the loins to authenticate the designs of Providence. Accordingly, the priest and the wife decide to wrest anointment by sheer force of will; once reconciled to this attitude, they no longer find their vocations burdensome. It is a particularly acute story, carefully composed and transparently honest; it is also a departure from simplistic norms that usually governed the handling of such materials. Other writings of Miss Taggart are more formulated or more original, but all show independence of mind and imagination and convey a convincing feel for the materials of her culture.

The last writer to be mentioned here is a priest and novelist, Father William McDermott, who came closer to writing emancipated prose than any of the Catholics of this group. An Irish immigrant, Father McDermott began working as a newspaper reporter in Chicago at age seventeen, then taught in a Catholic college. Somewhat later in life he began studies for the priesthood. He served out his last years as pastor of a parish in the Adirondacks. His life attracted scant attention from contemporaries and subsequent literary historians, but his few works qualify him for a position of eminence among the writers of his faith. Perhaps what most distinguish his work are the results of his journalistic experience and five years spent in the tenement districts of New York and other great cities.[13]

Father McDermott wrote several short stories and four novels,

12. See Smith, *Solitary Island* (New York, 1887); and Conway, *Lalors Maples* (New York, 1899).

13. William McDermott, "Maurice Egan," p. 187. Further biographical details, although scarce, are available in Patricia Feiten, "A Survey of Catholic Americana and Catholic Book Publishing in the United States, 1896–1900," (master's thesis, Catholic University of America, 1958), pp. 14–15.

most of which were first published in Catholic magazines. Nearly all the stories are set in rural communities in the Adirondacks, a fact which might seem to render McDermott's years as a reporter in the urban slums inconsequential. However, it is his journalistic training that accounts for the distinguishing character of his work, for pastoral prose it is not; McDermott's stories crackle with tensions observable only to a shrewd analyst of class structures and antipathies common to rural and urban areas. In most of his fiction he sets up rather simple confrontations between the village establishment and a band of "riffraff"—transient farmers, miners, and handymen. The basic decency and independence of mind of the latter stand out in sharp contrast to the village do-gooders, including the curate, who are proper and proprietary, sanctimonious, and intolerant of effronteries to convention or class.

McDermott's most successful novel was *Billy Buttons* (1896), a story about rural folk, with just enough melodramatic eventfulness to accommodate a rich array of crackerbarrel and homespun—slices of regional realism that compare not at all unfavorably with Bret Harte's fiction. More important than the Populist bias running through the fiction, however, is the casual pervasiveness of the religious point of view. He treats arrogant sectarian manifestations, whether Catholic or Protestant, with healthy cynicism if not contempt. His sympathies fall to the honest and unassuming, the decent little folk whose distinctive mode of religious behavior is the fellowship they show for others. Most often they are Catholics; but what identifies their religious commitment is not devotionalism, churchgoing, or exaggerated precautions to avoid Protestant contamination; rather it is their fundamental decency and compassion. Moreover, McDermott accomplishes all of this with no suggestion of sentimentality.

Father McDermott's ability to break through genteel literary conventions and prejudices and adopt without condescension the point of view of the common man, and his talent for naturally and unobtrusively injecting moral and religious insight, entitled him to leadership of Catholic writers seeking to develop a creative and productive nationalism. But his influence on subsequent generations appears to have been slight. He remains a symbol of the unrealized potentialities of Catholic fiction at the turn of the century.

Perhaps the most revealing and ultimately effective materials serving as simple reinforcement of community and ecclesiastical norms are to be seen in children's literature. The cultivation of proper sentiments, indoctrination in the articles of Catholic faith, and the inculcation of a veritable Catholic folklore of the young were important Church objectives, and children's fiction was a most important part of this development. In fact, children's literature earned respectability long before the adult variety, for the didactic fable appeared to be an effective means of introducing Catholic values to the young.

During the post–Civil War period, Catholic children's literature came into its own for much the same reasons as adult fiction did. Most of the writers considered in this study, in fact, wrote children's literature as well as adult fiction. Nevertheless, by 1890 a separate cadre of writers had emerged whose reputations were based on their children's stories. To classify these works is in effect to underline their social utility. Lightly structured travelogues, such as the novels of Mary Nixon-Roulet, acquainted the young with foreign lands and peoples as well as with the universality of Catholic beliefs and practices. Excursions into the past honored both the Church and America, the fictional saints of the heroic age of Christendom supplying a mirror image of the heroes of American history. Mary G. Bonesteel, wife of an Army officer, wrote half a dozen novels during the 1890s dramatizing the crucial but unsung roles Catholic soldiers played at decisive moments of national danger. A New York woman, Mary E. Mannix, wrote novels rather patently modeled on those of Horatio Alger but with a Catholic twist.[14] The novel of adventure set in the American West was more slow to develop, presumably owing to the lack of an available Catholic social history to support Catholic versions of the dime novel. But by 1890 two priests, John Talbot Smith and Henry S. Spalding, were writing in this genre, which Maurice F. Egan called "fresh-air" fiction. Spalding, for example, used a narrative premise based on the travels by raft of two white boys and a Negro to describe early Catholic missionary activities.[15] The sole difference between these and better known works

14. See, for example, her novel *Michael O'Donnell* (Boston, 1900).
15. Henry S. Spalding, *Sheriff of Beech Fork* (New York, 1894), and *The Cave by the Beech Fork* (New York, 1899).

of adventure fiction, according to Egan, was the absence of Ben Franklin "utilitarianism," an omission which he and the faithful celebrated.[16] Smith's works, which are much better than Spalding's, are located on stages of the advancing frontier in western New York. They are peopled with a rich array of stock native characters who convincingly wear their Catholic faith in buckskin and muslin.[17] For the most part these genres are familiar ones (Protestant minister Jacob Abbott had invented most of the narrative possibilities of the children's religious novel in his Rollo books in the 1860s); issued with the *imprimatur,* they represent one more example of the baptismal sanctification of secular and Protestant forms.

A type of fiction for Catholic children which earned a special distinction for infusing the genre with new possibilities was the novel of boarding-school life. The writer usually associated with these stories, who came to be a virtual one-man institution, was Father Francis Finn. Undoubtedly the best-known writer of juveniles for at least two generations of Catholic youth, Father Finn worked his magic in twenty novels and numerous short stories.

Father Finn described the beginning of his writing career as an accident, the outgrowth of a series of moralistic fables he wrote for his students at the Jesuit prep school in St. Mary's, Kansas.[18] Accident or not, he fell upon a simple but ingenious narrative formula. The secret of the story for young people has long been recognized as a matter of getting youthful heroes out of a context of conventional domestic life and into a world where young people dominate. Thus the orphan, the runaway, and the displaced have for generations been favorite types for writers of children's fiction. These devices, however, pose a difficulty for Catholic writers: models of Catholic behavior practice a regularized devotionalism, their life in the Church conforming to institutional patterns which are identical to adult norms. It is very hard to imagine Huck Finn carrying a rosary or serving Mass. Yet Father Finn managed to bring together a believable child's world, free of the impingements of ordinary adult life, and the full paraphernalia of orthodox religion. The Catholic

16. Egan, quoted in "Catholic Authors in Modern Literature, 1880–1930," *The Mariale,* vol. 6 (Loretto, Pa., 1930), p. 184.

17. See Smith, *Prairie Boy: A Story of the West* (New York, 1888).

18. Francis J. Finn, "The Boy and the Story" in *Fiction by Its Makers,* pp. 191–92.

boarding school gave Father Finn this environment—a child-centered world governed by rules growing out of peer-group associations on a twenty-four-hour-a-day basis. In this context, and given their ministerial vocation, the priest–teachers are regarded not as emissaries from the adult world—i.e., functionaries for the inculcation of an adult value system—but rather as pure versions of the most sacred boyhood ideals. The priest, because of his celibacy and his other-worldly commitment, can move into this milieu and be totally accepted by it.

A second advantage of this locale in which the priestly presence is fully integrated into the life of the place is a convenient and easily available solution to the problem of moral classifications by sex—a problem which dominated both secular and religious fiction of the time. The priest, though himself male, displays characteristics that in the lay world are associated with pious women—purity of expression, delicacy of mind, intellectual modesty, asceticism, and passive or unassertive beatitude—yet suffers no challenge to his masculinity. In other words the priest can express the full range of familiar and conventional religious behavior.

The boarding school was, then, a self-contained world where mythic confrontations between good and evil could be played out in a manageable, comprehensible, and, it was believed, salutary fashion. The priests portray both masculine and feminine virtues; but in nearly every story the hero is a young man who fulfills in flawless detail the national ideal of awakening manhood: he is intelligent, articulate, athletic, irresistibly popular with both his schoolmates and tutors, and instinctively fair-minded and generous. But Father Finn, like other Catholics, was suspicious of the active virtues so characteristic of his time. He reveals his discomfort by, in nearly every story, developing a secondary hero who is the epitome of passivity and acquiescence, in whose manner and characteristic expression we recognize the equivalent of the feminine in adult fiction. The principal conflicts of his stories, internal conflicts within the heroes, center around the issue of these two modes of moral perfection.

Tom Playfair is the most famous of the novels. Written in 1892, it portrays a thoroughly delightful title character whose one failing is assertiveness. Tom is all things to all boys; but to his spiritual confessor and eventually to himself, he lacks the perfection lent by a certain degree of modesty. While the logical equations worked out by the novels always require the triumph of the cloistered and virginal heart, the emotional bias favors the side of action and experience. The result is an uncertain resolution. Father Finn created a boys' paradise; but in his garden also lived the serpent of experience. He argues for a vocation to the life of holy-card innocence, and in this child's world he can give that ideal cogency. But the conflict is never finally laid to rest.

The reason, I suspect, is to be assigned in part to the divided loyalties, the divided cultures, of ancient Church and modern state. The all-American Catholic boy comes very close to being schizophrenic. For example, *Claude Lightfoot* (1893), another popular novel, has as its main character the son of a Canadian immigrant. The father is so obsessed with the issue of Americanization that initially he will not allow his son to attend the Catholic school for fear it will undermine the boy's national loyalties. Claude is a second Tom Playfair; his problem is to learn to subdue his impetuosity and enthusiasm. He brings these qualities with him to the Catholic school, unaware that they are flaws. Under the tutelage of his priest–teacher and moved by the prospect of receiving his First Communion, he becomes transformed and entirely subdued to the virtuous life.

It is not wholly speculative to say that Father Finn was responding to cultural divisions of two kinds. On the one hand, he dramatized the problem of the Catholic imagination, the conflicting ideals of native individualism and self-realization and an inherited bias in favor of submissiveness, docility, and obedience. In a second but very similar way, Father Finn reflects a conflict that runs deep into American culture, the polar claims of community virtues and the autonomous man. Significantly, Father Finn appears to have been satisfied that he kept control over his myth. A reader looking back at these works of eighty years ago will not share his conviction. Pleasant as they are, the stories leave one with the sense of an unsettled debate.

Father McDermott, whose opinion of Maurice Egan was cited earlier in this discussion, concluded that critique with these words: "He (Egan) is invited to lecture on all kinds of subjects. A clique grows around him, whose duty it is to puff the master. The reasons, frankly adduced, have limited the scope and dwarfed the really fine genius of Maurice Egan."[19] This judgment could suitably apply to the great majority of Catholic fiction writers; the mechanism of institutional absorption described in Chapter 4 is precisely what McDermott was referring to. Even within that institutionalized body there were, however, significant differences of kind and degree. What is important to recognize at this point is not that the talents of promising writers either flowered or wilted in the Catholic environment. Such talent, consciously perfected, was in some measure responsible for the extended range of possibilities open to the Catholic writer. The phenomenon of immediate social importance is the *fact* of a domestic fiction, a fiction that by the early 1890s had a momentum of its own.

19. McDermott, "Egan," p. 188.

6 Cosmopolitan Expressions

When Maurice Egan stated that he took for his special task the "rehabilitation" of the American Catholic imagination, he was, in effect, referring to its domestication. In contrasting the work he hoped to do with that of Huntington and Mrs. Sadlier, Egan allied himself with Brownson, Hecker, and John Ireland.[1] The tradition he repudiated, however, proved to be powerfully durable, a tradition here named Cosmopolitan.

For the Catholic writer living in America, the task of constructing imaginative fiction was complicated by conflicting allegiances—feelings resulting from a mixture of nationalism, aesthetics, and theology. The cultural antecedents of both his faith and his art lay in Europe. Not only the Church international but Catholic art too was rooted in the old-world environment; and America often seemed hostile to both. Some writers were able to resolve the conflict only by physical expatriation. Others, although they remained loyal citizens of America, created a special kind of literature.

The significance of expatriation, both as an imaginative and a physical act, has gone largely unnoticed in the annals of Catholic history. The story of the American artist who left his native country to seek out the roots of his art in Europe and who wound up living there, is a familiar one. Rarely, however, has notice been taken of the number of American Catholic writers who moved to Europe during the years after 1880. One can infer the same reasons for these as for their non-Catholic countrymen: desire for a more cos-

1. Egan's literary rationale is discussed in chap. 5.

mopolitan environment and contact with the cultural centers of the world. For the Catholic writer these factors seem even more significant, for to him Europe represented the conjunction of art and religion.

The group of Catholic expatriates was small, but their reputation and talents were large, and their works offer significant insight into the nature of American Catholicism. Although as a group they were much more competent artistically than the Tiernans and Sadliers who remained in America, they were nevertheless concerned with the same general themes and the same cultural conflicts growing out of the confrontation of the modern and the antique, of the European and the American. For that reason it is the act of expatriation which is the significant factor, an objective correlative of that remark frequently made by American Catholics that home is Europe—for religion, for art and literature, for culture in general.

The expatriates literally could not work, could not write on American soil. Henry James left Boston and took up permanent residence in Europe not only because he felt personally alienated from the cultural environment of America, but also because London and Paris had become important as capitals of avant-garde literary movements. Similarly, American Catholic Louise Guiney was both repelled by America and attracted to the Old World. Unable to find sufficient inspiration for her work in New England, she looked to England to provide that inspiration. But for Miss Guiney, the motive force was *both* religious and artistic, and the connection between the two was neither idle nor incidental. This relationship is best demonstrated by a cultural colony gravitating around a London-based publication called *The Yellow Book,* a colony with which several American Catholic expatriates affiliated themselves.

First published in 1894, *The Yellow Book* gathered under its masthead a rare and nearly undefinable blend of the daring and the decadent, who found their closest cultural antecedent in the pre-Raphaelite school of art and poetry. Loudly avant-garde in its claims, the magazine was yet curiously backward-looking in much of its content, especially its energetic rejections of utilitarianism, rationalism, and relativism. Factions from both extremes of the ideological spectrum—from the heterodox circle of Oscar Wilde to the respectable entourage of Catholic Alice Meynell—met in the pages of the magazine and discovered some peculiar cultural affinities. The coeditorship of Aubrey Beardsley and Henry Harland testifies to these contradictory impulses. While the magazine could hardly be called a Catholic front publication, it is significant that both editors and several contributors were converted to Catholicism during the run of the magazine or shortly thereafter.[2]

The Church in Europe offered varied attractions to this group. The color, movement, and incense of a Roman high mass made the Oscar Wilde of *Dorian Grey* swoon from a sense of overpowering sensuality;[3] for William Morris, Catholicism symbolized the medieval ideal of an organic society. Some responded to persistent strains of aristocracy and other antimodern tendencies in contemporary European Catholicism. But perhaps the most powerful attraction, seen from a twentieth-century and slightly Freudian point of view, was the fervid devotionalism that an English convert, priest, and aesthete, Father Francis Faber, made popular among English Catholics—an aesthetic religion in which the cult of the Virgin was central.

An example of this marriage of *fin-de-siècle* decadence and Roman Catholicism is a short story from the third volume of *The Yellow Book,* by the Englishman Ernest Dowson, himself a convert. The story, entitled "Apple-Blossom in Brittany," is obviously drawn from Dowson's life. He presents the plight of an English writer in love with his French ward. Despite an assurance of success if he would but plead his case, the lover chooses to relinquish her to a convent life, having decided that "any other ending to his love had been an impossible grossness, and that to lose her in just that fashion was the only way in which he could keep her always. And his acquiescence was without bitterness, and attended only by that indefinable sadness which to a man of his temper was but the last refinement of pleasure."[4] This was "mauve" Catholicism, the strangely pleasurable cultivation of denial, the gratifying style of despair, integrated with familiar elements of institutionalized belief.

The American expatriate name with the widest international

2. The most recent account of the magazine is Katherine Mix, *A Study in Yellow: "The Yellow Book" and Its Contributors* (Lawrence, Kansas, 1960).

3. James G. Huneker, American writer and apostate Catholic, captured this quality in describing his own attraction to Catholicism: "I love the odour of incense, the mystic bells, the music, the atmosphere of the altar." *Steeplejack* (New York, 1922), p. 55.

4. Ernest Dowson, "Apple-Blossom in Brittany," *Yellow Book* 3(1895):109.

currency is Henry Harland (1861–1905). Harland's fame rests on a widely read novel of the late nineties, *The Cardinal's Snuff-Box*. Having settled in London at twenty-six, Harland founded *The Yellow Book* with Aubrey Beardsley, was converted to Catholicism in 1897, and began thereafter to write novels with distinctly Catholic subjects.[5] *The Cardinal's Snuff-Box* is a charming story of love, art, the Italian countryside, of loyal but humorously obtuse peasant servants, elaborate domestic intrigues, and a wonderfully wise cardinal uncle who dispenses sweetness and light at the same time that he cunningly engineers the lovers' betrothal. The fable is delicately and wittily told, a genre piece of considerable merit, and contains a religious conversion that is convincingly motivated—no mean accomplishment in religious fiction. The anomalous reputation of Harland and *The Yellow Book*—"avant-garde reactionary"—is scored by critic Granville Hicks: "That a man who contributed so largely to the romantic deluge should also have been identified with the publication that most fully expressed the literary impulses of *fin-de-siècle* England points to the common basis of the sentimental and the sophisticated revolt."[6]

Another American, Pearl Marie Craigie (1867–1906), who wrote under the name "John Oliver Hobbes," was born in Massachusetts but went to England when quite young. Although she retained her citizenship until her marriage, she made only two brief trips back to America during her lifetime. In 1892, shortly after her divorce, she was converted to Catholicism. By the late nineties her novels and plays were beginning to develop Catholic themes, but these have no American content. Her stories abound in adventures of international intrigue and romance, with elaborate liturgical tableaux and theologically motivated confrontations—the conventional materials of the international Catholic novel. She was frequently mentioned as a member of the Aubrey Beardsley set and was among the contributors to the first edition of *The Yellow Book*.[7] Howells said of her: "She cannot be forgotten in any study of her time."[8]

An American with a religious pedigree quite different from those

5. For Harland's role in the *Yellow Book,* see Mix, *A Study in Yellow,* pp. 68–92.
6. Granville Hicks, *The Great Tradition* (New York, 1935), p. 156.
7. See Isabel C. Clarke, "Pearl Marie Craigie," *Six Portraits* (London, 1935); Mix, *A Study in Yellow,* p. 86. An example of Miss Craigie's post-conversion fiction is *School for Saints* (New York, 1898).
8. William Dean Howells, "Review," *North American Review* 183(1906):1251.

of Harland and Miss Craigie was Louise Imogen Guiney (1861–1920), perhaps the one literary genius among nineteenth century American Catholic writers. Born in Roxbury, Massachusetts, the daughter of a Civil War general, Miss Guiney did not lack for native roots. But before she was thirty she had determined to settle in Europe: "Not for excitement, not for vogue; but for the velvety feel of the Past under foot, like moss of the forest floor to a barefooted child."[9] Miss Guiney spent several years studying and writing about several Renaissance and seventeenth century British poets. Her discoveries, particularly in connection with the group known as the metaphysical poets, can reasonably be said to have anticipated the judgment and enthusiasm of critics like T. S. Eliot. Her own poetry was gem-hard and brilliant, fiercely restrained in subject and scope, but powerful nevertheless and always under control. She wrote two novels; not surprisingly they were both forays into the past—witty, lucid, but slightly anachronistic. The more famous of the two, *Monsieur Henri* (1892), had as its hero a leader of counter-revolutionary forces in the Vendée region of France. The peasant uprising central to the story is presented as a genuine grass-roots movement to restore the feudal authority of the province.

This short account of her work virtually exhausts the relevance of Miss Guiney for this study, even though one would like to make a great deal more of her. Her Yankee wit was observable throughout her life and her correspondence makes delightful reading. The letters also reflect something of the delighted complacency toward the political issues engaging American Catholics felt by expatriates. On the central political controversy of the time she wrote: "Nor do I look with edification on the Corrigan–Ireland civil wars [Archbishops Corrigan of New York and John Ireland of St. Paul] or on all the details of the entirely unimportant curriculum of the Plattsburgh Summer School." Of the energetic activities of Hecker's own order she wrote: "Schroder and the Paulists get into a temper over such local and transient trifles, that it always reminds me of the ancient Franciscan feuds about the shape of their founder's hood."[10] Her hero was Newman and with him as a model she literally remade herself into a British Catholic.

9. Quoted in E. M. Tenison, *Louise Imogen Guiney* (London, 1923), p. 215.
10. Louise Imogen Guiney, *Letters,* 2 vols. (London, 1928), 1:204,205.

The coincidence of expatriation and association with the aesthetes and mystics who gave buoyance to the British literary scene of the nineties has been seriously neglected by religious historians. These writers were Americans, after all, and at least Harland and Miss Guiney had deep Yankee connections, however much they wanted to sever them. Of course, their effect on American writing is difficult to assess because they chose fictional motifs which were then not uncommon in the writing of others. They belong with the cosmopolites, but they also represent something quite distinct. The choice Miss Guiney made is an understandable one, but it rendered her finally liable to a special criticism. While the Tiernans and the Skinners, and other writers who remained in America, were trying mightily to discover and proclaim a meaningful relationship between America and Catholicism; while they were developing a special literary strategy to persuade Americans of all faiths of the cultural claims of historical Catholicism—and thereby placed themselves in a position opposite to Egan and the other Americanists —Miss Guiney simply broke off the conversation. The ultimate effect of her work on American Catholicism was negligible even though critics and bibliographers rarely failed to exploit her fame in order to argue Catholic claims. As an example of one response to cultural conflict, however, Miss Guiney deserves a niche in the definitive story of the Church in America.

Henrietta Channing Dana Skinner was a member of another group of Cosmopolitan novelists who might be called the native romancers. Her life and works provide a profile of what was both a sect and a syndrome within American Catholicism. Important as the differences among them were, the group shared several significant characteristics, not the least of which was the assumption that religion is an important badge of breeding. As a class, these novelists were mostly women, their regional origins predominantly New England or Southern. Their family ties were at least mildly prestigious, and their American bloodlines reached back to the eighteenth century. As adults their lives were peripatetic, usually including an extended period of residence in a foreign country. Several of the group were converts to Catholicism, coming to the Church out of sympathy for the Oxford Movement or for reasons associated with the late-century liturgical revolution in the Anglican Church, itself shaped by the Oxonians. Their personal relationships went beyond Catholic boundaries, their circles religiously pluralistic and internationalist. By class and general inclination, this group would be called aristocratic; they resemble latter-day J. V. Huntingtons, distinguishable as much for class characteristics as by the overt content of their faith. Their identity within the institutional Church was somewhat ambiguous: on the one hand they enjoyed a certain celebrity among Catholics because of the public eminence of their lives; on the other hand, they lacked the parochialism of the more conventional American Catholic, which for the latter amounted to a special idiom and vernacular.

Mrs. Skinner, the daughter of Richard Henry Dana, was born into a storybook existence. Her family lived near the Longfellows and her brother married a daughter of the poet; her pedigree was Brahmin, her advantages rare. As a girl she professed her father's Anglican faith and attended services at the Boston Church of the Advent, which her father had helped build. Services there were conducted according to High Church ritualist formulae. The Dana family spent long periods in Europe, and a portion of Henrietta's education took place in a Paris convent. Although her father instructed the abbess not to proselytize his daughter, within a year Henrietta asked to be admitted into the Catholic Church. Hearing this, the father withdrew his daughter from school and for three years isolated her from all Catholic contact. At the end of the period, Henrietta remained convinced and was permitted to become a Catholic. The melodramatic cast of this narrative is misleading, for the girl was not ostracized from the society of her family and state because of her conversion; on the contrary, the pattern of her life continued to be much like that of any other similarly endowed New England lady: Radcliffe education, music study in Europe (under Cesar Franck), marriage (to Henry Skinner), and a life of travel and genteel refinement.[11]

The novels Mrs. Skinner wrote are interesting chiefly for the staple ingredients of aestheticism, international travel, monumental love affairs, and progress in the true faith. The novel *Espiritu Santo* (1899) is a fair example of her work. It could be called a vehicle for

11. This material is from Georgiana Pell Curtis, "Henrietta Dana Skinner," *Some Roads to Rome* (St. Louis, 1909).

exhibiting Mrs. Skinner's knowledge of European opera and society, as the plot follows the rising operatic careers of two Italian brothers. Two conflicts dominate the novel: the struggle of the older brother to withstand the attractions of hedonistic salon life and an ideological contest between traditional values and the new liberalism. Although Adriano at first succumbs to worldly ways, he is restored to the virtuous life through the agency of an American priest. On the political level, an opera critic expresses his Communist-bred hate for the aristocracy by attempting to destroy the brothers' reputation and to foment rebellion among the servant class. His ultimate failure permits the author to celebrate a traditional view of class behavior: servants should be loyal to their masters; masters should show a paternal love for servants. The classlessness of the critic Oeglaire's social vision is clearly abhorrent to Mrs. Skinner.

The religious ideal implicit in the novel is a demanding one. The more manifest criteria are fidelity to the laws of Moses and Rome; but the code can be said to pervade every least element of life, manners as well as morals. The potential confusion inherent in such a comprehensive code is demonstrated in one minor incident. Adriano, for a period, serves as a lay brother in a religious order in Algiers. His duties require him to spend a few hours a week looking after the needs of the parish. On one occasion he comes upon the heroine nearly dead from an accident and desperately needing help. Adriano, however, refuses, insisting that he must first complete his appointed rounds, a decision the author warmly applauds as the heroic triumph of duty over personal desires.

One may see in this narrative the attitudes common to the native romancers. They were most comfortable describing European settings and society; they took religion seriously, measuring all actions and sentiments in terms of religious affections. The religious spirit, however, was thoroughly interlaced with the spirit of class. Proper political beliefs and genteel behavior were, quite as much as correct theology, signs of grace. Villainy manifested itself as clearly by an offense against caste as by a violation of the Ten Commandments.

Invention being the very stuff of this fiction, one would expect melodrama to be the dominant narrative strategy. The preeminent Catholic potboiler of this period was a novel by Mary E. Smith, titled *Ambition's Contest* (1896). Miss Smith ("Christine Faber") was by birth a Southerner, but she spent her adult life teaching public school in New York City. The novel is a regular explosion of the imagination, a fabulous account of heroic struggles across two continents. It is also an instructive example of Cosmopolitan fiction.

Ambition's Contest, an extremely complicated story, is an account of a young man's struggle to curb his intellectual ambitions and submit to an external authority; the affairs of his badly divided family are also related. Howard Courtney (whose father has deserted his family for doubt of his wife's affections) is early pointed towards a brilliant intellectual career. An illness forces him to a convalescent journey to Europe where he impulsively enters a religious order. Finding religious life too confining, Howard joins a band of revolutionaries and writes a number of politically incendiary tracts that lead to his imprisonment. The shock of prison jars the young radical into a reevaluation of his beliefs; and after release he withdraws to a house of religious study and four years later emerges a priest. The subplot follows the hero's sister as she secretly watches over Howard, praying for his conversion and quietly extricating him from legal and personal difficulties. The denouement is one of those fantastic drawing-room scenes reminiscent of the nineteenth-century theater where one character after another advances, strips off his disguise and reveals himself as the lost father or uncle, brother, or domestic. Howard goes off to say his first Mass at the cathedral, manifesting every promise of clerical advancement and fulfillment.

Although one may be overwhelmed by the abundance of characters, the complexity of plot, and dramatic hyperbole, there remains in Miss Smith's story a body of materials that betrays a peculiar religious attitude. These include: the hysterical religiosity of the mother who would sacrifice the lives of her two children that a debt of honor might be paid; the conflict in Howard between Faustian intellectualism and the duty of obedience to an infallible Church; the seemingly irreconcilable claims of radical political theory and Christian orthodoxy; and the mystique of womanhood that would require Ellen to live a life of gratuitous self-denial in order to save Howard's faith.

Overriding all of these separate issues is the cultural conflict created by the interaction of America and Europe. Howard develops a hunger for ideas while growing up in America; his enthusiasm is, however, naïve and morally innocent. In Europe, among more sophisticated radical minds, Howard's rebelliousness begins to take on a Faustian character; his cause is social revolution, but the author makes it quite clear that Howard and his colleagues are in fact motivated by self-interest. The Europeans themselves, whether radical or conservative, are nearly all described as cunning, capable of all manner of treachery, monsters of intrigue, and steeped in centuries-old knowledge of good and evil. Only the priests—shadowy figures against backgrounds of gothic mystery—appear to have the necessary strength, wisdom, and goodness to actively combat the forces of continental duplicity.

Only the priests, that is, and pure women. Howard's sister has really no national character. She is the prototype of virtuous female passivity: instinctively recoiling from evil, giving way to egoistic demands all around her, intellectually modest to the point of stopping her ears to questionable ideas, and strong-willed in her selflessness—a prerogative, it seems, of the Victorian heroine. Ultimately, we are left with the following formulation: American culture is an inadequate environment for the nourishment of true spiritual wisdom; despite the decadence that dominates life on the Continent, experience of that life and discovery of true spiritual antecedents is an important source of wisdom and strength for the American. The marriage of Europe and America is an efficacious one, but it confers its blessings in greater abundance on the American.

Miss Smith and Mrs. Skinner suggest some of the more flamboyant characteristics of Cosmopolitan fiction. Within this broad category there are dozens of similar writers, but the possibilities for individuation were considerably inhibited by the genre. Mary Hartwell Catherwood and Mary Catherine Crowley enjoyed something of a distinction within the group, for their many novels were set in the American colonial period. However, their work is exclusively concerned with the period during which the French and Spanish were still active leaders in America's colonization. Both apparently found it difficult to write of the English or the "Americans"; of course, during the periods in which they were interested, the English were at war with Catholic France and Spain. They therefore confined their historical fiction to accounts of Catholic missionaries, French and Spanish settlements, and Indian relations. Miss Catherwood's *Romance of Dollard* is an account of the preservation of New France during a savage Iroquois attack; and Miss Crowley wrote a novel concerned with the time of Cadillac, called *Daughter of New France*.[12] Another variation is found in the work of the priest and bishop Charles Warren Currier, whose two novels drew on the events of early Christianity and the Counter Reformation.[13]

If there is one person who can by herself serve as an adequate foil for Maurice Egan and who best represents the persistence of the Huntington–Sadlier tradition, it is Mrs. Frances Tiernan (1846–1920), known to thousands of Catholics as "Christian Reid." One of the most influential and productive writers of her time, Mrs. Tiernan published over forty-one volumes of adult fiction during a career of forty years. Born to a Catholic mother and an Episcopalian father, she was raised as a Protestant. In 1868 she was converted to Catholicism, partly through the agency of Cardinal (then Father) Gibbons. Later she married F. C. Tiernan, lived in Mexico until his death in 1898, then resided alternately in Europe, Mexico, and the United States. She continued to write until shortly before her death in 1920. Respected for her vast popularity and for the consistent orthodoxy and purity of her novels, in 1909 she became the second woman to receive the University of Notre Dame Laetare Medal, an award annually offered to the Catholic who has contributed most significantly to Church and society.[14]

Collectively, Mrs. Tiernan's novels are a potpourri of locales, subjects, and historical periods. Their sequence provides a convenient classification, however, and in the classification lies a moral. The first group of novels was set in the Old South of plantations and small towns. Later, after a trip to Europe, her novels dealt with international materials. A third group of writings, comprising both

12. Mary H. Catherwood, *Romance of Dollard* (New York, 1898); Mary C. Crowley, *Daughter of New France* (New York, 1899).

13. See Currier's *Demetrius and Irene* (Baltimore, 1894), and *Rose of Alhambra* (New York, 1897).

14. M. F. Egan, "About Christian Reid," *Ave Maria* 47(1898):304–06; Annette S. Driscoll, "Christian Reid," *Literary Convert Women* (Manchester, N.H., 1928), pp. 97–108.

fiction and travelogues, have for a locus the Southwest and Mexico. The novels nearly exhaust the range of possibilities for depicting contemporary Catholic life, excepting urban America.

Child of Mary, first published in 1885, is the story of a post–Civil War Southern family trying to reclaim its wealth and self-respect in the face of advancing industrialization. The arrival of Renee, an orphaned niece whose French mother had raised her both French and Catholic, greatly complicates the lives of the Episcopalian Leighs. Of course, with the strength of Renee's religious purpose, the family is eventually converted from tepid Episcopalianism, but only after their minister shows himself to be intellectually dishonest by concealing certain doubts about his own church.

Apart from the lopsided battle for points in the Protestant–Catholic debate, a major interest of the story lies in its social geography. The town of Clarendon is made up of old family aristocrats, a new and commercial middle class, and a community of Irish immigrants who work in the town's new factory. The economic recovery of the town from the effects of the Civil War has been accomplished through the collaboration of the older families and northern industrialists. This rather remarkable relationship in no way compromises, however, the essentially pre-industrial coloration of village life. The immigrant Irish particularly live a life utterly circumscribed by the routine of work and worship, a rhythmic alternation as rigid as in an old-world manor. There is even a lady of the manor, the gracious Renee, to minister to the immigrants. She brings them, along with food and clothing, the Baltimore Catechism. She also subsidizes the visitations of a circuit-riding priest and eventually endows a chapel. As one would expect, the alliance of sentiment is established between planter, peasant, and the Roman Church. They reinforce one another; and, as long as the variable introduced by the new middle class can be contained, the arrangement has the appearance of permanence.

The variable in this social formula is most dramatically represented by an apostate Catholic and second-generation Irishman, who had come south to make his fortune. His fluid loyalties lead him first to deny his religion in order to further a career, then to promise a speedy return to the Church if Renee will marry him. Ferris represents a capitulation to pressures for which the author has a good deal of respect; in the face of such temptations, the alternatives are few and, under the circumstances, difficult of attainment. One of these is exemplified in the heroic stand against Mammon taken by a second suitor, a factory foreman. He too is Episcopalian until Renee inspires his conversion, a formula given plausibility by the young man's education, taste and breeding. For the ordinary Catholic, the Irish poor, Mrs. Tiernan seems to suggest the most sanguine course is to simply remain loyal to the Church. This point of view is the greatest moral weakness of the book, a disability that characterizes a great deal of fiction of this kind.

The Irish of Clarendon serve much the same function as a Negro element in earlier Southern fiction. They are quaint, picturesque, quiescent. In their dependence they find their rationale; in their helplessness they make the disinterested philanthropy of Renee seem positively lyrical. (It is of some importance to note that the Negro community is invisible in this novel.) The image of an ideal society pictured in this novel is one that is static, a sociological tableau.

Nearly the same formula was used in a novel by Mrs. Tiernan written fifteen years later, although the specific regional and national identities are altered. In *A Far-away Princess* (1900) a wealthy Protestant New York family is charmed into submission by the French-Catholic wife of their renegade son. The excitement of the novel is supplied by the bohemian inclinations of the artist-son and the stage career of his wife. Because of this element, the basic plot formula shows unexpected flexibility. The hostility of the American family toward Maria, the wife, dissolves with the discovery of her essential goodness and her impeccable and deeply held religious convictions. Not only is a stage career shown to be compatible with personal sanctity, Catholicism is discovered to be an important conservative force and thus a welcome ally of the anxious American aristocrats of the 1890s. The Harcourts, as a family, spend much of their time bemoaning the rapid decay of manners and morals and the triumph of a new and frightening barbarism. They are gradually led to see Catholicism as a powerful restraint upon social and moral change, a force, like their own community, with a vested interest in the past.

The international theme is given one further variation in a third novel, *Armine* (1884). Here Mrs. Tiernan reverses the direction, the principal characters leaving American soil (Louisiana) to live in France. The hero, D'Artignac, had returned to France to fight in the war of the Third Republic and suffered a disabling wound as an officer of the royalist forces. From his bed he acts as a father-confessor to Parisian intellectuals, counseling the old virtues of loyalty, order, obedience, duty to one's class, and chivalry. His antagonist—the villain of the story—is Duchesne, a fiery advocate of socialism. The character of Duchesne's daughter, Armine, torn between her own orthodox convictions and loyalty to her father, gives a certain poignancy to the story. Her dilemma supplies the focus for the novel's actions. When Duchesne dies, Armine joins a convent and thereby triggers the conversion of nearly the entire cast of characters.

In *Armine,* as in the other two novels, Mrs. Tiernan brings the old order into active confrontation with the new. In each case the threat of social dissolution hangs heavy over the traditionalists: a new and irreverent middle class in the American South; a bohemian spirit that strikes like a disease the heir of a New York family of ancient pedigree; the pernicious heresy of socialism that attacks the rotted underpinnings of continental culture. In each case, the force which works the defeat of heterodoxy is the Roman Church. So long as conservatism recognizes the Church as its ally and mainstay, civilization will endure. Mrs. Tiernan's novels repeat this formulation in dozens of ways. Identities change, but the functional elements remain the same.

This is the imaginary world of Mrs. Tiernan, a world of precious if not brilliant drawing-room conversations and issues, of contented peasants and domestics, of pure maidens and altruistic young men, of fiery radicals and besotted merchants—in short, of moral transparencies and philosophic simplicities. But in that world there is also a grim presence: the imminence of cataclysmic change. This presence the author does not directly face, much less exorcise. Her defense is to draw the lines of orthodoxy ever more tightly, ever more narrowly around an inflexible Church and a privileged class —the force, she would say, that informs Western civilization itself. In this calculus, one can find no dialogue between her values and those of the America of the day; the direction of influence is all one way. While John Ireland was urging the efficacy of American democracy and individualism as a prop for decaying continental Catholicism, his fellow countryman was arguing the antithesis: that the Western world could survive only by a league of conservative forces, cross and scepter. And Mrs. Tiernan was, by standards not exactly liberal, very successful at merchandising this view. Egan himself repeatedly invoked her name and her work as a standard of excellence. Her most enthusiastic biographer claimed for her a distinction that may well have represented a Catholic consensus: Mrs. Tiernan, Annette Driscoll declared, "never wrote a line that could soil a Christian soul." [15] The sales of her books were spectacular, considering the size of her potential audience. Although reviews of her novels were generally limited to the Catholic press, she was undoubtedly read by non-Catholics as well, since only about half of her ten publishers were Catholic.

Perhaps the most brilliant contemporary analysis of the cultural themes implicit in Cosmopolitan fiction was developed in a novel by a non-Catholic, *The Damnation of Theron Ware* by Harold Frederic (1896). Frederic's novel is the story of a Methodist minister who is overwhelmed by the beauty, the intellectual sophistication, and the urbanity of Catholicism in the persons of a priest and an Irish girl. A product of small-town Protestantism, Theron had been introduced to the Irish-Catholic through the Populist images of blue-collar revolutionaries, black-robed Bible burners, and urban drunks. His first Catholic acquaintance, however, the Catholic pastor Father Forbes, is a man of wide learning, elegant manners, and impeccable taste. Although the priest predicts a day when "his church—with the Italian element thrown out . . . will be the church of America," a day when the Church will be Americanized and America turned Catholic, he stands for Europe, in the Jamesian equation. In his conversations with Theron, Father Forbes describes the Church as the repository of the ancient wisdom of Western civilization, a gigantic force to which American Protestantism must eventually succumb. His own peculiar role as a genial skeptic is akin to that of the Grand Inquisitor. Ideologically, the novel develops a counterforce for Father Forbes in the folk figure of Sister Soulsby—an adult Huck Finn, a non-intellectual whose faith is based

15. Egan, "About Christian Reid," p. 305; Driscoll, "Christian Reid," p. 101.

on no religion other than love of humanity. But that part of the story is of no concern here. What is important for this study is to recognize Frederic's insight into the potential effects of a large Catholic element in American society; effects, significantly, on American culture rather than American religion. Henry James took his innocents abroad to find the cauldron of experience; Frederic alone of major American writers found the same possibilities on American soil, in the Catholic presence. The difference between Frederic and the Catholic cosmopolites is a difference of awareness. Frederic knew his subject was culture, not religion.

Altogether the writers discussed in this chapter represent both a positive and a negative reaction to the effort of American Catholics to accommodate their faith to American life. Measured by one set of norms, this reaction was benighted and utterly reprehensible, for the Cosmopolitans fed the Catholic reader a steady diet of irrelevant and anachronistic versions of reality—or at best, a version that prolonged hostility, inhibited a healthy acceptance of life in America, and was calculated to subvert the process of Americanization. According to this point of view, Egan and company were entirely correct in their attempts to domesticate Catholic literature.

Nonetheless, tempting as this conclusion is, it encourages an inadequate understanding of the dynamics of acculturation and its effect on the health of society. The potential effect of a wholesale acceptance of the formulation that Catholics must Americanize to the point of rejecting their European heritage and the forms of historical Catholicism is the development that H. Richard Neibuhr calls "denominationalism," the gradual overwhelming of the religious subculture until it no longer owns a separate, much less transcendent, identity. What Catholicism brought to America, to a degree greater than any other American religion, was its international character and profound historical consciousness. These qualities help to explain the survival of the Faith, the astonishing loyalty of Catholic laymen, and the even more astounding growth of the Church. Perhaps from this point of view the cosmopolitan literature was something other than benighted historicism. It performed a singular service for Catholics and ultimately for American life; that is, it communicated to Catholic readers an image of themselves and their spiritual legacy of cultural richness and depth. As such it served to create a healthy resistance to the spirit of Gallicanism, or religious nationalism, which is one interpretation of the Americanist movement.

Finally, one must recognize a regressive element in the extreme expressions of both Americanists and Cosmopolitans. At that point, descriptive genres become normative genres: the internationalist reinforces the cultural ghetto, the nationalist allows the fragile Word to be contaminated by the secular culture. The cosmopolitan becomes narrowly parochial, the parochial becomes secularized; both bear the marks of the mysterious beast of the Apocalypse, that frightening and ubiquitous monster of religious history who appears every time man mistakes a particular cultural form for the authentic gospel.

If this language appears familiar, it is because this study began with an account of the theoretical and historical polarizations of the secular and sacral within the Roman Catholic Church, an account that is freighted with these same assumptions. What emerges from this theoretical discussion is the suggestion that the ideal presence of the Church in time and in place is characterized by a working synthesis of these disparate and even antithetical forces—the forces for continuity and the forces for change. A political diagnosis of the Church of the eighties and nineties would show that the Americanist and internationalist positions were eventually polarized to the point where meaningful communication between them was no longer possible and that conditions were ripe for schism. That a break did *not* occur, that it was in fact unthinkable for the vast majority of American Catholics, is eloquent testimony to processes that were taking place below the level of hierarchical factionalism. These processes were aided and abetted by the imaginative literature of both the Parochials and the Cosmopolitans.

While the Irelands and Corrigans found themselves bitterly divided and demanded of their followers a degree of partisan loyalty that was nearly absolute, the analogous literary positions do not appear to have reflected or nurtured an equally self-conscious partisanship; instead the traditions of Brownson and Huntington flourished side by side, in the magazines, on publishers' lists, in the recommended-reading catalogs of numberless critics and reviewers.

Egan alone of the major writers seems to have clearly recognized the division. From the perspective of seventy years, this coexistence suggests either a critical ambivalence among American Catholic readers and editors or a lack of rigidity, perhaps both. In any case, it is clear that a largely silent dialogue was going on in the popular mind.

7 Catholic Fiction: Literary Anomalies and Excommunicates

As a generic term "Catholic novel" is severely restrictive as it has been used up to this point; in this narrow sense, the phrase refers to a work by an American Catholic novelist who wrote for an American Catholic audience, employing specifically Catholic materials, from a Catholic point of view. The four parts of the proposition are equally important: the credentials of the writer, no less than the overt character of the work; the makeup of the audience, no less than the interior bias of the fiction. The social phenomenon can almost be regarded as a single act; for the cultural significance of a particular work depends as much on the identity of the readership as it does on the writer's orthodoxy and the ideological content of the work. A novel that is extraordinarily sensitive, for example, but that has no noticeable Catholic bias, is not as important to this study as a less perceptive novel which is Catholic in viewpoint and enjoyed the favor of Catholic readers. Furthermore, the same distinction was persistently invoked by contemporary Catholic reviewers and bibliographers.[1]

The distinction is itself revealing of a particular and parochial point of view. But while it is instructive and provides a ready-made category of materials, the student of Catholic literature must also be familiar with the work of those few Catholic writers whose work did not conform, consciously or unconsciously, to the institu-

1. Frequently, Catholic historians and bibliographers have claimed as "Catholics" well-known writers and public figures whose connections with the Church were tenuous at best. See Appendix.

tional design. As a group they appear to have nothing else in common; that fact is both symptom and cause of their special distinction and supplies adequate justification for a discussion of their lives and work. Let it then be said for all of them that they were good and loyal Catholics and serious, dedicated writers who handled their materials with professional impartiality. They are important to this study because of their independence, the reception accorded them by fellow Catholics, and, most important, because of the attitudes revealed in their works.

Richard Malcolm Johnson, a teacher, lawyer, and writer, was the son of a Baptist preacher and grew up in pre–Civil War Georgia; he was a friend and neighbor of Alexander Stephens, who was later the vice-president of the Confederacy. After teaching and practicing law for a number of years, Johnson founded his own school in Georgia, later moving it to Baltimore. His life as a Catholic dates from his conversion in 1875. Encouraged to write by Sidney Lanier, Johnson began to publish short stories and sketches in the early eighties; before his death he had written six novels.[2] All of Johnson's fiction deals with regional characters and events of antebellum Georgia. His literary distinction lies in an unerring ear for the dialect and sentiments of the Georgia Negro, a rich but unsentimental compassion for his characters, and a vital sense of humor. Generally suggestive of the works of Joel Chandler Harris, his stories evoke nostalgia for a simple, uncluttered past; they are unpretentious, and uncontroversial, but, within limits set by the author, successful nevertheless. During the twenty years of his life as a Catholic, his fiction and criticism won loving, almost reverent tributes from fellow Catholics. Yet he remains something of an anomaly, for in all the many volumes of fiction he wrote, the word "Catholic" does not once appear!

There is little to say about the works of Colonel Johnson as the product of a Catholic imagination, devoid as they are of material touching on religious or social subjects. That he felt no compulsion to exhibit his faith in the explicit manner characteristic of so many Catholic writers, that he worked his materials according to the dictates of craft and his own personal experience, and that he found

2. *Autobiography of Colonel Richard Malcolm Johnson* (Washington, 1900); Frances Taylor Long, "RMJ," *DAB* 10:148–49.

no conflict in this position—these are significant facts. Catholic reviewers, moreover, responded to his work with unqualified praise.[3] This reception was at least partly the result of Johnson's choice of materials: he dealt with Negroes and with the past and did not raise sensitive questions of institutional loyalty.

In contrast, the life and work of John Boyle O'Reilly was as volatile and as controversial as any in American Catholic history, and the reaction of the faithful was understandably mixed. O'Reilly was a storybook character, one of the few people whose lives are adequately described in the inflated vocabulary of the Gilded Age. Born in Ireland and educated at the National School, O'Reilly enlisted in the army, joined the Fenian movement and, as a result of his revolutionary activities, was court-martialed and sentenced to death. The sentence was commuted to life imprisonment at the Australian penal colony, from which he escaped after two years and made his way to America, arriving in 1869. A year later he joined the staff of the Boston *Pilot,* a Catholic weekly, and soon became managing editor. Thereafter, his columns and speeches became familiar to an entire generation of Irish–American Catholics.[4]

His highly idiosyncratic personality loomed large over the terrain of postwar Catholicism. In a lifetime of memorable deeds—as publicist, Irish nationalist, Catholic apologist, organizer, poet, and novelist—one act stands out in contrast to the patterns with which this study is so much concerned. In 1889 O'Reilly refused to accept the chairmanship of a committee planning a national congress of Catholic laymen, and he resigned his membership on the committee as well. In his letter of resignation, he chided the other committee members for participating in a course which he thought wrong for both the Church and the nation. Religious conventions, he wrote, injure Catholicism by promoting divisiveness. Other unions, formed to promote the welfare of immigrants, to encourage temperance, to discuss and lobby for matters of political and economic moment, were, he said, legitimate concerns of Catholic laymen; but religious unions in themselves could only antagonize non-Catholics.[5]

Given this independence of mind, it is not surprising that when

3. See "Richard Malcolm Johnson," *Catholic World* 42(1885):91–102.
4. Joseph F. Wickman, "John Boyle O'Reilly," *America* 13(1915):425–26; and W. C. Schofield, *Seek for a Hero* (New York, 1956).
5. Katherine E. Conway, "John Boyle O'Reilly," *Catholic World* 52(1891):215–17.

the publicist turned to imaginative literature he bent the materials to his own purposes. The one novel he wrote, *Moondyne,* is not a literary masterpiece; it is, however, a powerfully original work and utterly dissimilar to all other Catholic fiction of the period. *Moondyne* (1885) is a barely disguised utopian novel concerned with a whole range of economic and social questions. The narrative follows Moondyne Joe, an escaped convict, as he miraculously acquires great wealth and becomes a philanthropist and social reformer. As governor of Australia, Joe sets about establishing a model community based on an economic democracy that would make political democracy viable. Describing a social scheme owing much to Marx, Joe calls for a radical redistribution of wealth and the abolition of class privileges. The golden age would arrive when society had learned to exist and prosper without laws. In the meantime, the forces of law were to be directed toward the protection of human, not property, rights. Joe's proposals closely resembled the ideas of Henry George and, like George, he argued his theory as a Christian response to the ills of society. Men must recognize the claims of brotherhood in Christ as superior to a set of values based on inhuman mechanisms. But, after expounding this revolutionary view with clarity and persuasiveness, the author surrendered to the characteristic weakness of genteel fiction: he assigned the source of remedial power to the traditional image of womanhood.

As the work of an American Catholic, the novel is an unusual document. Not only does it present an extreme position on matters of social reform, it also minimizes the role of institutional religion in achieving these reforms. For both these reasons, Catholic reviewers were reluctant to concede any virtues to the novel. The editor of the *Freeman's Journal,* for example, called *Moondyne* a failure because neither its chief character nor its spirit was Catholic. O'Reilly replied to these charges in a typically unorthodox manner: "To demand of a Catholic author that his chief character be Catholic is absurd. A novelist must study types as they exist." [6] This liberality of mind, this freedom from the sectarian mode of conception, marks O'Reilly as one of the precursors of an attitude some years in the future, when religious men were to assert that the sacral and the secular could not only coexist but could in fact

6. Ibid., p. 215.

reinforce one another. Yet O'Reilly was as much a part of the Catholic establishment as any layman in America; significantly, his influence seems not to have been diminished by *Moondyne*.

The most prolific and popular Catholic writer of the last quarter of the century, F. Marion Crawford (1854–1909), also avoided parochial preachments. Crawford's novels, turned out on the average of two a year, achieved celebration greater than those of any other Catholic writer of the period. At least four of them merited a listing among those Mott calls the "better sellers." [7]

Crawford's background combined native American advantages with cosmopolitan and Catholic experiences. His father was a sculptor who created some of the public monuments of this country. His mother was a sister of Julia Ward Howe, and Crawford was a favorite of his aunt throughout her life. His classmates for three years at a Boston school were Oliver Wister and John Jay Chapman.[8] To this list of influences should be added a European education and a wife who was converted to Catholicism.

Crawford's loyalty to the Catholic faith after his conversion in 1879 is unquestionable. He always proclaimed a deep devotion to the Church; and he demonstrated his concern for Catholic letters in 1898 by becoming a charter member of the Guild of Catholic Writers and by giving the first lecture at the new Columbian Reading Union of New Orleans.[9] His fiction, however, does not bear the conventional marks of the Catholic writer. His subjects were both religious and secular, contemporary and historical. He displayed a special reverence for materials sympathetic to the historical Church —tradition, Europe, and aristocracy. But when he did develop specifically Catholic materials, he seems to have exploited the melodramatic characteristics of Catholicism as freely and as opportunistically as Monk Lewis might have done. For example, his *Adam Johnstone's Son* (1896) gained its excitement mainly from a violated vow of religious celibacy and from divorce. *Taquisara* (1896) has a plot which turns on some questionable ecclesiastical legalisms about the validity of sacramental rites, the seal of confession, and deacons' powers. On the other hand, novels like *Three Fates* (1892),

7. Mott, *Golden Multitudes*, pp. 323–24.
8. Maud Howe Elliott, *My Cousin F. Marion Crawford* (New York, 1934), pp. 2–5,22.
9. *Publishers' Weekly* 53(1898):63; "Columbian Reading Union," *Catholic World* 67(1898):141.

The Ralstons (1899), *Paul Patoff* (1887), and *The American Politician* (1885) have no explicit religious content. This thematic ubiquity led one exasperated Catholic reviewer to exclaim: "Before reading the books of Mr. Crawford we had been under the impression, derived from sources apparently reliable, that he was a good Catholic, but his writings bear no internal evidence of the fact." [10] Nonetheless, no compiler of a checklist of Catholic authors and their works failed to include Crawford.

What appeared as an anomalous discrepancy to the reviewer quoted, to others smacked of a sell-out to commercial success. Whatever the explanation, it appears that, by the standards of institutional reviewers, the few Catholic writers who gained a measure of popular success beyond a Catholic audience frequently tailored their theology to a less sectarian readership. Crawford himself provided the summary comment on this question. Reacting angrily to the comments of fellow Catholics, he described himself as "a staunch adherent to the faith and a conscientious observer of prescribed duties." [11] To the editor of the *Ave Maria*, however, Crawford revealed the pressures under which he wrote by remarking that he had an expensive family to support. [12] Crawford's writings are therefore notable less for their content than for the pained response they produced among Catholic literati. The typical reviewer wanted desperately to claim Crawford for the Church and to exploit his eminence as evidence of the cultural superiority of Catholicism. His readers, however, could not translate his statements into easily recognized apologetics.

By contrast, Thomas Allibone Janvier (1849–1913), like Crawford a Cosmopolitan, took on the most urgent questions posed by his faith and his sense of history. Janvier was the son of a poet-father, a novelist-mother, and was married to an author and translator. Although he had little formal education, by the time he was barely twenty he was a staff member of the Philadelphia *Evening Bulletin*. Between 1880 and 1900 he traveled to the Southwest, Mexico,

10. J. M. Faust, "Two New Novelists," *Catholic World* 38(1884):790.

11. F. M. Crawford to Margaret Terry, September 18, 1882, in John Pilkington Jr., *Francis Marion Crawford* (New York, 1964), p. 87.

12. For a candid contemporary account of this chronic dilemma of the Catholic novelist, see Frank H. Spearman, "The Catholic Novelist," in Francis X. Talbot, ed., *Fiction by its Makers* (New York, 1926), pp. 102–12.

England, and France, writing news dispatches, a series of travelogues, and adventure novels.[13] Among all these writings only one piece, a critical introduction, was written about and for an explicitly Catholic subject and audience.[14] The novels, however, are worthy of careful study for their literary merit as well as for their insights into cultural conflicts in the Spanish Southwest and Mexico.

The Aztec Treasure House, published in 1890, is an adventure story about the discovery of a lost Aztec civilization by an American archeologist and an assorted crew. The central theme of the story is the nature of the Indian society. The archeological team is made up of several unattached American technicians and a Mexican priest, embodying the familiar stereotypes of Yankee resourcefulness, practicality, and attractive irreverence on one side, and Assisi-like simplicity and mildness on the other. A rather strong racist element also runs through the novel (e.g., "Anglo-Saxon hearts are found to be the strongest in the heat of battle"), but the relationship between priest and invader is not so simply described. The simple shepherd of Christ, hungering for martyrdom, moves the Yankees to admiration; at a critical moment, when all appear to be minutes from death, he prays with them and gains their full if temporary assent: "There was no word of doctrine in all his discourse. Rather was what he said a simple setting forth of that primitive Christianity which has its beginning and its ending in a simple faith in an all-pervading, all-protecting love."[15] The Americans appear to accept the piety of the Catholic priest and to acknowledge the efficacy of his ministry, but only in this anachronistic setting. There is no fundamental dialectic here, only a momentary exchange between a vital and energetic Americanism and a picturesque, pastoral survival from the past. Although both cultures are rendered sympathetically, Janvier makes it clear that he could see no effective halt to the spread of American industrialism and could not imaginatively find a workable synthesis of Catholic and American cultural attributes.

Janvier had opened a vein, and its rich suggestiveness would hold him fascinated for some time. The sparest and most clearcut ex-

13. Material taken from Archibald L. Bouton, "Thomas Allibone Janvier," *DAB* 9:615.
14. Preface to a novel, *Maria,* by Isaac Jogues (New York, 1898).
15. Thomas A. Janvier, *The Aztec Treasure House* (New York, 1890), pp. 69,151.

pression of Janvier's concern occurs in his short stories, particularly in the collection entitled *Stories of Old and New Spain*.[16] Here the writer's tendency to multiply adventure ad infinitum is checked by the economy of the short story, concentrating a novel's worth of meaning and emotional energy into one brief vignette. Three of the stories develop the cultural theme, what might be called an American pastoral. All three take place in the Southwest or Mexico, and all involve the effect of the railroad and ancillary forces on native life.

In one story, a New Mexican aristocrat, Don Jose, betrays the code of his class and calling to speculate in land with a Yankee partner, buying cheap from his countrymen and selling to the railroad. This violation of his people works disastrously for Don Jose, but his eventual reformation only leads to his murder, the assassin escaping all legal consequences. The Americans of the story are depicted as money-grubbers, cynical, rootless men whose way of life and whose railroad are inimical to Mexican culture. The adventurers who follow the train cheat the native out of his savings, rape the land, and leave as payment only their vices.

Another story, "Flower of Death," is gothic in its atmosphere but nevertheless full of familiar realities of the late nineteenth century. It carries the cultural interaction a step further with a love relationship between a Mexican girl and an American railroad engineer. The engineer, a New Englander married to a Massachusetts woman, has in his pedigree a Latin grandmother. Alone in Mexico, cut off from his Yankee environment, he succumbs to the call of blood and falls helplessly in love with the native life. Living with the girl, the engineer loses his usual vigor and becomes listless and unambitious. With a desperate effort, he makes plans to leave the country, but is poisoned by the girl before he can get away. Once again, the railroad appears as the nemesis of Latin culture, although Janvier is not willing to assign moral superiority to either side. Change appears as an inevitable force, lamentable perhaps but not to be avoided. Religion is represented as a cultural factor and Roman Catholicism as an indistinguishable part of the fabric of village life.

A third story in the collection, "Ninita," is more richly symbolic than the others. Again the plot brings together an American rail-

16. Janvier, *Stories of Old and New Spain* (New York, 1891).

road engineer and a Mexican girl, but the scope is considerably enlarged and the conflicting value systems more pointedly identified. The Mexicans regard the building of the railroad as a barely disguised act of U.S. imperialism, indistinguishable from the invasion of 1848. Restrained by the Mexican government from opposing the railroad, the Mexicans passively but knowingly witness the change and eventual collapse of village life. The girl, momentarily infatuated with an engineer, resolves to remain with her Mexican lover; but her parting gesture toward the American is misinterpreted by her father, a veteran of the Mexican-American War. Determined to offset his daughter's disgrace, he leads a suicidal mission against the railroad workers. When the bodies of the dead Mexicans are brutally dragged back to the village by the Americans, the girl kills herself by walking in front of the train. In the concluding vignette, Janvier describes the scene in a railroad car at the moment of the girl's death, the Americans arguing whether or not the train's pause was caused by a goat on the tracks. Here Janvier's sympathy is wholly with the villagers, although the American characters are not unfeelingly described. Grant, the pure Anglo-Saxon, casually accepts the affections of the girl and writes patronizing descriptions of the Mexicans to his Boston friends. He nonetheless conducts himself with great care for his honor. Religion is again depicted as an essential part of the pastoral culture and, implicitly at least, incompatible with the ways of the invader.

The works of Janvier are remarkable in a number of ways. The absence of jingoism is itself an extraordinary event in fiction that had a strong popular appeal. This absence, however, is less an independent element of a writing technique than a symptom of a deeper awareness of cultural norms; although, needless to say, Janvier's position is often ambiguous. He appears as the unwilling observer of a struggle that can only end in annihilation for one side and the loser is foreordained. But for all his fascination with the death struggle, he is able to identify emotionally with both parties as they await the triumph of a force over which there is no control. Janvier's is no effete lament over the steady erosion of genteel mores and the triumph of the new barbarism that respects neither custom nor title. His achievement is to have discovered a nearly perfect locus where the forces of the Virgin and the Dynamo can act out their conflict in a thoroughly believable yet symbolically powerful way.

As a Catholic, his singularity lies in the fact that he took the issue of culture conflict out of a strictly American or European setting—from the former, where accommodation followed the pattern of dissociation of religion and culture; from the latter, where Americanism was a clearly subordinate force. When Yankee confronts Mexican, the Yankee is not domesticated nor converted, nor is the Mexican invigorated with the values of opportunism, discipline, and the pragmatic use of power.

In one sense Janvier continued the tradition of J. V. Huntington, who found the only workable social context for an American Catholic tale to be in a society of Indian converts in primitive, frontier America. Like Huntington, he was unable to conceive of a culturally viable compound of the American and the Catholic. But Janvier was not led as a consequence to turn his back on history and to repudiate the American value system, and this is his distinction. It is not too much to claim that had Janvier had a larger influence on his fellow Catholic writers, he might well have led them into a more forceful awareness of the real dangers and potentialities of the environment in which they worked. As it was, however, his work appears only to have invoked indifference.

Earlier chapters in this study have focused on writers and writings that conformed to rigid canons enunciated by a Catholic literary establishment. One recurring implication of these discussions is that Catholic fiction was a form of "groupspeak," that individuation was possible only in matters incidental to the main concerns of the novelist, and that in fact the novelist was just another species of apologist. Such a generalization makes the subject manageable and makes possible a picture of American Catholicism as a neatly interwoven subculture. The judgment is not completely accurate, however, as the careers of O'Reilly and Janvier demonstrate. One can find considerable fluctuation, if only on the part of a small number of writers. And, if the point is insufficiently made by the foregoing examples—or even if there had been no Janvier, O'Reilly, Crawford, or Johnson—the range of possibilities for an American Catholic could still have been demonstrated by the next and final writer to be discussed.

Mary Agnes Tincker was at once the most quixotic of Catholic novelists and the one who best illustrates the currents of thought and feeling that give shape to this discussion of Catholic literary anomalies. In a larger sense, her life may say a great deal more about nineteenth century America than about the Catholic subculture. Miss Tincker never married but lived the life of a solitary pilgrim; her mind was constantly on pivot, moving through all the available stances possible to a sensitive and earnest seeker. Like Brownson, she ran the gamut of philosophical affiliations; also like Brownson, she found her ultimate haven in orthodox Catholicism. Her chronicle is recorded not in letters or essays or biography, however, but in works of the imagination.

Mary Agnes Tincker was born in Ellsworth, Maine, in 1831, the daughter of middle-class Protestant parents. Briefly educated, she began teaching at the age of thirteen in the public school of Ellsworth. At twenty she was converted to Catholicism and, with the outbreak of the Civil War, moved to Washington to serve as a volunteer nurse in Union hospitals. At the war's end she resumed teaching, in Catholic schools; but by then she was testing her skills in anonymous contributions to *Harper's* and *Putnam's* magazines. Her first novel, *House of York,* ran serially in the *Catholic World,* then was published in 1872. A second novel, *Grapes and Thorns,* appeared shortly thereafter and was also serialized. After these two novels had established her reputation and currency among Catholic readers, Miss Tincker left America and lived in Italy for the next fifteen years (1873–1887). During her years abroad she continued to write novels, but her ideas and literary habits changed considerably. Eventually she left the Church. Returning to the United States, she lived in Boston, wrote more novels, and exasperated Catholic reviewers with the ambiguity of her convictions. Well before her death in 1907, however, she had reestablished her religious credentials and, as one biographer wrote, died serenely in the company of relatives and clergy.[17]

This pilgrimage, so briefly sketched, is a faithful summary of the available accounts of Miss Tincker's life. The absence of detail is the result of inadequate scholarship and, more importantly, the

17. Driscoll, "Mary Agnes Tincker," *Literary Convert Women,* pp. 43–55; Harry Shaw, Jr., "Mary Agnes Tincker," *DAB* 18:560; "Obituary," *Boston Transcript,* November 30, 1907.

author's earnest efforts to avoid public life. One need not abandon the search, however; for Miss Tincker left a rich spiritual biography in her remarkable novels.

Her first novel, *House of York,* is rather freely constructed on an incident in American Church history, the brutal tarring and feathering of a French priest, Father Bapst, in the town of Ellsworth, Maine. Around this episode the author weaves an elaborate romance with elements that later became stock materials in Catholic fiction. The heroine, an orphan whose parents were disinherited because of anti-Catholic prejudice, returns to her father's family, her faith the source of family conflict and eventual conversion. Here the plot divides into two parts, the progress of true love and the war for sanity and tolerance among the villagers of Seaton, the fictional setting.

The triangular love interest is further complicated by the fact that one suitor is Protestant but well born, while the second is Catholic but lower class. Miss Tincker solves the problem of orthodoxy and social propriety by converting the gentleman and sending his competitor to the priesthood. Know-Nothing political agitation and the presence of a community of Irish laborers cause controversy in the village. The nativists commence a spree of violence against the Church and its priest that causes wholesale destruction before running its course. The warring factions eventually achieve some semblance of *détente;* but the reader is led to understand that the barbarians have not only won the day but also the future as long as American society is bent on a course of constant social mobility. Most telling in this assessment is the ineffectual reaction of the local aristocracy to the riot. Either they remain silent or attempt to dictate policy on claims no longer meaningful to the citizenry—namely the patent of gentility. The story plainly sketches the loss of leadership by the older families and the political ascendancy of commercial interests.

In this first novel Miss Tincker showed that she had well understood one of the significant images of contemporary Catholicism: the Irish peasants present a convincing if sentimental picture of a feudal community clinging to its faith with intense, simple loyalties. They are served by selfless priest-missionaries and sympathetic ladies of wealth. The Protestant majority, especially the townsmen, fear them, while the more settled farmers and country gentlemen see no harm in them. According to the logic of the social environment, Catholic and Protestant meet and touch only as respective members of the laboring class and the aristocracy. Squire York and his family, therefore, have only mild difficulties accepting Edith or the Irish immigrants. Between the laborers and the Protestant townsmen, however, there exists what appears to be a condition of permanent impasse.

Although Orestes Brownson claimed to have discovered the taint of transcendentalism in the novel (and he was perhaps right if by that he meant a certain vaporous romanticism which threatens to overwhelm the doctrinal orthodoxy of the piece), most Catholic reviewers saw promise of greatness. Twenty years later another novelist, Kate Conway, called it "the best novel written by an American Catholic." [18]

Grapes and Thorns (1874) confirmed in most critics' minds the promise of the first novel. Seizing on the dramatic possibilities of one of the more sensational articles of Catholic faith—the seal of the confessional—Miss Tincker fabricated a melodrama of compelling ingredients. Subsequently, that device became a popular implement to Catholic writers of fiction and won a place in Catholic folklore for several generations.

In the novel, the priest of a small New England parish is robbed, and his mother, who is his housekeeper, is killed. The murderer confesses his crime to the priest, but because Church law binds the priest to secrecy on confessional matters, he (and the reader) must sit idly by as an innocent suspect is identified, brought to trial, convicted and sentenced to be hanged. Needless to say, justice is eventually upheld, and the innocent man is set free. Before that happens, however, a community is fragmented by misplaced self-righteousness, anti-Semitism, and a stultifying class prejudice.

The relationship between Honora, the heroine, and Shoeninger, a Jewish musician who is accused of the crime, is the real center of the story; and its denouement, in which they marry, is a daring one indeed, even with his conversion to Catholicism. Miss Tincker

18. Brownson, "House of York," *Works*, 19:564; Conway in Driscoll, *Literary Convert Women*, p. 48.

appears to have abandoned in this work the convenient sociology of the first novel in order to attempt a statement on American Catholicism considerably more thoughtful and energetic than anything heretofore hazarded in imaginative literature. Honora, it is true, insists that Shoeninger become a Catholic; and Miss Tincker makes sure that no violence is done to conventional norms of class decorum. But the gentile does marry the Jew, and in their union work a diminution of the classical antipathies that were being daily multiplied on American soil. The Catholic religion is the solvent of these antipathies, and it is clearly the fond expectation of the author and her characters that the same solvent will work a society-wide reconciliation. The most revealing single statement in the novel is given to the Jew Shoeninger, who voices a sentiment and a prophecy, both of which were to have striking currency 25 years later: "I always admire most the Catholicism of America, or what the Catholicism of America is going to be. It is more intelligent, noble, and reverent. It isn't a sort of devotion that expresses itself in tawdry paper flowers. Indeed, I believe that America is destined to show the world a Catholicism morally more grand than any it has yet seen—a worship of the heart and intellect where children shall be delighted and yet common sense find nothing to regret."[19] *Grapes and Thorns* thus represents the first significant expression of the Americanist proposition in a literary context, and the language of that statement might well have been dictated by Isaac Hecker.

Not long after writing *Grapes and Thorns,* Miss Tincker went to Italy and, life there being congenial, stayed several years. During this phase of her writing career, her novels moved gradually away from American subjects and from the uncompromisingly Catholic point of view. Two of these later works are worth mentioning to show the direction of Miss Tincker's thought. *Signor Monaldini's Niece* (1879) is a skillfully written potboiler that incorporates gothic effects and spiritualism into an Italian romance. Technically the novel ranges from brilliant passages of description (particularly of the settings) to unrestrained evocations of the preternatural. The climax to a narrative which includes murder, deception, and fortuitous revelations of complicated relationships, is a miraculous

19. Tincker, *Grapes and Thorns* (New York, 1874), p. 237.

recalling of the heroine from the dead! Miss Tincker describes Italian Catholicism as a mixture of orthodox formalities and mysterious feelings and motivations that suggest a folk religion.

Another Tincker novel of this period reverses the Henry James motif, pitting American resourcefulness against Italian impotence. The novel, *Two Cornets* (1887), traces the lives of two girls—one heiress to an Italian dukedom out of which she is cheated, the other an American girl who accidentally becomes involved in the heiress's predicament. Most significant in the moral structure of the narrative is the implied superiority of the American Protestant woman to Italian Catholic culture. And that superiority wins the day. This fact was enough to set Catholic reviewers on edge and one, writing for the *Catholic World,* expressed horror that Miss Tincker could allow such a formulation to dominate her book. He goes on to label both Italian novels inferior to her earlier works and charges the author with pandering to commercial tastes.[20]

The pattern so far, although vaguely sketched, suggests Miss Tincker's growing disaffection with the conventional rubrics of Catholic fiction. Between those two "European" novels is another with less pronounced ideological and artistic shifts (*By the Tiber,* 1881) which shows a more secular turn of mind. To the literary historian, it bears striking resemblance to Hawthorne's *Marble Faun;* but to the religious historian, it offers a narrative tapestry in which formal religious configurations are very nearly incidental.

Thus, by the time Miss Tincker returned to America, she was an enigma to her fellow Catholics. The enigma was only temporarily resolved with the publication of a literary bombshell, *San Salvador,* in 1893. This novel offered a full-blown Utopia and a searching analysis of contemporary religious, political, and economic attitudes. Although the plot is unwieldy and frequently becomes lost in tangential conversations, the author manages to describe a perfect community.

The life of a young Spanish girl, Elena, is used to describe a secret community hidden in the mountains of Spain. Here the inhabitants live a communal life and develop plans to evangelize the world. The novel's interest centers on the history, attitudes, and structures of the community. For this study, however, the concern is with the

20. 'Talk about New Books," *Catholic World* 43(1889):250.

specifically religious character of the community. And, as San Salvador is a theocracy, nearly all aspects of public life bear directly or indirectly on the communal theology. Specific credal positions are given no official endorsement; and community members share a general belief that all Christian faiths have a content of truth. The goal of life is to rediscover the simplicity and purity of primitive Christianity and, by study and self-discipline, to achieve a higher Christianity purified of institutional forms and complex theologies. Although monogamy and the family remain sacred institutions, the social organization is communal. The text is rich in suggestive associations on nearly every issue confronting society in the 1890s.

The novel is saved from being merely a curiosity of utopian fantasy by the character of Iona, directress of education in San Salvador. An extremely intelligent woman, she has become, in adulthood, a virtual machine. Her ambitions, although dedicated to the welfare of the state, have rendered her nearly inhuman. Her goal is a world-wide theocracy, a New Jerusalem, in which the element of her enormous egoism is apparent. Deftly, the author exposes this paradox—the corruption of Messianic ambitions, the selfishness of total dedication, and the inhumanity implicit in this apparently most humane person. Iona at the end of the novel discovers that she has not only dehumanized but desexed herself as well—not for love of Christ but for love of self.

The creation of Iona is Miss Tincker's stroke of genius in the novel. Not only is her character executed with great psychological subtlety, but it also shows a delicate understanding of religious motivation. The novel ends without a convincing program for redeeming the world. There is no easy release from the inexorable contingencies of history; San Salvador remains an isolated island retreat from which influence modestly radiates. Even so, because of its restraint, the reader is convinced of the integrity of the vision.

This novel is certainly one of the most remarkable documents in American Catholic annals. It incorporates and projects much of the American sensibility, past and contemporary; but it is also a reflection of an imagination profoundly influenced by a Catholic experience. Perhaps no one else in her lifetime managed a more perfect synthesis of the American and the Catholic than Mary Agnes Tincker; and yet to achieve this rare integration she had to adopt the voice and the materials of neither Catholicism nor America. *San Salvador* is an extravaganza, but it is also as thoughtful, as well written, and ultimately as prophetic of time both past and future as either of the more famous utopian novels of Bellamy and Donnelly.

Theologically, the message of *San Salvador* closely resembles the position called "modernism" which gained vogue among European Catholics ten years later. To the author's American Catholic contemporaries, however, *San Salvador* was simply unacceptable. The preachments of one of the principal characters, Professor Mora, were an affront to orthodox Catholics, and the Christian transcendentalism of the San Salvador community was incomprehensible. The reviewers for both *Ave Maria* and the *Catholic World* expressed bemusement, the more especially as the author continued to be regarded as a Catholic.[21]

The reviewers' painful recognition that a valued sheep had gone astray brought its own form of ritual excommunication. From that point on, the name of Mary Agnes Tincker virtually ceases to appear in Catholic literary records; nor can one find it today in even the most comprehensive and inclusive checklist of Catholic books. One exception to this, an exception difficult to explain, is a short story that appeared in the *Catholic World* a year after the reviews of *San Salvador*. "Two Little Roman Beggars" is a harmless but quaint tale on the level of tourist impressions. The story is credited to Mary Agnes Tincker.[22]

As mentioned earlier, one biographer claimed that Miss Tincker repented her apostasy and returned to the fold some years before her death in 1908. The author herself, however, remains silent on these matters. During the last fifteen years of her life two more novels appeared. Their content, even better than extraliterary comments by the author, testifies to a mellowing of attitudes: the later novels are conventional in subject, quiet in tone, and theologically orthodox in theme.

Miss Tincker's work provides perhaps too convenient an example of the cross-currents in American Catholic fiction. For, although her pilgrimage had a direction, the resulting design is *sui generis*. Nonetheless, there is profound social import in her work, however idio-

21. Ibid. 53(1892):286–89; "San Salvador," *Ave Maria* 34(1892):442.
22. Tincker, "Two Little Roman Beggars," *Catholic World* 56(1893):609–21.

syncratic her vision. The novels and short stories run the gamut of the ideological spectrum of belief—from a simple and transparent faith in an Americanized Catholicism to a hope for a society purified of the dross of both nationalism and creed. Hers was a lonely journey; and despite the prophetic force of her work, she earned no particular following. She does represent, however, a development implicit in the American situation—a potential that required another four generations to take root.

In summary, the bulk of Catholic imaginative literature of the 1880s and 1890s falls into several broad classifications, which reflect the various tensions and conflicts among the members of the Church. The first and most obvious division emerged from the exacting standards by which a writer and his work were adjudged to be Catholic or not. These standards were simple ones and in themselves a comment on the level of sophistication of institutional criticism. But, however narrow the criteria and however false and misleading particular judgments were, the important point is that the institution was beginning to mobilize its resources to control and shape its own myth, by authorizing and encouraging an approved version and carefully excluding those works which did not conform to that version. This is by no means to suggest that a conscious or deliberate conspiracy of exclusion was in operation; but norms, distinguishing characteristics, did evolve that took on a rigid, almost sacrosanct character. And behind the norms was the weight of an ever more formidable institution, the Church in America.

The range of flexibility in Catholic fiction was thereby gradually narrowed to what was transparently Catholic. Within that range, however, there was still room for conflict over which was the appropriate self-image—the Cosmopolitan or the Parochial. Beyond that range, influenced but not bound by it, were the mavericks, working out their own syntheses of art and belief.

8 Catholic Literature: A Topical Analysis

The characteristic responses of Catholic writers to contemporary reality during the 1880s and 1890s resulted in the development of several broad categories of Catholic fiction, as the previous three chapters have demonstrated. The categories are, of course, limited by the same qualities that give them their strength, namely the weaving together of a multitude of biographical and narrative threads into an essentially impressionistic design. The present chapter will consider much of the same material in the form of a topical analysis. A few words of explanation on the process are therefore in order.

From the hundreds of works that make up the corpus of late-nineteenth-century American Catholic fiction one could extract the numerous narrative components and arrange them according to several significant classifications. By a simple calculation based on the assumption that incidence equals significance, one could then construct a composite of the corporate Catholic mind. For example, by a casual survey of over a hundred novels and short stories with an American subject matter, it is estimated that above ninety per cent of the priests who appeared were of Irish ancestry. The remainder were either English or of unidentified national origin. This statistic could lead to a number of inferences: that the Catholic conception of leadership was molded in an image of Irish Americanism; that readers therefore conventionally associated the idea of the clergy with Irish nationality; and that the judgment of most historians that Irish influence prevailed over the minds of American Catholics during this period is essentially correct. Introducing and weighting factors such as the popularity of the author or a particular work would require only simple adjustments of the formula to give an impression of greater sophistication. This process would seem to be a legitimate one.

The purpose here, however, is to use the phenomena somewhat less mechanically to clarify, by means of a topical analysis, two kinds of issues, whether directly or indirectly expressed: those which are broadly representative of writers and audiences alike; and those which offer exceptions to the norm, exceptions that express something more than an accident of choice. In this respect, patterns, indices of thought and feeling, of an oblique as well as forthright nature, will be considered.

Moreover, the topics themselves were chosen less for statistical convenience than for their overtones of covert values and attitudes. To continue with the above example, what seemed more important in an examination of the role of the clergy in Catholic fiction was not the *number* of Irish-American priests, but the fact that the authors invariably assigned them roles outside the center of action. They may have important functions in the stories—most often they serve as *dei ex machina,* superhuman figures called in to resolve a complicated dilemma or act as an ombudsman with power to intercede for the hero with his god. While the explanation of this phenomenon is rather simple, its meaning is a complex index to Catholic values. A priest, as the direct agent of a divine institution, was rendered free of psychological or moral conflict; his character was consequently undramatic. Unless a writer looked elsewhere for a subject, he would have no story. A priest, whether poor or well-off, in hostile or congenial territory, asked to neutralize a mob or baptize an infant, walked serenely through his appointed rounds. That conception of the priesthood appears to have dominated readers, who were aware of their own fragile defenses, as well as writers charged with the duty to present the institution and its agents felicitously.

In this chapter a number of subjects and themes relevant to both American and Catholic attitudes of the period are discussed along with judgments on the significance of separate religious, political, and cultural categories of story materials. In a concluding statement, these discrete discussions are brought together in an effort to form a composite picture of American Catholics.

Catholic fiction, in its self-consciously didactic form, was concerned throughout the eighties and nineties with a variety of religious subjects that can be grouped under headings of (1) doctrine, (2) moral conduct, and (3) the devotional life. Presumably the issues which were pursued most frequently and energetically were the ones about which American Catholics felt most apprehensive. According to this hypothesis, the preeminent doctrinal concern of Catholic fiction was religious authority. The term refers not only to the claims to authenticity of the Roman Catholic Church, but also, and more importantly, to the claim to an unerring and indisputable agency for fathoming and interpreting divine truth—a claim embodied in the doctrine of papal infallibility. The first American Catholic novel by Father Pise dealt directly with this question; as the century wore on, the fictional debate became louder and more strident.

One should not be surprised that this article of faith lay so heavily on the minds of novelists who were apologists for American Catholicism. A society which had no experience with divine-right rulers, which was aggressively egalitarian and suspicious of any control over the private conscience, and which had moreover deep roots in the Protestant Reformation, would have found religious authoritarianism distasteful even without a history of anti-Catholic bias. Yet, almost without exception, American Catholic writers endorsed the claims of contemporary Catholic theology to absolute and infallible authority for the Church in matters of faith and morals and for the hierarchical structure through which that authority flowed. This endorsement revealed itself not only in their considerations of the conflict between Catholic authority and the claims of competing religious bodies, but also of that between the Church authority and private conscience. The implications of the belief are apparent also in the typical behavioral norm of docility and in certain conventional relations—for example, those between clergy and laity.

The usual tactical approach of the Catholic novelist to this issue was to present a direct debate, often between a Protestant and a

Catholic. Frequently the polemic was reinforced by a brief narrative segment which demonstrated the anarchic and destructive consequences of religious individualism. Egan's novel *The Vocation of Edward Conway* exemplifies this method in its more transparent form. The novel is structured as a debate tournament, with the protagonists representing the entire range of attitudes toward religious authority—from the incipient permissiveness of a High Church Episcopalian to the antinomian individualism of a rural transcendentalist. For the most part these representations were free of subtlety; they differed only in the extent of their doctrinal elaboration. The Cosmopolitans, of course, found the orthodox structure of religious authority an obvious model for all human relationships, political and social. Other Catholic writers, for example Ella Dorsey in *Midshipman Bob,* exploited the affinity between military discipline and church discipline to argue the cogency of the Catholic position. The same military model sometimes appeared in the catechizing of candidates for religious orders, as in Lelia Hardin Bugg's *Orchids.*[1]

If not in the form of a debate, the explication of this doctrinal issue often took the form of a spiritual odyssey. As the protagonists journeyed from non-belief to belief, the intermediate stages of their progress were marked by reductions in the degree of individual choice available to them. Thus Marion Ames Taggart demonstrated the theological confusion produced by certain environments in two stories. In "Rome via England," the individualism characteristic of Unitarianism eventually drives a young man into the Roman Church. In "A Round Year," an intellectually promiscuous family life propels another youth through all the intermediate positions from humanistic agnosticism to Catholicism.[2]

The most skillful example of the spiritual odyssey is Mrs. Elizabeth G. Martin's novel *Katherine* (1886). This novel also develops and clarifies an intellectual accommodation only hinted at in numerous other works, by displaying both the paradox and the resolution Catholics experienced. The accommodation was extended into other areas of church and culture contact as the novel develops the thesis that unqualified freedom is disastrous to human fulfillment. The

1. Ella Dorsey, *Midshipman Bob* (Notre Dame, Ind., 1886); Lelia Hardin Bugg, *Orchids* (St. Louis, 1894).
2. Marion Ames Taggart, "Rome via England," *Catholic World* 60(1894):636–52; idem, ibid. 62(1895):362–76.

heroine, Katherine, moves with deliberate care along a spiraling route beginning with her parent's New England Methodism, progressing through Unitarianism to agnosticism, and at last ending when the heroine, exhausted and spiritually bewildered, finds comfort in Catholicism. Apart from a mild satirization of a Unitarian minister, Mrs. Martin takes no undue liberties in the prosecution of her theme; the tone of the novel is respectful to all those religious convictions which fall short of Romanism.

The novel is most remarkable for the carefully developed cultural context in which the argument is located. Mrs. Martin does not urge that religious individualism is inherently wrong; on the contrary, examples of Protestant and non-religious goodness abound throughout the novel. The character of contemporary American culture, which she also presents favorably, enforces the claims of Catholicism. The radical dislocations of persons, ideas, and things which characterize political, social, and philosophical life in America, she says, place intolerable burdens on the human personality. Under such conditions, the individual needs a haven of stability, of security, of absolute trust. The Catholic Church could not only provide these qualities, she argues, but it could also give the individual the strength to enter more fully, more daringly, and with greater abandon into the life of such a society.

Whatever the merits of this psychological intuition, it spoke directly to the most serious apprehensions of Americans of that time. By endorsing the native predilection for change, innovation, and freedom from absolutes, Mrs. Martin strengthened the appeal of faith in an absolute religious authority by picturing it as a necessary reinforcement of these predilections. To the Catholic reader, her novel offered a blueprint for the adjustment of Catholic faith to American ways; it promised the best of both worlds on the assumption that they reinforced one another. Accordingly it stands high among the documents of accommodation.

The necessity of a living and completely authoritative agent for divine truth was argued, of course, as but one pillar of the theological edifice. A corollary to the claim of infallibility was the idea of ecclesiastical exclusiveness. The proposition that outside the Church there is no salvation was also especially abrasive in a society which was committed, in fact if not yet in explicit policy, to religious pluralism. Catholic commentators handled this theme variously, depending largely on their partisan identification within the Church. Theologians had long since provided relief for certain unbelievers through the concept of "invincible ignorance." Interpreting the criteria which assigned unbelievers to that class became a major preoccupation of Church spokesmen. Thus, John Ireland employed a liberal definition for the edification of his non-Catholic fellow citizens; conservatives, on the other hand, imagined an enormous population regularly filing into hell for want of proper credentials.

In Catholic fiction a number of narrative ploys designed to deal with this issue rapidly became conventions, if not clichés. Although writers rarely faced the problem head-on, their intent is clear from what happened to non-Catholics. In a majority of cases, they either were converted or found wanting in character. Non-Catholics appeared as men of bad or weak characters or persons suffering from some grave impediment to the workings of grace. In the latter cases, a Catholic friend or lover induced the conversion of the nonbeliever. Most often the agent of grace was a chaste and devout woman who would not consent to marry someone not of the true faith. An alternative convention was the miracle, the recognition of which stripped the veil from the eyes of the benighted. Writers reserved their strongest criticism for apostates. They represented defectors, either as opportunists for whom the ties of Church membership were an obstacle to success, or as persons moved simply by lust. Nowhere in the fiction is there a single example of apostasy explained in any way other than by assigning the character a severe moral deficiency.

Given the grim inflexibility of this position, it is not surprising that a favorite device of novelists was the deathbed conversion or recantation. They apparently recognized two distinct uses for this convention: to relieve the story of its terror, and to generate suspense. Some writers exploited the convention cunningly, delaying the moment of truth and complicating the movement toward conversion with obstacle heaped on obstacle.

Although the overwhelming majority of Catholic novels treat this subject narrowly, there were significant exceptions; these, however, say more about the individual writer than about the institution. William McDermott, for example, in nearly all his stories, credited non-Catholics with intelligence, sensitivity, and unassailable integrity. This is not to say that conversion was not a central event in his works, but rather that he did not pander to his readers' tastes by denigrating non-Catholics. John Talbot Smith also dared to describe Protestantism with good will. His moving short story, "A Voice from the Wilderness," tells of a Baptist fisherman who raises an orphaned Catholic boy to be true to his heritage and fights both small-town bigotry and the boy's own willfulness to keep the youngster loyal to his faith.[3] It is significant that capturing the reader's sympathy does not depend on the conversion of the non-Catholic. Both McDermott and Smith were proponents of more tolerant relations between America's Christian communions; they were also among those writers labeled the Parochials.

A position of equal tolerance, although of a different kind, appeared in some of the fiction of the Cosmopolitans. As noted earlier, these writers classified behavior as much by characteristics of social class as by religious belief. Thus, for example, Mrs. Tiernan described a cultural synthesis of breeding, taste, and ideological convictions, an alliance that included not only Catholics but Protestants as well.

The range of attitudes toward the non-Catholic, nonetheless, was relatively narrow. According to most Catholic writers, the non-Catholic must either be converted or suffer eternal damnation. Exceptions did appear, however, in the two camps with the least similarities. As minority voices, they suggest an accommodation to American life more liberal than that found in the strictly expository discussions of Church doctrines. Since the narrowness of the official range of tolerance caused one of the more serious conflicts between American Catholic and non-Catholic, the existence of a body of sentiment favorable to the non-Catholic—however slight in volume and modest in its range—is quiet testimony to a gradual enlargement of thinking on the subject.

Problems of ecclesiastical structure and discipline, of all the strictly doctrinal questions raised, received the greatest emphasis in fiction. Still another doctrinal concern which yields insight into Catholic attitudes is the theology of grace or the sacramental system. Both of these subjects admit of a hard and a soft line and thus

3. John Talbot Smith, "A Voice from the Wilderness," ibid. 43(1886):485–504.

represent possible barriers or avenues to interfaith dialogue. Hecker, at one time, seemed to suggest that natural virtue responded to and called for divine grace and that the good life was sacramental even though agencies outside the formal structure of the Roman Catholic Church nurtured it. This sentiment, which Hecker's apologists hotly denied during the controversy over his biography in 1898, was an inevitable area of contention, tied as it was to questions of authority and exclusiveness. I have found no place in the fiction, with the single exception of Miss Tincker's *San Salvador,* where a writer directly proposed a freely functioning economy of grace. In some instances, however, writers acknowledged and addressed the question in their general attitude toward non-Catholics. Fathers Smith and McDermott again sound the conventional limits of non-Catholic beatitude. For most writers of fiction, however, the issue was simply not a live one. For them, the life of virtue was a life of divine grace; and the life of grace was lived only within the Roman communion.

Besides the question of the availability of divine grace, the sacramental or liturgical life of the American Catholic received much attention. Perhaps the best way to introduce this subject is through the account of a return to the Faith in Father Francis Finn's story "Sacred Majesty." [4] This story tells of a family's efforts to persuade the father to perform his Easter duty (confession and communion). Although they pray a great deal, plant reminders, and talk around the subject, he remains obstinate. His difficulty, vaguely described, appears to be simply a spiritual block in the face of which the family is helpless. What brings him around is the death of a child whose last wish is that her father be reconciled to the Church. This grief brings the father to the door of the confessional; but what happens then is not explainable by natural causes. The man is, during this brief experience, transformed into a devout Catholic, an effect one is led to believe is permanent.

This narrative is typical of hundreds of similar stories. What they have in common is at once paradoxical and revealing. First of all the sacramental effect is instantaneous and complete. Second, there is no apparent relationship between the effect and the natural patterns and environment of one's life. Third, the process itself is one

4. Francis Finn, "A Sacred Majesty," in *Mostly Boys* (New York, 1895).

that follows an exact formulation. And fourth, the process is characterized by highly exotic elements. In this example, the father walks into the confessional to pay a debt to a dead child. He walks out filled with an awareness of spiritual forces. The instruments of his miraculous change, the box enclosure, the rites of formal penance, and the priest-confessor, form a special mixture of the mystical and the legalistic; they combine to create a charged, other-worldly atmosphere, where the true presence is signaled by emotional transport. For dramatic purposes, such moments often form the climax of a spiritual adventure.

The magical character of the religious life is not, however, confined to the sacraments; it permeates all public and private devotions of Catholics in the fiction. The authentication of the Mass as a religious experience, for example, arises from qualities which are discontinuous with life outside the church building. Soft lights, angelic voices, stylized movements, richly colored vestments, the smell of incense, and the murmur of Latin phrases approximate, one is led to think, the expected afterlife. Private devotions played perhaps a larger part in the religious life of the nineteenth century Catholic than the Mass and sacraments, according to fictional accounts. To begin with, it is the rare hero or heroine who does not practice a special devotion to a saint or to one of the anatomical mysteries of Christ; and this devotion is frequently the badge of special sanctity. Moral identification is not the only function of devotions, however; they also serve as talismans. The Catholic who says the rosary daily, who makes the nine First Fridays, or who prays to St. Anthony, can expect anything, from protection against physical harm to reconciliation with an estranged husband or material success. Thus, in one short story an army sergeant who has fallen away from the Church, wears from habit a badge of the Sacred Heart and is by that gesture led back to the Faith. In another story, a boy who is about to succumb to the temptations of drink is, because he has made the nine First Fridays, given the grace to resist. A prayer to St. Anthony leads to the discovery of a lost waif. A medal of the Blessed Virgin protects a Civil War soldier from the effects of a bullet.[5]

5. Mary E. Bonesteel, "The Sergeant's Mission," *Messenger of the Sacred Heart* 8(1893): 520–34; Finn, "He Kept it White," ibid. 8(1893):118–30; Anna Dorsey, "Little Gladys,"

The life of worship for the fictional Catholic was, then, lived amidst incense and vigil lights, elaborate rituals and indulgences, charms and invocations, a peculiar combination of mystical faith and pragmatic calculation. In another terminology, it was a form of spiritual numerology based on precise units of grace-giving words and deeds.

The exact meaning of these observations as evidence in a study of patterns of Americanization is difficult to assess. Austin Warren, a brilliant analyst of literature and culture, discovered virtually the same devotional characteristics in the religion of British Catholics during the Counter Reformation. He explained these phenomena as symptoms of temporal and cultural dislocation.[6] Oscar Handlin found that similar elements were prominent in the devotional life of first-generation-American immigrants and explained their presence and power by reference to their origin in the folk religion of European peasants. Acts of devotion thus served to link the displaced immigrant with his personal and social past, to provide him with a sense of cultural continuity, and thereby to cushion the psychological shock of acculturation.[7]

These explanations are not incompatible, but they need to be extended. It strikes me that the peculiar devotional life of the American Catholic is to be understood less as a process of reinforcing the ghetto mentality than as a phenomenon designed to cope with the anxieties attendant upon rapid social change. Americans of whatever color and stripe developed during the post-Civil War period a variety of liturgies, all of them far removed from the real character of American conditions. The pious rituals of nationalism, success, racism, as well as the mysteries of investiture into the fraternal societies—secret and public—suggest an urgent and widespread need to fabricate a sacred order, however divergent that order might be from the secular order. Perhaps the divisiveness promoted by the exoticism of Catholic devotions is less important ultimately than the fact that such behavior had its parallel in other realms of American experience.

Ave Maria 21(1885):553–56,574–77; Ella Dorsey, *Jet the War Mule* (Notre Dame, Ind., 1894).

6. Austin Warren, *Richard Crashaw, A Study in Baroque Sensibility* (Baton Rouge, 1939).
7. Oscar Handlin, *The Uprooted* (New York, 1951).

Moral preachments in Catholic fiction were confined largely to conventional problems of love and career, but these separate subjects found a common theme in the question of loyalty to the Church. Discussions of sexual morality, for example, often dealt with the threats to purity from feminine immodesty; but the writers aimed their heavy artillery almost exclusively at the dangers to faith of marriage with a non-Catholic. The disasters that accompanied mixed marriage were sufficiently numerous and variant to justify their own special cataolgue. These engagements were tolerated when, as in Mary Meline's *The Mobrays and the Harringtons,* they led to the conversion of the non-Catholic. Occasionally, canon law supplied an agreeable solution, as in the case of Father John Talbot Smith's *The Art of Disappearing.* In his story, the husband deserted a bad marriage, found a good Catholic woman, and by virtue of the Pauline privilege (based on the assumption that unions of unbaptized persons are not true marriages) was received into the Church.[8]

More orthodox courtships and marriage seem not to have greatly interested the writers of Catholic fiction. When they did, the writer frequently drew on a convention from secular fiction, thus evading the problem of depicting mature sexual relationships. The untimely death of the heroine or her removal to a convent were familiar conclusions to the Catholic romance. William Seton, in his story "The Solitary Baron," described a singularly platonic passion between a wealthy land owner and a poor farm girl. Conveniently, the girl dies before the marriage, a disaster which confirms the Baron in a life of philanthropy.[9] One of Egan's novels, *The Success of Patrick Desmond,* ends with the disillusionment of the heroine and her withdrawal into a convent. A novel discussed earlier, Mrs. Tiernan's *Armine,* has a similar ending.

If the content of the fiction is an accurate guide, the greatest threat to the faith of the Catholic layman, other than mixed marriage, stemmed from the ambition for worldly success. This was a thoroughly understandable concern, particularly in a business climate thought to be aggressively hostile to Catholics. With few ex-

8. Mary Meline, *The Mobrays and the Harringtons* (Notre Dame, Ind., 1893); John Talbot Smith, *The Art of Disappearing* (New York, 1899).
9. William Seton, "The Solitary Baron," *Catholic World* 43:(1886):240–59.

ceptions, stories which deal with this problem follow the Horatio Alger pattern; but the Catholic Alger is different from his secular counterpart, particularly in his relations to the religious institution. According to the implicit logic of these narratives, a poor Catholic boy faced the same great obstacles to his worldly well-being as others, but with the added handicap of his faith. He had therefore to practice all the virtues of the traditional rags-to-riches candidate —patience, humility, sobriety, loyalty, temperance, honesty, and instinctive good timing—plus a special steadfastness against the apparent rewards for apostasy. Miles Gilligan and Patrick Desmond, two of Egan's characters discussed previously, retreated to nominal Catholicism in order to move ahead in the worlds of business and politics. Their fate was to fail in both worldly and spiritual careers. A variation on this theme was the story of the reclaimed, penitent apostate who captured, with his belated integrity, a comfortable position or legacy or some other prospect of a rewarding career. An anonymously written story in *The Catholic Keepsake,* a giftbook of 1893, tells of a man who deliberately leaves the Church in order to make his fortune in a Protestant business establishment. He bankrupts himself and is thereby stirred to confess to a priest. With his return to the fold, he receives a loan and starts over, becoming one of the "wealthiest and most respectable men in town." [10]

One further adaptation of a secular convention, more closely tied to the Alger tradition, was the fable of urban waifs. B. J. Reilly wrote a story about a pious New York newsboy whose death prompted all his rowdy friends to return to the sacraments and to resolve to lead holy lives modeled on his. All of them subsequently achieve a measure of worldly success. Ella Dorsey worked a similar vein in "The Wharf Rat's Christmas," a story about a crippled orphan who is discovered on Christmas Eve by a priest and started on a promising business career.[11]

One can make a number of points about this theme. First of all, the amount of attention devoted to the temptations of worldly ambition would suggest that it was seen as one of the most serious threats to religious loyalty. To counter the threat, the Catholic writer

10. Anonymous, "The Apostate Saved," in *Catholic Keepsake* (Baltimore, 1890), pp. 89–93.
11. B. J. Reilly, "How a New York Newsboy Died," *Messenger of the Sacred Heart* 30(1895):412–24; Ella Dorsey, "The Wharf Rat's Christmas," *Jet,* pp. 272–93.

argued an enlightened opportunism: the Catholic true to his faith would reap appropriate rewards of spiritual and material well-being. The suggestion appears often that one's Catholicism would, with patience and forebearance, eventually lead to a more successful material life. This being the characteristic bias of the stories, it is hardly surprising that the economic and social system should enjoy hearty approbation. While writers implied that people who were hostile to Catholics and Catholicism controlled economic power in America and placed numerous and frustrating obstacles before the enterprising Catholic, they also implied that the virtues of loyal churchmen would eventually insure them a competitive advantage. It is appropriate to infer from these examples that Catholic fiction served the established economic and social order quite as well as secular fiction did. No doubt Catholic success fantasies stifled discontent and encouraged a certain ready acceptance of one's initial lot, however sorry it might be. The reader need not think, however, that exceptions to this affirmation never occurred. The success ethic was challenged, sometimes severely; but in nearly all the cases, the renunciation of that goal was a sign of candidacy for the religious life. The young woman in Lelia Hardin Bugg's novel *Orchids* goes into the convent to demonstrate her freedom from the urgings of wealth. Egan's Conway is a similar case, a bright and ambitious young man who, on the threshold of a fine business career, withdraws from the world to become a priest. Laymen, however, are not called to such a life of renunciation, but instead are invited to enter the arena and demonstrate that they are the equals if not the superiors of non-Catholics.

The problem of drink was a somewhat less prominent concern of Catholic fiction. Temperance appears to have been important principally in treatments of immigrant life, although stories of this sort were few. Egan alone realized the important social function the saloon filled in the life of the immigrant; nonetheless he could not justify the institution and called for a more forceful parish life to offset its attractions. Other, less knowledgeable, writers regarded drink as a simple cause of failure and degradation, rather than as one symptom of a more profound disease. The conception that drink was an active agent for evil was certainly not peculiar to Catholic

writers; in fact, the handling of the subject by non-Catholic enthusi-
asts was practically identical. This viewpoint was apparent in spite
of the fact that large numbers of non-Irish immigrants were unfamiliar with such an idea.

As moral issues gained in force and persuasiveness in Catholic
fiction according to the extent of the threat they posed to religious
loyalty, the subject of racism was a very minor theme. Writers
treated ethnic discrimination as an evil, particularly when it combined with anti-Catholic prejudices against, for example, the Irish.
Catholic authors gave Negroes and Jews no special advocacy; when
members of these minorities appeared, they were treated perfunc-
torily and according to prevailing stereotypes. As noted earlier, Mrs.
Tiernan wrote an elaborate novel of southern society without once
mentioning the presence of Negroes. A prominent character in
Mary Agnes Tincker's *Grapes and Thorns* is a Jew who, although
treated respectfully, gains full acceptance only when he is converted
to Catholicism. F. C. Farinholt's short story "Dat Freed-man's Bureau" is typical of fiction with Negro characters.[12] Less vicious than
Thomas Dixon's *The Klansman* but equally condescending toward
the Negro, Farinholt told of a Negro freedman who is whipped by
his Southern employer for malingering. When the Negro complains
to the Freedman's Bureau manager, a Yankee, he becomes the instrument by which his employer and the Northerner become close
friends—partly on the strength of the Yankee's discovery that the
Negro is dishonorable. The recognition of Negro perfidy was, of
course, the familiar price of sectional reconciliation during Recon-
struction. This treatment is also consistent with general attitudes
and policies of the Catholic hierarchy at the time, an attitude reflected in the fact that at the Catholic Columbian celebration of
1893, the Negro contingent was required to meet separately.

Racial stereotypes figure even more prominently in fiction dealing
with Indian, Mexican and South American cultures, as indicated
in earlier discussions of Thomas Janvier and Mrs. Tiernan. These
writers, however, extended a measure of respect beyond tolerance
to the non-American peoples, respect partially explained by the Catholicism of the Spanish-American.

12. *Catholic World* 42(1886):488–95.

Any one of these several areas of Catholic morality deserves a longer and more systematic analysis; the code of personal and social behavior, insofar as it can be educed from the oblique testaments of narrative prose, is a richly suggestive tangle of contradictions and paradoxes. For my purposes, however, this brief discussion is sufficient to point up two crucial principles of the writers: the urgency and intensity of a moral issue was measured, by the threat it raised to fidelity to the Church; and secondly, conduct urged on Catholics was for the most part compatible with the morality of secular American life.

The political issues that found their way into Catholic fiction were few; and works with a primary interest in American politics were rare. From the broadest perspective, of course, all fiction deals in some sense and to some degree with political problems; that is, all of it is concerned with social relations and the structures and institutions within which these relations develop. Partly because of this interconnection, partly because there are numerous works which encounter the political in a minor way, one can identify certain significant attitudes. Two kinds of problems should be distinguished at the outset: areas of potential conflict clearly related to the official posture of the Church in secular society; and attitudes crucial to the political identity of Catholics within American society but somewhat incidental to their dogmatic position.

The overriding theoretical concern of Catholic leaders during the nineteenth century and for a long time thereafter, was the relationship of the Church to government. The literary response to this question was of two kinds, depending largely on authorship and fictional setting. The Europeanized Cosmopolitans saw no viable future in continental disestablishmentarianism. For Mrs. Tiernan and her fellows, the secularization of government was an unmixed evil, a thinly disguised attack on the Church by the nefarious forces of liberalism. This attitude was not confined to Europe, but extended to Latin American politics as well. In one of her stories, "The Hacienda," Mrs. Tiernan assigned to a patrician landholder a long diagnosis of the malaise of Mexican life; according to him, contemporary social demoralization in Mexico was the result of a policy of economic socialization and ecclesiastical separation. With the elimination of the official presence of Catholicism, he argued, life in Mexico had become ever more inhuman.[13] Such attitudes are to be expected, their antipathies directed toward what Catholics on both sides of the Atlantic and Rio Grande took to be a virulent, aggressive anticlericalism.

If these societies historically linked by law to ecclesiastical authority were ungrateful despoilers of an essential birthright, and if Catholic novelists and characters alike indulged a nostalgia for the *ancien régime,* no such animus characterized the Catholic regard for American church–state relations. Catholics appear to have blessed the First Amendment with all the fervor of the Founding Fathers. They regarded the neutrality of the state toward religion as a policy favorable to the Catholic minority. Not surprisingly, men as separated in time and sentiment as John Carroll, John Hughes, and John Courtney Murray, have celebrated this constitutional protection. Certain corollaries to this position, however, bespeak a solicitude for the ecclesiastical institution as well as for the state. One such corollary is the conviction that in an environment free of legal privilege, the divinely sanctioned Church must triumph. A second proposition, one that Brownson asserted midway in the nineteenth century, holds that the Church is utterly necessary to the American public, that the growth of Catholic influence alone would assure the health of the American government. This argument depended on the assumption that the American political process was a mixture of the permanent and the transient, the Constitution being the unchanging element, majority rule the ephemeral. Catholic theorists like Brownson considered the Constitution much as they did Holy Scripture, a deposit of political truth of permanent validity but infinitely various in its interpretation. Given the mechanism of democracy, society required a stabilizing force, an island of certitude in the maelstrom. This force was to be provided by the unchanging Roman Catholic Church. The Church, therefore, far from being subversive of democratic principles, was rather their reinforcement.[14]

In the fiction, this assumption appears for the most part in explicit debates between Catholic apologists and non-Catholics who were suspicious of the Catholic presence in America. In answer to the

13. Mrs. F. C. S. Tiernan, "The Hacienda," Mother Seraphine, ed., *Immortelles of Catholic Columbian Literature* (New York, 1897).

14. See Brownson's political treatise, *The American Republic* (New York, 1865).

charge that he could not be a loyal citizen, that he was under direct political control of the Vatican, the Catholic character would typically respond that there was no conflict between the Faith and American nationalism. The American believer who studiously practiced his religion was both a better American and a better Christian, loyalty to one's country being a touchstone of that faith. If that were not enough, the apologist would recite the honor roll of American Catholics who had performed important services for the Republic.[15]

In addition to the larger theoretical problems of politics, Catholic fiction occasionally reflected particular areas of conflict in social legislation, such as education, divorce, the exemption of priests from courtroom testimony, tax-exemption of church property, and temperance. Already described is Miss Tincker's novel, *Grapes and Thorns,* which dealt with the difficult legal problem stemming from the church law forbidding priests to reveal information learned in confession. No other work of fiction assigns a central position to that or similar Church-law conflicts. Occasional conversations include a lamentation on the permissive divorce laws of the state, a defense of the Catholic school system, or a plea for more stringent controls over the merchandising of spirits. But for the most part the literature gives the impression that American law is basically benign and congenial to Catholics. Public office was a worthy goal for young men, and the machinery of democracy appears again and again as a divinely ordained instrument of human perfection. Difficulties are seen to stem more from the failure of individuals than from the structure of government. This favorable attitude is not surprising; it only confirmed the position which Catholic spokesmen took in innumerable expository essays.

The specter of Tammany crowded the pages of Catholic fiction, and the reactions to it were surprisingly varied. Considering the age and the special condition of the mass of Catholics, a major political concern of many Americans was the survival of traditional values in the face of an ever-growing immigrant electorate and the expansion of new urban power blocs under machine politicians. As one response, one finds in Miss Tincker's novel *House of York* a frank admission that the traditional leaders of society, the landed

15. See for example Bugg, *The Prodigal Daughter,* and Egan, "How Perseus Became a Star."

aristocracy, are constitutionally incapable of dealing effectively with the new class of entrepreneurs; Miss Tincker applauded Squire York's decision to retire from political life to escape involvement in political affairs. In Mrs. Tiernan's vision of social realities, the old leadership and the immigrants had to forge an alliance in order to sustain enlightened government. Given the immigrant's old-country habits and the influence of the Catholic Church, he would, according to Mrs. Tiernan, actually spurn association with the new business interests and turn instinctively for leadership to the more traditional establishment. Mrs. Tiernan argued through all her American stories that the forces of social dissolution could be checked only by the cultivation of this union of the oldest and newest social elements. She dramatized this conviction in her stories of the post–Civil War South and East, and she urged on her Brahmin characters a ready acceptance of the Catholic immigrant as a natural ally in their efforts to withstand the economic and political barbarians, and to conserve the established order.

Maurice Egan took a somewhat different view, more knowledgeable as well because closer to the realities of urban life. He satirized the city machine in two novels, and he extracted pathos from numerous short stories of immigrant exploitation by urban bosses. His finest political creation was Miles Gilligan, Irish slum dweller, who translates a gift for street-corner oratory into a state office. Miles never rose above simple, transparent opportunism; and while Egan cast him in a comic role and therefore kept a certain degree of emotional distance from his dilemma, he obviously regarded his hero as a victim of the acculturation process. In Egan's urban slum, the prospect of humanizing the political and economic institutions was long range and depended on individual conversion rather than an alteration of the "system." His was a Progressive's response to the social problems of the time. He looked to the government to perform certain regulatory functions in order to prevent business establishments and party opportunists from exploiting the poor; and he looked to the religious institutions to instruct the faithful in their social responsibilities.

Egan's position is dead center on the spectrum of Catholic political attitudes reflected in the fiction. Two writers, John Talbot Smith and Molly Elliot Sewell, represent those left of center in their responses to the new political alignments of the 1890s. Father Smith wrote a few stories with direct political themes. One, *Solitary Island* (1888), is a melodrama whose elaborate plot involves a Russian prince, an assassination, mixed marriage, and gross political corruption. What is significant is his method for solving the dilemma of the Catholic politician. Young Florian Wallace leaves a small town to pursue a political career in New York City. His success is accompanied by moral and religious infidelity. Awakened to his corrupt condition, Florian retires to a hermit's existence on an island. He is finally persuaded that integrity is possible for a Catholic in public life and that the life of monastic withdrawal is a luxury fraught with its own dangers. He returns to politics, but insures his purity by retaining residence in his home town and by cultivating a life of rigorous personal discipline, including voluntary poverty and celibacy.

This critique of the morality of withdrawal and isolation suggests a new and important development in Catholic political thought. A parallel plot in the novel hinges on the decisions of a young woman to solve her crises of love and religion, first by going into the convent; then, after thinking through the alternative rationales of the worldly and cloistered vocations, by returning to secular life and marriage. Father Smith thus worked out a celebration of the life of the layman which contrasts nicely with the dominant practice of novelists who sent the characters with the most heroic moral and spiritual qualities off to the seminary or convent.

Another story of Smith's, "The Baron of Cherubisco," is a clearer account of a new politics.[16] The Baron is a political boss of a New England town whose wealth and organizational methods have won him nearly complete power over town government. He runs the community like a big-city boss, principally because a majority of the population is made up of immigrant poor. In a critical election, the local curate works against the Baron and persuades the Catholic immigrants not to sell their votes. In the contest, both leaders undergo a powerful learning experience. The Baron loses some of his arrogance and agrees to consult the poor directly on their needs rather than to simply trust his own judgment. The priest discovers

16. *Catholic World* 42(1885):25–51.

that the image of the Baron publicized by the older establishment of the town is a distortion and that he is in fact a compassionate person. Moreover, he learns that the system of political patronage can provide an efficient and humane welfare program for the poor, effecting a good in society that could not accept an official program of welfare. This is an overstatement of Smith's case, of course, his point being necessarily muted. However, it is not incorrect to claim for him an anticipation of those revised and favorable evaluations of machine politics that have gained currency in our own time.

If Smith's defense of a political boss is somewhat timid, Molly Elliot Sewell's account of the new political alignments is more clear-cut. Her novel *Despotism and Democracy* (1900) is a comprehensive account of Washington politics at the turn of the century. (Miss Sewell was herself a member of a prominent family and worked professionally as a political journalist in Washington.)[17] The novel depicts the day-to-day workings of government: legislative committees, cloakroom negotiations, and the long-drawn-out process of moving bills through Congress. Well-drawn characterizations and drawing-room intrigues relieve the tedium. The lines of action in the novel develop from the relationship of the two central characters: one is an old and venerable veteran of the Senate, without wealth, who doggedly pursues his career with a modest amount of vision and much old-fashioned determination. In contrast is a young man new to politics who loses his moral equilibrium nearly as soon as he is seated in Congress and embarks on a career of quick advancement through office patronage. This conventional study in contrasts has some peculiar developments. Thorndyke, the devoted senator who refuses to serve his own interests, represents a traditional ideal of disinterested dedication—not because of family or class origins, but because of a wholly individualized morality. His opposite, Crane, is quick to exploit opportunities to further his advancement, and in the course of building a career throws off his wife, family, and all other ties which might impede his progress. The main difference between the two is a capacity for personal loyalty—to the electorate, to family, to friends, and to religion. Curiously, Crane's most offensive crime is his betrayal of the party boss

17. Mother Seraphine, "Molly Elliott Sewell," *Immortelles of Catholic Columbian Literature*, p. 482.

of his own district by allying himself with the state governor to subvert the boss's authority. This is curious because Crane is persuaded to reform himself only when he becomes convinced that the machine is the one legitimate instrument for assessing and expressing the will of the people. This mixture of old-fashioned personal idealism and endorsement of machine politics is an unusual phenomenon in Catholic fiction of that period or any other.

The fictional representation of Catholic political thought suggests, then, that it was a much more complex ideology than most historical accounts imply. It was, for one thing, heavily affected by unstated but powerful differences in the norms governing reactions to European and to American politics. Assessments of the American situation displayed a range of theoretical positions broad enough to include at one end an endorsement of a hereditary class system and at the other an approval of machine politics. Common to all these positions, however, was the assumption that American political traditions and institutions were congenial to the health and progress of the Catholic faith. Commentary on international politics was, by contrast, scant. The idea of a world order appeared as a prospect only through the process of religious conversion. No writer posed the possibility of political solutions to international disputes.

By nearly unanimous agreement, Catholic writers identified the two most powerful forces at work in the world as liberalism and Christianity. Under the former title was grouped all that was nefarious: agnosticism, socialism, and hatred for the Church and other religious bodies, a force subversive of national and personal integrity alike. John Boyle O'Reilly and Mary Agnes Tincker provided, it is true, sympathetic versions of socialistic communities, but both significantly located their utopias in environments which were not only foreign but "virgin land" as well. In other words, neither attached his vision of a new world-order to existing political forces either in America or elsewhere. In addition, both described what could only be called genteel socialism (like that of Englishman William Morris) based on a conception of medieval society: paternalistic, patriarchal, dependent on a shared religious belief and an organically related society. The single sympathetic treatment of a native socialism, *John Van Alstyne's Factory,* is discussed below.

In more conventional fiction, advocates of economic and political liberalism were frequently caricatured, and their positions were rarely taken seriously. If not personally ludicrous, the fictional socialist was a venal person, ideological heresy being but a confirmation of moral corruption. In any story with a concern for contemporary theological issues, the freethinker or agnostic position was usually depicted in a satirical tone. Dozens of characters were given a superficial resemblance to Colonel Robert Ingersoll, the allusiveness producing cheap witticisms more often than serious examination.[18]

Henry O'Brien displayed a mature understanding of the threat to orthodoxy posed by contemporary liberalism which went beyond the level of cartoon caricature. His story, "Van Horne's Way," examines the freethinker position with respect and sympathy.[19] Van Horne is a wealthy dilettante who, in the name of scientific inquiry, conducts a study of the beliefs and behavior of his Irish Catholic domestic and her son. Van Horne assumes that Catholicism is simply one of several symbolic systems that serve various natural human needs. The son's life follows a pattern of failure: an orthodox childhood, a brief period in a seminary, apostasy, alcoholism, and violent death. A death-bed repentance, however, convinces the agnostic that a supernatural force has entered the situation; and the boy's transformation triggers Van Horne's own conversion.

Van Horne is a benevolent agnostic; like a William James or Ingersoll, he comes to the problem of faith in the attitude of a sincere seeker. The hero, who tells the story himself, offers an image of life without faith which can stand as a judgment shared by most American Catholics, a judgment on philosophical skepticism if not on the intellectual life generally. However honestly arrived at one's personal convictions, however disinterested one's approach to philosophical truth, the life of the skeptic is seen as a soul-withering experience. Like Brownson's "Spirit-rapper," the free-thinker wanders the waterless deserts of speculation and suffers in the process the drying up of the natural juices of trust and affection.

In its various expressions, liberalism provided a convenient demonology for American Catholics. Insofar as this "evil" occupied a

18. See, for example, the principal adult character in Francis Finn's *His First and Last Appearance* (New York, 1900); and the slapstick performance of the agnostic in M. F. Egan, *The Vocation of Edward Conway* (Notre Dame, Ind., 1896).

19. Henry O'Brien, "Van Horne's Way," *Catholic World* 51 (1890):584–605.

similar position in non-Catholic American thought, it provided a crucial link between Catholics and non-Catholics. Romanism, of course, continued to be a pernicious force in the nativist view of things; but such diminution of anti-Catholic feeling as did occur was at least partly the result of shared objects of distrust. Catholic fiction served an important role in supplying imaginative referents for this sentiment.[20]

Fictional representations of Catholic doctrine, morality, the devotional life, political thought, and attitudes toward liberalism provide, then, a crude index to Catholic thought. Treatment of the twin themes of industrialization and urbanization by Catholic writers of fiction serve to flesh out this profile. In the main, the movement of American economic life toward greater industrialization, like the growth of urban centers of population, seems not to have caused the same anguish for Catholic writers as it did for secular prophets like Howells, Norris, and Crane. Factory life was rarely described, and its influence on the quality of the social environment inspired neither muckraking nor praise. It was, rather, a given fact of contemporary existence, an instrument, with no special moral value in itself. Rural and small-town life too seemed to call forth no special feelings in stories with American locales. Fiction with European or Latin settings developed a heavy bias in favor of the rural retreat; but the center of interest in such fiction was the country estate rather than the herdsman's cottage.

On the whole, the image of American society in Catholic fiction is more balanced than what appears in secular fiction, if only because Catholic writers were less influenced by an agrarian cultural bias. They were, of course, affected by the "fresh air" fiction of secular writers, an influence reinforced by a pastoralism traditional in Christian imagery. But they were also influenced by the facts of American Catholic demography, and the majority of Catholics lived in cities. Occasionally a writer depicted both the factory and a rural location, the two adjacent to one another and generating a certain amount of tension. Frequently the manners and morals of the old-fashioned community would stand as mute critics of the careless destructiveness of the machine and its managers. Writers

20. For an account of this anomaly, see John Higham, *Strangers In the Land*, (New Brunswick, N.J., 1963), pp. 35–105.

did form themselves into identifiable groups, now familiar, on the basis of their cultural assumptions and the depth of their perceptions.

One group of writers employed its energies to retard action. Mrs. Tiernan especially seemed determined to hold back the forces of social change, employing her characters in a fruitless but romantically satisfying task of confronting the monsters of modern civilization with the weapons of bell, book, and candle. Her bias was almost medieval, her ideal image of a social order an updated version of the manorial complex.

In other treatments of this cultural conflict, particularly the work of Thomas Janvier, the motif is tragic. Janvier accepted the inevitable triumph of the new entrepreneurial spirit and the necessary destruction of the traditional community and its values. While reporting these changes and paying genuine respect to both value systems, Janvier saw no prospect for the survival of the spirit once the traditional structures had been destroyed. Like Henry Adams, he would not even speculate on the character of modern spirituality.

The only other writer to meet the problem of radical social reorganization in contemporary America head-on was Elizabeth Martin. Her novel *John Van Alstyne's Factory* (1888) is a carefully engineered account of one man's vision of social renewal and the hostile reactions of his community. Van Alstyne owns a factory which employs most of the inhabitants of a small New York town. Somewhat late in life he conceives of an extraordinary and—for the local establishment—frightening plan to offer his employees a chance to buy into the company. Calling his plan "centralized communism," he proposes the eventuality of complete worker-ownership. He also develops a program of home ownership for his employees, which proves for his defenders that he is not a socialist. Van Alstyne has few defenders, however, even within his own family. When he cites Christianity and the principle of distributive justice to reinforce his position, his enemies accuse him of blasphemy. The novel does not end with a glorious promise of social redemption; the community remains confirmed in its recalcitrance. Only one disciple, a factory foreman, gives promise of carrying on Van Alstyne's social gospel.

Mrs. Martin developed a restrained, mildly ironic, but hopeful examination of American social reality, much as she did in *Katherine*. At the same time, her obvious sympathy with Van Alstyne suggests a social vision more radical than anything being expressed by her fellow American Catholics. The combination—a radical social proposal and a rhetoric conditioned by sober expectations—is worthy of remark. It suggests a mature and historically conditioned sense of possibility; and like Father Smith's work, it foreshadows the chastened enthusiasm of the Catholic avant-garde of the mid-twentieth century.

Two oblique but interesting departures from the usual responses to industrialization—singular and yet more than incidental—are developed in stories by William Seton and Miss M. T. Elder. Seton was the nephew of a major religious figure in America, Mother Elizabeth Seton, foundress of the Sisters of Charity; and he was himself a scientist of some repute among Catholics. His story, "Wicked Number Seven," concerns a locomotive and the men who tend it.[21] One engineer is convinced, because of numerous accidents which have occurred under mysterious circumstances, that the engine is possessed by a devil. His partner, a skeptic by nature, scoffs at the idea but is subsequently thrown off the train following a brake signal that could have been activated by no human agent. Afterwards the locomotive blows up.

Reinforcing the narrative suggesting mysterious forces is a long discussion among the characters, two men and a woman, on the credibility of supernatural events in an age of scientific and technological expansion. The most forceful of the discussants argues that science has not dispelled mystery from life, that there are forces at work in the universe that cannot be rationally understood because they have no natural origins—forces for good and evil that influence or inhabit people or things and even direct the course of events. One interesting aspect of this argument, offered with great seriousness, is the attack by such forces on the arrogance of science; but more important is the association of traditional Catholic ontology with the suggestion of animism. The particular repository of the evil genius in the story is not a tree or an animal, not a witch, but a locomotive, the perennial symbol for the nineteenth-century notion of the machine as monser. The implications of this story for this study are

21. William Seton, "Wicked Number Seven," *Catholic World* 38(1884):505–23.

only incidental, largely because the example is so singular. But the plot, the didactic comment, and the play of fearsome images seem to qualify "Wicked Number Seven" for a place in studies of American reactions to industrialization.

A story with an even heavier allegorical content is a work by Miss M. T. Elder, "Mother Nature's Revenge." [22] Miss Elder was herself an interesting personality, something of a gadfly to various Catholic interest groups. She was the niece of an archbishop of Cincinnati and a frequent contributor to Catholic journals. As a commentator, she was a frequent and outspoken critic of various developments within the Church, but her position was often confusing. For example, she wrote an article for the *Catholic World,* " 'Put Money in Thy Purse'," in which she invoked Iago's line, without apparent ironic intent, to extoll the virtues of acquisitiveness and to criticize Catholic laymen for not pursuing wealth with "gumption." [23] In contrast, her story is a thin little fantasy in which Mother Nature is depicted as rendering a fatal judgment on urban life. Finding the city deficient in qualities necessary for a healthy environment—it is filled with smoke and noise, overflowing with humanity, bereft of the graces, and moved by motives of greed and exploitation— Nature announces to a young poet her plans to destroy the earth. During the ensuing debate, beginning in the city and moving to a scene of pastoral serenity, the poet persuades Nature to delay her plan; he describes an urban environment redeemed of its physical and moral evil, a garden city that will become the model of the future. The imagery of this story, if not the argument itself, is of a highly conventional order. More unconventional are the apocalyptic urgency of the story and the thesis that the urban world can be humanized. It is true that this story is a marginal work, almost trivial; but it is also one of the very few direct considerations of this critical American theme by a Catholic writer.

The changes in American life caused by large-scale industrialization during the eighties and nineties, the move to the cities, and the replacement of the traditional social leaders by an oligarchy of wealth evoked some apprehension among Catholic writers (although nothing quite so severe as that expressed by the secular Jeremiahs

22. M. T. Elder, "Mother Nature's Revenge," ibid. 55(1892):707–15.
23. Elder, "Put Money in Thy Purse," ibid. 50(1890):618–28.

of the day). The different reaction reflects the atypical condition of Catholics, particularly their concentration in cities, as well as the intuitions of original minds, as in Father Smith's unusual sketches of a theology for an industrialized society. Beyond similarities and dissimilarities among Catholic writers, however, a state of fluidity and variety prevailed—an attempt, often barely discernible, to develop fictional metaphors adequate to contemporary life. This flexibility appears more forcefully in imaginative literature than elsewhere in the expressions of Church attitudes.

9 Varieties of Accommodation

Americanism has three faces in Catholic fiction, corresponding to attitudes which prevailed among significant numbers of American Catholics. The same images found in the institution's literature are at least loosely analogous to the typology described in the Introduction—the behavioral variations represented by the three Catholic principals to the Democratic Convention of 1968 (Daley, McCarthy, and Kennedy) and the separate traditions they express. The first of these is an image of an America in which the Church is a cultural seed-bearer, exerting an influence like that of ancient missionaries upon the pagans, bringing the noble heritage of Western civilization to a barbarian race. At the point of contact, the two traditions—American and European Catholic—become one, the peculiarly American elements being muted and absorbed by the cultural forms of Western Europe. Numerous works of fiction dramatized this point of view. The attitude bespeaks a kind of cultural imperialism on the part of the Catholic writer of this persuasion and had its counterpart in the ingrained but inconspicuous sympathy for European traditions which existed in the consciousness of large numbers of non-Catholic Americans.

A second image, pragmatic and eclectic, projects Americanism as a mixture, but not an integration, of two traditions. According to the Egan school, the American Catholic has a dual, compartmentalized spiritual consciousness. He can be a cowboy, a farmer, a city laborer, an entrepreneur, or an impoverished slum dweller. He can fight a war, join a gold rush, or wage a political campaign. He can embrace all the varieties of American occupations, express all varieties of American manners, speak the idiom of all regional and ethnic types, and hold within himself all the aspirations formed by the native folklore. Yet, in all these roles and activities, his religion will provide security and strength and free him to engage fully in all aspects of American life with an abandon, a recklessness that gives him the advantage over others. Faith, in short, permits the Catholic to be *more* American than anyone else.

But this religion that works his release, what of it? Institutional Catholicism for the Parochials was an ecclesiastical structure, a body of doctrine, liturgy and devotions tied even more inflexibility to the past than the religion of the Cosmopolitans. The authoritarian structure of the Church, its Latin rituals, the paternalism of its clergy, the harsh theology of Trent and Vatican I, the mysterious baroque devotions—these all seem, on the surface, to have promised bitter conflict for progressive Catholics seeking an accommodation with the secular forms of American life. On the contrary, however, the very anachronism of idea, object, and gesture appears to have supplied the Catholic with a sense of certitude and confirmed the permanence and stability of his faith. Paradoxical as this point may seem, the easy adjustment of ex-transcendentalist Isaac Hecker to the doctrine of Papal Infallibility illustrates its force. His adjustment was perhaps the first clear-cut signal of the way in which many Catholics would come to find their special identity in America.

Before describing the third face of American Catholicism, I want to cite two models of social behavior that seem to validate the two images described above. One is George Santayana's analysis of the Genteel Tradition; the second is Marcus Hansen's theory of the stages of acculturation. Both are imaginative analyses of social groups caught between two worlds and attempting to deal with both.

Santayana defined the Genteel Tradition in America as the result of a division of thought and feeling between eighteenth century idealism and post–Civil War social realities.[1] The division prevented the integration of personality for turn-of-the-century Americans. Once it becomes habitual, this fragmentation, Santayana said, si-

1. George Santayana, "The Genteel Tradition in American Philosophy," in *Winds of Doctrine* (New York, 1912).

phoned off psychic energy into the worship of old gods and prevented a healthy and productive apprehension of contemporary problems. Although Santayana's account excludes American Catholics, their experience provides a necessary correction to his conclusions. What he failed to see is the necessary and salutary, albeit unselfconscious, reasons for the cultural lag. The spiritual legacy which survived the Civil War was a necessary support for Catholics and non-Catholics caught in the whiplash of events. The ideological remains supplied emotional ballast, a hold on the past, and a sense of continuity so necessary to the beleaguered and the dislocated. American Catholics also exploited their history, real or imagined, in this way. For a further understanding, I turned to the work of Marcus Hansen.[2]

Hansen described the process of adjustment to a new culture as a sequential movement through three generations. The immigrant of the first generation, caught between two cultures, reached back to his old world traditions, language, and particularly his religion, to find the security of a special cultural identity in the New World. His offspring, a member of the second generation, was impatient to take advantage of opportunities available to the American. Convinced that ethnic loyalty restricted his possibilities, he broke away, sometimes violently, from his cultural origins and became an unattached citizen of the nation. He soon discovered, however, that to reject his subculture was to risk anomie and to lose his social identity altogether. The third generation, witness to the dangers of the inner-directed life and driven by a hunger for social identity, worked his way back to the remnants of his cultural birthright: religion, an ethnic fraternity, a neighborhood association.

The relevance of this model to what is apparent in the behavior of American Catholics seems obvious. But it strikes me that the process for Catholics was not so much sequential as it was simultaneous. By that I mean that the Church afforded the American Catholic at once an image of himself and a means to interiorize that image which permitted both an ethnic and an American iden-

---

2. Marcus Lee Hansen, *The Immigrant in American History* (Cambridge, Mass., 1940). My own knowledge of Hansen is mediated by an acquaintance with two writings of Oscar Handlin and Will Herberg. See Handlin, *The Uprooted;* and Herberg, *Protestant-Catholic-Jew* (Garden City, N.Y., 1955).

tity. The writers of Catholic fiction contributed greatly to the fabrication and the reinforcement of that self-image.

But for me the most compelling explanation of this period of Catholic history comes not from the theoretical inferences of the social historian, but from an event of modern times that has yet to run its course. That event is the public debate over and private adjustments to the deliberate cultivation of Afro-American culture, or Black Power.[3] If that debate does not illuminate the past, it does encourage one to view his materials in a new perspective. The parallels to the case of American Catholics are clear: to give himself a place in the sun, the American Catholic required a mythology of his own, a history, a pedigree, a cultural heritage, as well as a special and exclusive membership. The esoteric rituals of communion and the arrogant claims to all that is best in the development of Western civilization were expressions of desperate necessity, not imperialistic ravings.

The differences between Catholics and Blacks is first of all that the Catholic had an immediately available old-world heritage to draw on and an international organization to exploit. A more significant difference, perhaps, is that the Catholic adjustment was unselfconscious and ingenuous for the most part; it had a natural and evolutionary quality. The Black, however, has been forced to fashion a racial consciousness with great deliberation from the scattered fragments of his history and a tradition formed of little more than a shared misery and oppression. In the long run, however, these differences may work to the advantage of the Black.

For the Afro-American caught between two worlds, white and black, aware of the process of culture-building as artifice and yet convinced that the needs of his people cannot be adequately served by the manipulations of social engineering alone, the present period of transition is very nearly an intolerable one. He bears the most awesome burden of Ralph Ellison's Invisible Man, stripped to a core of individual sensibility beyond racial consciousness and faced with the prospect—the urgent need—to reconstruct a personality by immersion in time and place or hazard total paralysis. For him the element of conscious risk is much greater than for the Catholic of the nineteenth century, but his chances for escaping cultural

3. Stokely Carmichael and Charles V. Hamilton, *Black Power* (New York, 1967).

entrapment are also greater; for the curse of selfconsciousness is his one hedge against the long, dark night of ethnocentrism. For the larger society this drama certainly has more than aesthetic or speculative interest; as the Black community resolves its dilemma, the entire society calculates its chances for survival.

The third face of Catholicism was masked in metaphor, sometimes terrifying, sometimes glorious, but never complacent or static; and it was genuinely poetic if not prophetic. As molded by Thomas Janvier, it is a tragic face, reflecting the anguish of an eyewitness to catastrophe, an eyewitness who could find no basis for hope for the integration of Catholicism in the modern world. Mary Agnes Tincker and John Boyle O'Reilly, although less pessimistic than Janvier, nevertheless cast their visions of a renewed social order—a democratized and Christianized world in fantastic Utopias. For this reason their testimonials to the future are perhaps even less heartening than Janvier's. Miss Tincker appeared at one time in her writing career to have developed viable symbols of a Catholic-American synthesis; but circumstances, including her lifelong infatuation with antinomianism, prevented the maturation of this development.

This leaves only a handful of writers to complete the profile, writers minor in their impact, who appear to have salvaged something of an authentic voice for prophecy, and may be regarded as the legitimate precursors of the post-World War II Catholics who achieved an art of relevance and integrity. In the language of political classification of the time, they were neither mugwumps nor Populists, nor old-guard aristocrats, but a little bit of each and something more. Influenced by the same native forces as the others, they were yet sometimes able to view reality without the blinders of parochialism. For them, for Fathers Smith and McDermott and Mrs. Martin, America symbolized a new social reality. And that reality required a new and relevant religious expression: a Catholicism that reflected the social forces shaping America; a Church conscious of itself as movement rather than institution; a Church which expresses itself through the full idiomatic range of the secular world but is never absorbed by that world.

Americanism in Catholic fiction then has a variety of forms and a great number of nuances. In the main, however, one can say that for most writers the problem of adaptation was a comfortable one. By 1900 the basic narrative stratagems had been worked out, formulas that would do for the next several generations of Catholic readers and writers. The variables had been virtually exhausted. To read twentieth century Catholic fiction is to see reenacted the basic motifs of the eighties and nineties.

By the standards of simple social functionalism, the techniques for creating and preserving a Catholic identity worked; and Catholics did assimilate. There is almost no example of cultural integration in American history quite so spectacular as that of Catholicism; and the institutional Church hastened the process. To say that it worked, however, is not to canonize the process, to confer on it acclaim based on higher criteria. Social assimilation is not the primary objective of a religious institution. Nevertheless, for a generation at least the balance of effects shows a bias on the side of liberation. After that brief and creative period, success itself became nemesis. Those literary inventions of the nineteenth century, intuitive fabrications born of the desperation of intense need, became the rigid and undeviating formulas of the twentieth century. The myth that was shaped, puny and graceless as it was, to provide the means of cultural freedom for the Catholic of one era, became the instrument of entrapment and constraint for his descendants.

This study, however, is neither an account of failure nor an exercise in the obvious. Catholic fiction served a purpose, a crucial one: as an instrument of cultural adjustment it was more important in some ways than the magnificent edifices of worship that rose in every urban ghetto. It gave American Catholics a special identity, anchored to the unique circumstances of American life. It filled their minds with images of a glorious past which they could claim as a personal legacy, and with models of success that spoke to their most immediate needs.

Appendix

There was a category of bogus Catholics who won a certain significance as a group, not for what they did nor wrote, but because they
were included on the official rosters of Catholic writers. In the interest
of winning souls as well as defending against charges of cultural
impoverishment, many questionable claims were made by Catholic
historians and bibliographers. Often important public figures were
claimed for the Church, and a great deal of research was devoted to
gathering and publishing this material. Frequently the association of
these figures with the Church was such, had it been known or admitted, as to make their polemical value slight.

Examples of misleading claims occurred as recently as 1940 in *The
Guide to Catholic Literature,* compiled by Walter Romig (Detroit,
1940). The list contains, for example, the name of Joel Chandler
Harris (p. 947). Harris married a French-Canadian Catholic, Esther
LaRose, but not until a week before his death was Harris himself
baptized into the Church. (See Julia Collier Harris, *Life and Letters
of Joel Chandler Harris,* Boston, 1918, pp. 123, 581.) This same guide
lists Kate Chopin, whose regional fiction earned her a considerable
reputation. But Miss Chopin, although born a Catholic and educated
in Catholic schools, had left the Church by the time her professional
life began. (Cf. Daniel S. Rankin, *Kate Chopin and Her Creole Stories,*
Philadelphia, 1932.) Miss Chopin never publicly repudiated the
Faith; she simply did not practice it. A somewhat more vociferous
apostate who was nonetheless also cited was James G. Huneker, the

avant-garde critic (Feiten, "Catholic Americana," p. 87). Huneker might have been the man to lead American Catholic writers out of their wilderness, but he chose instead to cut himself off from the institution. Huneker, who was a friend of Egan, was inclined toward the ritual and aesthetic props of Roman Catholic ceremony (see chap. 6, note 3). He at least had a Catholic boyhood, but Ignatius Donnelly (Romig, p. 325), the Minnesota Populist, got no further than infant baptism in his relationship with the Church. (See John D. Hicks, *DAB* 5: 260–61.) An even more serious mistake, however, was committed by the bibliographers who claimed Finley Peter Dunne for the glory of the Church (Romig, p. 342; Feiten, p. 19). Dunne's Mr. Dooley was one of the most celebrated newspaper characterizations of all time; but only at his author's baptism and at his funeral was there any overt relationship with the Catholic Church. Dunne himself claimed to be an agnostic, and his son and biographer speculated ironically at the embarrassment those last ecclesiastical rites would have caused his father. (See Finley Peter Dunne, *Mr. Dooley Remembers,* edited by Philip Dunne, Boston, 1963, pp. 13–16.)

Bibliography

This bibliography is intended to be selective rather than exhaustive and to serve as a general accounting for help received as well as offering suggestions for further investigation. Many published and unpublished works have stimulated or confirmed the ideas developed in this study. Listed here are four separate kinds of sources relevant to the subject.

The first section lists general and historical documents and interpretations relevant to an understanding of the Catholic experience in America. A second section contains material concerned with American and American Catholic publishing history, literary theories, and criticism. A third section, of special value to the scholar interested in the primary documents of Catholic literature, lists sources for a bibliography of Catholic fiction; and a final section provides a checklist of representative novels and short stories published during the period of the study.

HISTORICAL AND SOCIOLOGICAL DOCUMENTS AND
INTERPRETATIONS

Abell, Aaron. *American Catholicism and Social Action: A Search for Social Justice, 1865–1950.* Garden City, N.Y.: Doubleday and Co., 1960.
Altholz, Josef L. *The Liberal Catholic Movement in England: "The Rambler" and Its Contributors, 1848–1864.* London: Burns and Oates, 1962.
Bain, John A. *The New Reformation.* Edinburgh: T. and T. Clark, 1906.
Barrows, John Henry, ed. *World's Parliament of Religions.* Chicago: Parliament Publishing Co., 1893.
Barry, Coleman. *The Catholic Church and German–Americans.* Milwaukee: Bruce Publishing Co., 1953.
Blanshard, Paul. *American Freedom and Catholic Power.* Boston: Beacon Press, 1949.
Browne, Henry J. *The Catholic Church and the Knights of Labor.* Washington: Catholic University of America Press, 1949.
Brownson, Henry Francis. *Orestes Augustine Brownson's Life.* 3 vols. Detroit: H. F. Brownson, 1898–1900.
Brownson, Orestes A. *Works.* Edited by Henry F. Brownson. Detroit: Nourse, 1882–87.
Burr, Nelson R. "A Critical Bibliography in Religion." In *Religion in American Life,*

edited by J. Ward Smith and A. Leland Jamison, vol. 4. Princeton: Princeton University Press, 1961.

Carmichael, Stokely, and Charles V. Hamilton. *Black Power.* New York: Random House, 1967.

Commager, Henry Steele. *The American Mind: An Interpretation of American Thought and Character since the 1880's.* New Haven: Yale University Press, 1950.

Conway, Joseph P. *The Question of the Hour: A Survey of the Position and Influence of the Catholic Church in the United States.* New York: McBride, 1909.

Cross, Robert D. *The Emergence of Liberal Catholicism in America.* Cambridge: Harvard University Press, 1958.

Dohen, Dorothy. *Nationalism and American Catholicism.* New York: Sheed and Ward, 1967.

Elliott, Walter. *Life of Father Hecker.* New York: Columbus Press, 1891.

Ellis, John Tracy. *American Catholics and the Intellectual Life.* Chicago: Heritage Foundation, 1956.

———. *American Catholicism.* Chicago: Rand McNally and Co., 1956.

———. *Documents of American Catholic History.* Milwaukee: Bruce Publishing Co., 1956.

———. *Life of James Cardinal Gibbons.* Milwaukee: Bruce Publishing Co., 1952.

———. *Select Bibliography of the History of the Catholic Church in the United States.* New York: Macmillan Co., 1947.

———. *The Formative Years of the Catholic Universtiy of America.* Washington: American Catholic Historical Association, 1946.

Garrison, Winfred. *Catholicism and the American Mind.* Chicago: Willett-Clark-Colby, 1928.

Gleason, Philip, ed. *Contemporary Catholicism in America.* Notre Dame, Ind.: University of Notre Dame Press, 1969.

Greeley, Andrew M. *The Catholic Experience.* Garden City, N.Y.: Doubleday and Co., 1967.

Guilday, Peter. *A History of the Councils of Baltimore.* New York: Macmillan Co., 1932.

———, ed. *The National Pastorals of the American Hierarchy.* Washington: National Catholic Welfare Council, 1923.

Herr, Dan and Wells, Joel. *Through Other Eyes: Some Impressions of American Catholicism by Foreign Visitors from 1877 to the Present.* Westminster, Md.: Newman Press, 1965.

Handlin, Oscar. *The Uprooted: The Epic Story of the Great Migrations that Made the American People.* Boston: Little, Brown and Co., 1951.

Hansen, Marcus Lee. *The Immigrant in American History.* Cambridge: Harvard University Press, 1940.

Herberg, Will. *Protestant, Catholic, Jew: An Essay in American Religious Sociology.* Garden City, N.Y.: Doubleday and Co., 1955.

Higham, John. *Strangers in the Land: Patterns of American Nativism, 1865–1925.* New Brunswick, N.J.: Rutgers University Press, 1955.

Houghton, Walter R., ed. *Neely's History of the Parliament of Religions.* Chicago: Neely, 1893.

Ireland, John. *The Church and Modern Society: Lectures and Addresses.* 2 vols. Chicago: McBride, 1896.

Kinsman, Frederick J. *Americanism and Catholicism.* New York: Longmans-Green, 1924.

Klein, Felix. *Americanism: A Phantom Heresy.* Cranford, N.J.: Aquin Book Shop, 1949.

Lenski, Gerhard. *The Religious Factor*. Garden City, N.Y.: Doubleday and Co., 1961.
Leo XIII. *The Great Encyclical Letters of Pope Leo XIII*. Edited by John J. Wynne. New York: Benziger Bros., 1903.
Lord, Robert H., Sexton, John E., Harrington, Edward T. *The History of the Archdiocese of Boston in Various Stages of its Development, 1604–1943*. New York: Sheed and Ward, 1944.
McAvoy, Thomas T. *The Great Crisis in American Catholic History*. Chicago: Henry Regnery Co., 1957.
———. "The Catholic Minority after the Americanist Controversy, 1899–1917: A Survey." *Review of Politics* 21 (1959):53–82.
———, ed. *Roman Catholicism and the American Way of Life*. Notre Dame, Ind.: University of Notre Dame Press, 1960.
May, Henry. *End of American Innocence*. New York: Alfred A. Knopf, 1959.
———. *The Protestant Church and Industrial America*. New York: Harper and Bros., 1949.
Maynard, Theodore. *The Catholic Church and the American Idea*. New York: Appleton-Century-Crofts, 1953.
———. *The Story of American Catholicism*. New York: Macmillan Co., 1941.
Moberg, David O. *The Church as Social Institution*. Englewood Cliffs, N.J.: Prentice-Hall, 1962.
Moynihan, James H. *Life of Archbishop John Ireland*. New York: Harper and Bros., 1953.
Murray, John Courtney. *We Hold These Truths*. New York: Sheed and Ward, 1960.
Niebuhr, H. Richard. *The Kingdom of God in America*. New York: Harper and Bros., 1937.
———. *The Social Sources of Denominationalism*. Hamden, Conn.: Shoestring Press, 1929.
O'Dea, Thomas F. *American Catholic Dilemma*. New York: Sheed and Ward, 1958.
O'Faolain, Sean. *Newman's Way*. London: Devin-Adair, 1952.
Official Proceedings of the Catholic Congress. Detroit: Hughes, 1889.
Ong, Walter. *American Catholic Crossroads*. New York: Macmillan Co., 1959.
———. *Frontiers in American Catholicism*. New York: Macmillan Co., 1957.
Putz, Louis, ed. *The Catholic Church, U.S.A.* Chicago: Fides Publishing Co., 1956.
Reilly, Daniel F. *The School Controversy, 1891–93*. Washington: Catholic University of America Press, 1943.
Roemer, Theodore. *The Catholic Church in the United States*. St. Louis: B. Herder Co., 1950.
Salisbury, W. Seward, ed. *Religion in American Culture: A Sociological Approach*. Homewood, Ill.: Dorsey Press, 1964.
Schlesinger, Arthur M., Sr. *The Rise of the City, 1878–1898*. History of American Life, vol. 10. New York: Macmillan Co., 1933.
Schlesinger, Arthur M., Jr. *Orestes A. Brownson: A Pilgrim's Progress*. Boston: Little, Brown and Co., 1939.
Shaughnessy, Gerald. *Has the Immigrant Kept the Faith?* New York: Macmillan Co., 1925.
Shea, John Gilmary. *A History of the Catholic Church in the United States*. 4 vols. New York: McBride, 1886–92.
Shuster, George N. *The Catholic Spirit in America*. New York: Dial Press, 1928.
Smith, H. Shelton; Handy, Robert T.; and Loetscher, Lefferts A. *American Christianity: A Historical Interpretation with Representative Documents*. 2 vols. New York: Charles Scribner's Sons, 1963.
Troeltsch, Ernst. *Social Teaching of the Christian Churches*. Translated by Olive Wyon. New York: Macmillan Co., 1931.

Walburg, A. H. *The Question of Nationality and Religion in Its Relations to the Catholic Church in the United States*. St. Louis: Herder, 1889.

World's Columbian Exposition Catholic Congress: The Columbian Jubilee, or Four Centuries of Catholicity in America. Chicago: T. S. Hyland, 1892.

Zurcher, George. *Foreign Ideas in the Catholic Church in America*. Buffalo: Roycroft Printing Co., 1896.

Zwierlein, Frederic J. "Americanism, Some Roots of the Controversy." *Social Justice Review* 52(1959):47–49.

WORKS ON CATHOLIC AND SECULAR LITERARY THEORY
AND PRACTICE

Brennan, Joseph X. "The American Catholic and American Literature." *Emerson Quarterly* 39(1965):85–93.

Britten, James. *Protestant Fiction*. London: Catholic Truth Society, 1899.

Brown, Herbert. *The Sentimental Novel in America, 1789–1860*. Durham, N.C.: Duke University Press, 1940.

Cavanaugh, John William. *The Reverend John Talbot Smith*. Notre Dame, Ind.: Ave Maria Press, 1924.

Cavanaugh, Sister Mary Stephana. "Catholic Book Publishing in the United States, 1784–1850." Master's thesis, University of Illinois, 1937.

Clarke, Isabel C. *Six Portraits*. London: Hutchinson, 1935.

Conway, Katherine. "John Boyle O'Reilly." *Catholic World* 53(1891):117–18.

Desmond, Humphrey J. *A Reading Circle Manual*. Milwaukee: The Citizen Co., 1903.

Driscoll, Annette S. *Literary Convert Women*. Manchester, N.H.: Magnificat Press, 1928.

Drummond, Edward J. "Catholic Criticism in America: Studies of Brownson, Azarias, and Egan, with an Essay for Catholic Critics." Ph.D. dissertation, University of Iowa, 1942.

Egan, Maurice F. "The Basis of the Catholic Novel." *Catholic World* 76(1902):316–27.

———. "Christian Reid, A Southern Lady." *America* 23(1885):496–500.

———. *Confessions of a Book Lover*. New York: Doubleday & Page, 1922.

———. *Modern Novels and Novelists*. New York: Sadlier, 1888.

Fiedler, Leslie A. *Love and Death in the American Novel*. 2d rev. ed. New York: Stein and Day, 1966.

Finn, Francis. *Story of His Life as Told by Himself*. New York: Benziger Bros., 1929.

Hart, James. *The Popular Book: A History of America's Literary Taste*. New York: Oxford University Press, 1950.

Hassard, J.R.G. "Catholic Literature and the Catholic Public." *Catholic World* 7(1870):399–407.

Healey, Robert C. *A Catholic Book Chronicle*. New York: P.J. Kenedy and Sons, 1951.

Lavelle, Francis. "Novels and Novel Writing." *Catholic World* 43(1886):521–22.

Martin, Terence. *The Instructed Vision: Scottish Common Sense Philosophy and the Origins of American Fiction*. Bloomington: Indiana University Press, 1961.

McDermott, William. *Down at Caxtons*. New York: Murphy, 1895.

McGuire, C. E., ed. *Catholic Builders of the Nation*. Boston: Continental Press, 1923.

McMillan, Thomas. "The Growth of Catholic Reading Circles." *Catholic World* 61(1895):709–12.

Meehan, Thomas. "House of Sadlier." *America* 47(1932):214–15.

———. "Catholic Literary New York, 1800–1840." *Catholic Historical Review* 4(1918): 399–414.

Merrill, William S. *Catholic Authorship in American Colonies Before 1774*. Washington: Catholic University of America Press, 1917.

Meyer, Kenneth J. "Social Class and Family Structure: Attitudes Revealed by the Earliest American Novels, 1789–1815." Ph.D. dissertation, University of Minnesota, 1965.

Miller, Perry. *The Raven and the Whale: The War of Words and Wits in the Era of Poe and Melville*. New York: Harcourt, Brace, 1956.

Mix, Katherine L. *A Study in Yellow, "The Yellow Book" and Its Contributors*. Lawrence, Kansas: University of Kansas Press, 1960.

Morse, Charles A. "The Priest in Fiction." *Catholic World* 65(1897):145–53.

Mullaney, Brother Azarias. *Books and Reading*. New York: Catholic Library Association, 1890.

———. *Philosophy of Literature*. Philadelphia: McVey, 1898.

O'Neill, Rev. James L. *Catholic Literature in Catholic Homes*. New York: P. O'Shea, 1894.

———. *Why, When, How, and What We Ought to Read*. Boston: Marlier, 1901.

Pallen, Condé B. "Catholic American Literature." In *Official Report of Proceedings of the Catholic Congress, 1889*. Detroit: Hughes, 1889.

Panovsky, Erwin. *Meaning in the Visual Arts*. Garden City, N.Y.: Doubleday & Co., 1955.

Pick, John. "The Renascence in American Catholic Letters." In *The Catholic Renascence in a Disintegrating World*, edited by Norman Weyand. Chicago: Loyola University Press, 1951.

Pilkington, John, Jr. *Francis Marion Crawford*. New York: Twayne, 1964.

"Prospectus of the Catholic Publishing Society." *Catholic World* 3(1886):278–83.

["RP"]. "Novel Writing as a Science." *Catholic World* 42(1885):277–85.

Sadlier, Anna T. "Christian Reid, A Tribute of a Fellow Worker." *Ave Maria* 11(1880):688–91.

Seraphine, Mother M., ed. *Immortelles of Catholic Columbian Literature*. New York: McBride, 1897.

Sheehan, Donald. *This Was Publishing*. Bloomington: Indiana University Press, 1952.

Smith, John Talbot. "Mary Agnes Tincker." *Ave Maria* 62(1907):32–33.

Summer School Essays Chicago: McBride, 1896.

Talbot, Francis X., ed. *Fiction by Its Makers*. New York: America Press, 1928.

Tenison, E. M. *Louise Imogen Guiney*. London: Macmillan Co., 1923.

Walsh, James J. "Father Hudson of the *Ave Maria*." *Catholic World* 139(1934):31–39.

Watt, Ian. *The Rise of the Novel*. London: Chatto and Windus, 1957.

Wegelin, Oscar. *Early American Fiction, 1774–1830*. New York: Peter Smith Co., 1929.

White, James A. "The Era of Good Intentions: A Survey of American Catholic Writing between the Years 1880–1915." Ph.D. dissertation, University of Notre Dame, 1956.

Wickham, Joseph F. "John Boyle O'Reilly." *America* 13(1915):425–26.

SOURCES OF A BIBLIOGRAPHY OF AMERICAN FICTION, 1884–1900

The standard checklists of Catholic literature, unrestricted as to era and nationality, are Walter Romig, *Guide to Catholic Literature* (Detroit: Romig, 1940) and Stephen J. Brown, *A Survey of Catholic Literature* (Milwaukee: Bruce Publishing Co., 1945). In addition to these sources, the following section includes bibliographical aids and checklists from contemporary books and journals, as well as lists of Catholic books carried on the shelves of public libraries in various cities. A series of bibliographical studies of Catholic publishing conducted at Catholic University of America (as masters' theses) are also valuable. Finally, the novels and short stories published in American Catholic magazines during the period of the study (especially *Ave Maria*,

Catholic World, and *Messenger of the Sacred Heart*) would be notable additions to any comprehensive bibliography.

Catalogue of All Catholic Books in English. New York: Benziger Bros., 1912.

Catalogue of Catholic Books in the Milwaukee Public Library. Milwaukee: Knights of Columbus, 1900.

Catalogue of Catholic Literature: No. 1, Fiction, with special reference to the Buffalo Catholic Institute and Library. Buffalo: Knights of Columbus, 1899.

Catholic World. "Columbian Reading Union." 50(1890):701–02. A checklist of Catholic boy's books.

————. 52(1890):340–41. A list of contemporary Catholic women novelists.

————. 53(1891):622–27. A checklist of Catholic authors for 1891.

————. 67(1898):380. A list of "choice" Catholic stories published in 1898 as Charles Wildermann's One-half Dime Library.

Cecil, Sister. *Selected Annotated List of Books and Magazines for Parochial School Libraries.* Westminster, Md.: Eckenrode, 1935. An annotated list, primarily of children's literature.

Chen, Josephine Ti Ti. "A Survey of Catholic Americana and Catholic Book Publishing in the United States, 1891–1895." Master's thesis, Catholic University of America, 1956.

Curtis, Georgiana Pell. *Some Roads to Rome.* St. Louis: Herder, 1909. Short biographies of noted Catholic converts.

David, Brother. *American Catholic Convert Authors, A Bibliography.* Detroit: Romig, 1944. Biographical accounts of convert authors.

Dawson, Avelina. "A Survey of Catholic Americana and Catholic Book Publishing in the United States, 1881–1885." Master's thesis, Catholic University of America, 1951.

Donnnelly, Eleanor C., ed. *Round Table of Representative American Catholic Novelists.* New York: Benziger Bros., 1896. An anthology.

————. "Women in Literature." In *World's Columbian Catholic Congress.* Chicago: Hyland, 1893. A list of Catholic women novelists.

Fahey, Margaret Ann. "A Survey of Catholic Americana and Catholic Book Publishing in the United States, 1876–1880." Master's thesis, Catholic University of America, 1954.

Feiten, Patricia. "A Survey of Catholic Americana and Catholic Book Publishing in the United States, 1896–1900." Master's thesis, Catholic University of America, 1958.

Fullam, Paul J. "A History of the Catholic Publication Society and Its Successors from 1866 to the Founding of the Catholic University of America." Master's thesis, Catholic University of America, 1956.

Gowney Literary Society. "Catholic Authors in Modern Literature, 1880–1930." In *The Mariale,* vol. 6. Loretto, Pa.: St. Francis Seminary Press, 1930.

Hughes, Thomas. *A Directive List of Catholic Books.* Baltimore: Murphy, 1890.

Library of Short Stories. New York: Benziger Bros., 1891. An anthology of stories by Catholic writers.

List of the Catholic Books in the Pratt Free Library of Baltimore. Compiled by Rev. John F. O'Donovan, S.J. Baltimore, 1900.

Lonergan, Joan Mary. "Publishing Trends Reflected in Works of Academy Members of the Gallery of Living Catholic Authors." Master's thesis, Catholic University of America, 1955.

Publishers' Weekly. "'Catholic Writers Guild.'" 53(1898):63. Aritcle contains the guild's charter membership list.

———. 54(1898):178. An advertisement for Benziger Brothers' weekly, *Our Boys' and Girls' Own,* which lists featured Catholic writers.

Ruskin, Mary Patricia. "A Survey of Catholic Americana and Catholic Book Publishing in the United States, 1886–1890." Master's thesis, Catholic University of America, 1952.

Seraphine, Mother, ed. *Immortelles of Catholic Columbian Literature.* New York: McBride, 1896. An anthology of works by and about contemporary Catholic women writers.

REPRESENTATIVE AMERICAN CATHOLIC WORKS OF FICTION, 1884–1900 (INCLUDING ALL NOVELS CITED IN THE TEXT)

ADULT FICTION

Adams, Henry Austin. *Westchester.* St. Louis: Herder, 1898.

Ames, F.S.D. *Wishes on Wings.* New York: Catholic Truth Society, 1888.

Barry, John D. *Mademoiselle Blanche.* New York: Stone & Kimball, 1896.

Bugg, Lelia Hardin. *Orchids.* St. Louis: Herder, 1894.

———. *People of Our Parish.* Boston: Marlier, 1900.

———. *The Prodigal's Daughter.* New York: Benziger Bros., 1898.

Catherwood, Mary Hartwell. *Romance of Dollard.* Boston: Houghton Mifflin and Co., 1898.

———. *White Islander.* Boston: Houghton Mifflin and Co., 1893.

Conway, Katherine. *Lalor's Maples.* Boston: Flynn, 1900.

Cox, Eleanor Rogers. *A Millionairess' Trials.* New York: P.J. Kenedy & Sons, 1894.

Craigie, Pearl Marie. *School for Saints.* New York: Macmillan Co., 1898.

Crawford, F. Marion. *Adam Johnstone's Son.* New York: Macmillan Co., 1896.

Currier, Rev. Charles W. *Dimitrios and Irene.* Baltimore: Gallery and McCann, 1893.

Donnelly, Eleanor C., ed. *Round Table of Representative American Catholic Novelists.* New York: Benziger Bros., 1896.

Dorsey, Anna H. *Warp and Woof.* Notre Dame, Ind.: Ave Maria Press, 1887.

Dorsey, Ella Loraine. *A Salem Witch.* New York: Benziger Bros., 1897.

Egan, Maurice F. *The Disappearance of John Longworthy.* Notre Dame, Ind.: Ave Maria Press, 1893.

———. *The Success of Patrick Desmond.* Notre Dame, Ind.: Ave Maria Press, 1893.

Guiney, Louise Imogen. *Monsier Henri.* New York: Harper and Bros., 1892.

Harland, Henry. *The Cardinal's Snuff-Box.* London: J. Lane, 1898.

Janvier, Thomas A. *The Aztec Treasure House.* New York: Harper and Bros., 1890.

———. *Stories of Old New Spain.* New York: D. Appleton and Co., 1891.

McDermott, William A. [Walter Lecky]. *Gremore: A Village Idyl.* New York: Sadlier, 1886.

———. *Mister Billy Buttons.* New York: Benziger Bros., 1896.

———. *Père Monier's Ward.* New York: Benziger Bros., 1898.

Martin, Elizabeth G. [Louis Dorsey]. *John Van Alstyne's Factory.* New York: Holt, 1886.

———. *Katherine.* Philadelphia: Holt, 1886.

Meline, Mary Miller. *Mobrays and the Harringtons: A Novel of American Life.* Baltimore: Baltimore Publishing Co., 1884.

O'Reilly, John Boyle. *Moondyne.* Boston: Pilot Publishing Co., 1885.

Pise, Charles Constantine. *Father Rowland.* Baltimore: Catholic Truth Society, 1829.

Reilly, Bernard J. *College Boy.* New York: Benziger Bros., 1899.

———. *Passing Shadows.* New York: Benziger Bros., 1897.

Reilly, Louis W. *A Blessed Peacemaker.* New York: C. Wildermann, 1898.

Seawell, Molly Elliott. *Despotism and Democracy.* New York: McClure-Phillips, 1900.
Seton, William. *A Poor Millionaire.* New York: P. O'Shea, 1884.
Skinner, Henrietta Dana. *Espirito Santo.* New York: Harper and Bros., 1899.
Smith, John Talbot. *Art of Disappearing.* New York: Benziger Bros., 1899.
———. *His Honor and Other Tales.* New York: Catholic Publication Society, 1891.
———. *Saranac.* New York: Benziger Bros., 1892.
———. *Solitary Island.* New York: W.H. Young, 1894.
———. *Woman of Culture.* New York: Catholic Publication Society, 1892.
Smith, Mary E. [Christian Faber]. *Chivalrous Deed.* New York: P.J. Kenedy & Sons, 1891.
———. *Ambition's Conquest.* New York: P.J. Kenedy & Sons, 1891.
Stoddard, Charles Warren. *For the Pleasure of His Company.* Notre Dame, Ind.: Ave Maria Press, 1887.
Taggart, Marion Ames. *The Blissylvania Post-Office.* New York: Benziger Bros., 1897.
———. *Loyal Blue and Royal Scarlet.* New York: Benziger Bros., 1899.
Tiernan, F. C. [Christian Reid]. *Armine.* New York: Catholic Publication Society, 1884.
———. *Child of Mary.* Notre Dame, Ind.: Ave Maria Press, 1885.
———. *A Far-Away Princess.* New York: Devin-Adair, 1900.
Tincker, Mary Agnes. *Grapes and Thorns.* New York: Catholic Publication Society, 1874.
———. *House of York.* New York: Catholic Publication Society, 1872.
———. *San Salvador.* Boston: Houghton Mifflin and Co., 1892.

CHILDREN'S FICTION

Bonesteel, Mary. *A Hostage of War.* New York: Benziger Bros., 1900.
Brown, Mary Josephine. [Marion J. Brunowe]. *Mad-cap Set at St. Anne's.* New York: Benziger Bros., 1898.
Copus, Rev. John, S.J. *Harry Russell.* New York: Benziger Bros., 1903.
Dahlgren, Sarah, M. *Secret Directory.* Philadelphia: Kilner, 1896.
Donnelly, Eleanor C. *A Klondike Picnic.* New York: Benziger Bros., 1898.
Dorsey, Anna H. *Beth's Promise.* Baltimore: Murphy, 1887.
Dorsey, Ella Loraine. *The Taming of Polly.* New York: Benziger Bros., 1887.
Finn, Rev. Francis, S.J. *Tom Playfair.* New York: Benziger Bros., 1892.
———. *Claude Lightfoot.* New York: Benziger Bros., 1893.
Juvenile Round Table. New York: Benziger Bros., 1891.
Mannix, Mary E. *Michael O'Donnell.* Boston: J. Flynn, 1900.
———. *Pancho and Panchita.* Newk York: Benziger Bros., 1899.
Nixon-Roulet, Mary. *Little Marshalls at the Lake.* New York: Benziger Bros., 1888.
O'Malley, Sallie Margaret. *Boys of the Prairie.* New York: Lathrop, 1888.
Sadlier, Agnes Laurette. *Marjorie's Adventures.* New York: Sadlier, 1889.
Smith, Rev. John Talbot. *Prairie Boy: A Story of the West.* New York: P.J. Kenedy & Sons, 1888.
Smith, Mary P. *A Jolly Good Summer.* Boston: Roberts Bros., 1895.
Spalding, Henry S. *Cave by the Beech Fork.* New York: Benziger Bros., 1900.
———. *Sheriff of Beech Fork.* New York: Benziger Bros., 1894.
Taggart, Marion Ames. *By Branscome River.* New York: Benziger Bros., 1891.
Waggaman, Mary Theresa. *Little Comrades.* Philadelphia: Kilner, 1894.
Whiteley, Isabel N. *The Falcon of Langeac.* Boston: Copeland and Day, 1897.
Wood, Julia. *Clare Loraine.* New York: Benziger Bros., 1893.

Index

Abbé Constantine, The (Halévy), 75
Adam Johnstone's Son (Crawford), 118
Adams, Henry, 155
Alban (Huntington), 41–42
Alden, Isabella, 73
Agnes of Sorrento (Stowe), 75
Alger, Horatio, 73, 87, 91, 143
Ambition's Contest (Mary E. Smith), 103–05
American Catholic expatriates, 96–97; and
  Yellow Book, 97–98
American Catholic fiction: "bogus" Catholic
  authors, 165–66; and Catholic culture, 21–
  22; children's fiction, 91–92; cosmopolitan
  fiction, 101–13; definition of, 114;
  didactic fable, 88; and doctrine of salvation,
  136–38; early, 38–49; of expatriates,
  96–100; general, 20–21; magazine criticism
  of, 65–67; and moral issues, 142–45;
  parochial, 80–81; and political themes,
  146–54; serial publication of, 69–70; and
  social change, 155–58; and theme of
  authority, 134–36; and theology of grace,
  138–41; theory and criticism of, 62–64;
  topical analysis, method of, 132–34
American Catholic literature: and publishing
  practices, 53–56; social function of, 64
American Catholic organizations, 58, 59;
  Catholic Summer School, 59, 60, 61, 64;
  Guild of Catholic Authors, 118; reading
  unions, 57–58; Young Men's Catholic
  Association, 59
American Catholics: and acculturation, 78–
  79; and Cahensley Affair, 6; and Civil War,
  50; conservative faction of, 5; liberal
  faction of, 4–5; and Parliament of
  Religions, 6–8; population, 50–51;
  post-Vatican II reactions of, xv–xviii; and
  publishing practices, 32–33; and school
  controversy, 5–6

American Ecclesiastical Review, 63
Americanism, 1 3, 4, 78–79, issues
  defining, 3–9
American literature: and attitudes toward
  Catholicism, 74–77; early nineteenth-
  century attitudes toward, 23–24;
  "*Graustark* fiction," 72; major themes and
  developments of, 71–77; religious themes
  in, 72–73; utopian fiction, 72
American Politician, The (Crawford), 119
American Protestant literature, 73–74
Armine (Tiernan), 109–10, 142
Art of Disappearing, The (John Talbot
  Smith), 142
Atala (Chateaubriand), 32
Ave Maria, 65, 70
Awful Disclosures (Monk), 74
Aztec Treasure House, The (Janvier), 120

Barry, John D., 88
Barry, William, *The New Antigone,* 63
Bazin, René, 77
Beardsley, Aubrey, 98, 99; and *The Yellow
  Book,* 99
Bellamy, Edward, *Looking Backward,* 72,
  74
Ben Hur (Wallace), 73
Benson, Robert Hugh, 77
Benziger Brothers, 55, 62, 70
Billy Buttons (McDermott), 90
Bingham, Caleb, 32
Black consciousness, 162–63
Bonesteel, Mary G., 91
Bourget, Paul, 77
Brownson, Orestes Augustus, 32, 34, 40, 44,
  48, 65, 81, 96, 112, 123, 126, 147, 153;
  Charles Elwood, 44–46; critical theory of,
  27–31; *The Spirit-Rapper,* 46–47
Bugg, Lelia Hardin, 87–88; *Orchids,* 144;

The People of Our Parish, 87; *The Prodigal's Daughter*, 88

Caesar's Column (Donnelly), 67, 72, 166
Cahensley Affair, 6
Cahensley, Peter, 6
Callista (Newman), 34–36
Cardinal's Snuff-Box, The (Harland), 99
Carey, Matthew, 32, 54
Catherwood, Mary Hartwell, 105; *Romance of Dollard*, 106
Catholic Church: and liberal-conservative dialectic, 3–4
Catholic Educational Union, 57, 59
Catholic Experience, The (Greeley), 11
Catholic fiction, European, 77–78. *See also* American Catholic fiction
Catholicism: conservative, 3–4; liberal, 3–4
Catholic Keepsake, The, 143
Catholic literature: traditions of, 22–23. *See also* American Catholic literature
Catholic Press Association, 54
Catholic Publication Society, 53, 54, 63
Catholic Publishers' Association, 55
Catholic Reading Circle Review, 57
Catholic Reading Union, 58
Catholic Summer School, 59, 61, 64
Catholic World, 2, 28, 52, 58, 65, 70
Charles Elwood (Brownson), 44–46
Chateaubriand, *Atala*, 32
Chautauqua, 59, 60
Chicago Exposition of 1893, 58
Child of Mary (Tiernan), 107–08
Children's fiction, 91, 92. *See also* American Catholic fiction
Chopin, Kate, 165
Cincinnati Telegraph, 71
Clarke, Isabel C., 67
Claude Lightfoot (Finn), 94
Columbian Reading Union, 57, 60, 61
Commager, Henry S., 12
Connecticut Yankee in King Arthur's Court (Twain), 75
Conway, Katherine, 59, 64, 88, 126
Cooper, James Fenimore, 74; *The Prairie*, 74, 75
Corrigan, Archbishop Michael, 5, 100, 112; and McGlynn Affair, 9
Cosmopolitan fiction, 101–13
Council of Baltimore of 1866, 51
Council of Baltimore of 1884, 51–52, 54, 57
Craigie, Pearl Marie, 100
Crane, Stephen, 71, 154
Crawford, F. Marion, 118–19, 123; *Adam Johnstone's Son*, 118; *The American Politician*, 119; *Paul Patoff*, 119; *The Ralstons*, 119; *Saracenesca*, 82; *Taquisara*, 118; *Three Fates*, 118
Cross, Robert, 11

Crowley, Mary Catherine, 105; *Daughter of New France*, 106
Currier, Charles Warren, 106

Daley, Richard, xiii–xiv, 159
Damnation of Theron Ware, The (Frederic), 110–11
Daughter of New France (Crowley), 106
Democratic Convention of 1968, xiii, 159
Despotism and Democracy (Sewell), 151–52
Dion and the Sibyls (Keon), 77
Disappearance of John Longworthy, The (Egan), 81, 83, 85–86
Dixon, Thomas, *The Klansman*, 145
Donahoe, Patrick, 33
Donnelly, Eleanor C., 67, 88
Donnelly, Ignatius, *Caesar's Column*, 67, 72, 166
Dorsey, Anna, 38
Dorsey, Ella, 143; *Midshipman Bob*, 135
Dowson, Ernest, 98
Dreiser, Theodore, 78
Driscoll, Annette, 110
Dunne, Finley Peter, 166
Dunnigan, Edward, 33

Egan, Maurice Francis, 38, 68, 81, 86–87, 91, 94, 96, 101, 106, 113, 149, 159; *The Disappearance of John Longworthy*, 85–86; literary theory of, 81, 83; *The Success of Patrick Desmond*, 84–85, 142; *The Vocation of Edward Conway*, 83–84, 135, 144
Elder, M. T., 156–57
Eliot, T. S., 100
Elliott, Walter, 4; and Hecker biography, 9
Ellison, Ralph, 162
Elsie Venner (Holmes), 75
England, Bishop John, 11
Espiritu Santo (Skinner), 102–03

Faber, Francis, 98
Fabiola (Wiseman), 36–37
Far-away Princess, A (Tiernan), 108
Farinholt, F. C., 145
Father Clement, 74
Father Rowland (Pise), 39–40
Fiedler, Leslie, 26
Finn, Francis, 92–93, 139; *Claude Lightfoot*, 94; *Tom Playfair*, 93–94
Foregone Conclusion, A (Howells), 76
Forest, The (Huntington), 42, 43
Frederic, Harold: *The Damnation of Theron Ware*, 110–11

Garland, Hamlin, 71
George, Henry, 9, 73, 117; *Progress and Poverty*, 74

Gibbons, James Cardinal, 1, 5, 51, 106; and
    Cahensley Affair, 6; and McGlynn Affair, 9
Gladden, Washington, 73
Globe-Review, The, 61
Grace Morton (Meany), 47–48
Grapes and Thorns (Tincker), 126–27, 145,
    148
"*Graustark* fiction." *See* American literature
Greeley, Andrew, 11
Guild of Catholic Writers, 59, 118
Guiney, Louise, 97, 100–01; *Monsieur Henri*,
    100

Halévy, Ludovic, *The Abbé Constantine*, 75
Handlin, Oscar, 141
Hansen, Marcus Lee, 160; on assimilation,
    161–62
Hardy, Thomas, 82
Harland, Henry, 98–99, 100, 101; *The
    Cardinal's Snuff-Box*, 99
Harris, Joel Chandler, 115, 165
Hawthorne, Nathaniel, 18, 46, 74, 75; *The
    Marble Faun*, 75, 128
Hecker, Isaac, 4, 28, 30, 53, 54, 57, 58, 62,
    63, 65, 96, 100, 127, 139, 160; and
    biography controversy, 9–10; and Vatican
    Council of 1869–70, 2–3
Hewit, Augustine, 4
Hicks, Granville, 99
Holmes, Oliver Wendell, *Elsie Venner*, 75
House of York (Tincker), 125–26, 148
Howells, William Dean, 66, 71, 76, 82, 83,
    99, 154; *A Foregone Conclusion*, 76; *The
    Quality of Mercy*, 75
Huneker, James, 82, 165
Huntington, Jedediah Vincent, 40–41, 43–44,
    83, 96, 102, 106, 112, 123; and *Alban*,
    41–42; and *The Forest*, 42, 43; and *Lady
    Alice*, 41

Index Librorum, 27
In His Steps (Sheldon), 74
Ireland, Archbishop John, 4, 96, 100, 110,
    112, 137; and Manifest Destiny, 12–14;
    and O'Connell correspondence, 12–14; and
    school controversy, 5–6; and Spanish-
    American War, 12

Jackson, Helen Hunt, *Ramona*, 75, 76
James, Henry, 46, 66, 82, 83, 97, 111, 128
Janvier, Thomas Allibone, 119–20, 122–23,
    145, 155, 163; *The Aztec Treasure House*,
    120; *Stories of Old and New Spain*,
    120–22
John XXIII, xvi
John Van Alstyne's Factory (Martin), 155–56
Johnson, Richard Malcomb, 115–16, 123

Katherine (Martin), 135–36

Keane, Monsignor John, 4
Kehoe, Lawrence, 53, 55
Kendrick, Archbishop, 54
Kenedy, P. J. and Sons, 55
Kennedy Family, xiv, xv
Kennedy, Edward, xiv–xv, 159
Kennedy, John F., xv
Keon, Miles G., *Dion and the Sibyls*, 77
Klansman, The (Dixon), 145
Klein, Abbé Felix, 9

Lady Alice (Huntington), 41
LaFarge, John, 11
Lanier, Sidney, 115
Leo XIII, 8; and *Testem Benevolentiae*, 1–3
Liberalism, 153–54
Library of Choice Catholic Stories (Wilder-
    man), 70
Literary sociology, 16–20
Literature: classical theory of, 25–27; and
    culture, 24–27, middle-class patterns of,
    25–27
Looking Backward (Bellamy), 72, 74
Lucerne Memorial, 6

McAvoy, Thomas T., 10–11
McCarthy, Eugene, xiv, 159
McCutcheon, George Barr, 72
McDermott, William, 66, 89–90, 94, 95, 137,
    138, 139, 163; *Billy Buttons*, 90
McGlynn, John: and Henry George, 9
Manifest Destiny, 12–14
Mannix, Mary, 64, 91
Marble Faun, The (Hawthorne), 75, 128
Martin, Mrs. Elizabeth G., 163; *John Van
    Alstyne's Factory*, 155–56; *Katherine*,
    135–36
May, Henry, 78
Maynard, Theodore, 10
Meany, Mary L., *Grace Morton*, 47–48
Meline, Mary, *The Mobrays and the
    Harringtons*, 142
Messenger of the Sacred Heart, 65, 67, 70
Meynell, Alice
Midshipman Bob (Ella Dorsey), 135
Miller, Emily Clark, 73
Mobrays and the Harringtons, The (Meline),
    142
Monk, Maria, *Awful Disclosures*, 74
Monsieur Henri (Guiney), 100
Moondyne (O'Reilly), 117–18, 123
Morris, William, 98, 152
Mott, Frank Luther, 72
Mullaney, Brother Azarias, 65; literary theory
    of, 68–69

New Antigone, The (William Barry), 63
Newman, John Henry Cardinal, 33–34, 77,
    83, 100; and *Callista*, 34–36; literary

influence of, 37–38
Niebuhr, H. Richard, 111
Nixon-Roulet, Mary, 91
Norris, Frank, 66, 71, 154
Northwestern Chronicle, 71

O'Brien, Henry, 153
O'Connell, Denis, 5, 12–14
Orchids (Bugg), 144
O'Reilly, John Boyle, 116, 152, 163;
    Moondyne, 117–18, 123
Our Boys and Girls' Own, 70
Ozanam Reading Union, 57

Pallen, Condé B., 69
Panovsky, Erwin, 18
Papal infallibility, 2
Parliament of Religions, 6–8, 58
Parochial fiction, Catholic: analysis, 80–81;
    children's, 91–92; didactic fable, 88
Paulist Order, 2
Paul Patoff (Crawford), 119
People of Our Parish, The (Bugg), 87
Pick, John, 69
Picture of Dorian Gray, The (Wilde), 98
Pilot (Boston), 33, 116
Pise, Charles Constantine, 23, 38, 39;
    Father Rowland, 39–40
Popular literature and culture, 16–21
Prairie, The (Cooper), 74, 75
Preuss, Arthur, 61
Prodigal's Daughter, The (Bugg), 88
Progress and Poverty (George), 74

Quality of Mercy, The (Howells), 75
Quo Vadis (Sienkiewicz), 73

Ralstons, The (Crawford), 119
Ramona (Jackson), 75, 76
Rauschenbusch, Walter, 73
Reilly, Bernard J., 143
Review, The (St. Louis), 61
Roe, E. P., 72
Romance of Dollard (Catherwood), 106
Roosevelt, Theodore, 82
Ryan, John A., 11, 63

Sadlier, Dennis and James, 33, 106
Sadlier, Mrs. James, 33, 83, 96
Sadlier, Mary Ann, 38
St. Raphael Society, 6
San Salvador (Tincker), 128–30, 139
Santayana, George, on the Genteel Tradition
    in America, 160–61
Saracenesca (Crawford), 82
Saranac (John Talbot Smith), 66
Satolli, Archbishop Francisco, and Parliament
    of Religions, 7–8

School controversy, 5–6. *See also* American
    Catholics
Seton, William, 142, 156–57
Sewell, Molly Elliot, 151; *Despotism and
    Democracy*, 151–52
Shea, John Gilmary, 23
Sheed, Wilfred, 61
Sheldon, Charles, *In His Steps*, 74
Sienkiewicz, Henryk, *Quo Vadis*, 73
Skinner, Henrietta Dana, 101–02;
    Espiritu Santo, 102–03
Smith, Henry Nash, 19
Smith, Father John Talbot, 88, 91, 138, 139,
    149, 150–51, 156, 158, 163; *The Art of
    Disappearing*, 142; *Saranac*, 66; *Solitary
    Island*, 150
Smith, Mary E., *Ambition's Contest*, 103–05
Solitary Island (John Talbot Smith), 150
Spalding, Henry S., 91
Spalding, Bishop John Lancaster, 4
Spalding, Archbishop Martin J., 54
Spearman, Frank H., 67
Spirit-Rapper, The (Brownson), 46–47
Stories of Old and New Spain (Janvier),
    120–22
Stowe, Harriet Beecher, *Agnes of Sorrento*, 75
Success of Patrick Desmond, The (Egan),
    84–85, 142

Taggart, Marion Ames, 89, 135
Taquisara (Crawford), 118
Tarkington, Booth, 82
Testem Benevolentiae, 1–2, 14
Thorne, William Henry, 61–62
Three Fates (Crawford), 118
Tiernan, Mrs. Frances, 101, 106–07, 138, 145,
    146, 149, 155; *Armine*, 109–10, 142;
    Child of Mary, 107–08; *A Far-away
    Princess*, 108
Tincker, Mary Agnes, 124, 130–31, 149, 152,
    163; and European novels, 127–28; *Grapes
    and Thorns*, 126–27, 145, 148; *House of
    York*, 125–26, 148; *San Salvador*, 128–30,
    139
Tom Playfair (Finn), 93–94
Twain, Mark, 82; *A Connecticut Yankee in
    King Arthur's Court*, 75

Ultramontanism, 4
Utopian fiction. *See* American literature

Vatican Council, First, 2
Vatican Council, Second, xvi
Vocation of Edward Conway, The (Egan),
    83–84, 135, 144

Wallace, Lew, *Ben Hur*, 73
Warren, Austin, 141
Watt, Ian, 25

Whitman, Walt, 82
Wilde, Oscar, *The Picture of Dorian Gray,* 98
Wilderman, Charles, Library of Choice
    Catholic Stories, 70
Wiseman, Nicholas Cardinal, 33, 36, 77, 83;
    and *Fabiola,* 36–37; literary influence of,
37–38
World's Catholic Columbian Congress, 8

Yellow Book, The, 97–99
Young Catholic, The, 60
Young Men's Catholic Association, 59, 60